JAMES B. MURPHY is Assistant Professor of History at Southern Illinois University. A native of Rome, Georgia, he received his M.A. at Emory University and his Ph.D. at Louisiana State University. At present, he is researching the history of the Appalachian South.

SOUTHERN BIOGRAPHY SERIES

Titles in the SOUTHERN BIOGRAPHY SERIES

Edited by Fred C. Cole and Wendell H. Stephenson

Edited by T. Harry Williams

L. Q. C. LAMAR

MURPHY, James B. L. Q. C. Lamar, pragmatic patriot. Louisiana State, 1973. 294p bibl (Southern biography series) 72-94150. 11.95. ISBN 0-8071-0217-2
Lucius Lamar's political career spanned some 40 years of Mississippi history from the 1850 Compromise, through secession, the Civil War, and Reconstruction to the Bourbon restoration. Congressman, Senator, Secretary of Interior and Supreme Court Justice, he was a spokesman for what he conceived to be Southern interests. Defender of secession and the Confederacy, he adjusted somewhat to the changing reality of the postwar world. He urged reconciliation with the North, supported the political rights of the newly enfranchised blacks, and advocated federal aid for railroads and rivers. At all times he linked his position with Southern interests. Murphy in this judicious biography places the famous Sumner eulogy and Lamar's role in the political settlement of 1877 in the context of a man urging a nationalist approach in order to improve the South's position in the Union. A shallow person, Lamar never approaches greatness as the author suggests in his subtitle. *L. Q. C. Lamar* belongs with A. D. Kirwan's *Revolt of the rednecks* (1964) and Vernon L. Wharton's *The Negro in Mississippi* (1965) as the standard works on the Bourbon period in the state. This well-researched volume has an extensive bibliography in both primary and secondary sources. Belongs in all undergraduate and graduate libraries.

L. Q. C. LAMAR

Pragmatic Patriot

JAMES B. MURPHY

LOUISIANA STATE UNIVERSITY PRESS   Baton Rouge

ISBN 0–8071–0217–2
Library of Congress Catalog Card Number 72–94150
Copyright © 1973 by Louisiana State University Press
All rights reserved
Manufactured in the United States of America
Printed by The TJM Corporation, Baton Rouge, Louisiana
Designed by Albert R. Crochet

for PAUL LOWREY MURPHY

Contents

L. Q. C. LAMAR

Prologue

A scion of the Lamar family born in the early nineteenth century contracted certain privileges, obligations, and even burdens derived from the clan's almost two centuries' experience in America. Responsibility for the family's honor and future and its commitment to public service was imposed at birth. No Lamar had accepted less since the immigrants Thomas and Peter settled in Virginia and Maryland about 1660. From Huguenot France, they had boldly struck out for a different destiny in the New World and had committed following generations to that destiny.

The Lamars moved with the advancing line of civilization into the Carolinas and Georgia. As successive generations built their fortunes and altered the countryside, they substituted a vital connection with the American community for the now quite distant European background. By the time of the Revolution the Lamars were prepared to fight for American independence. Some paid the ultimate price for rebellion, but others returned to their homes laden with glory and pride which they passed down to their sons.

In time, commitment to America developed strong sectional overtones. As the family moved south in its restlessness it completely absorbed the peculiar qualities of the region. Economic and cultural acquisitions bound the Lamars to the section's destiny; and to a lesser degree the relationship also worked in reverse—the family shared responsibility for the South's history.

The bonds forged between family and section would survive the ultimate test of the Civil War, and the habit of leadership and responsibility would persist.[1]

In many aspects of this heritage, Lucius Quintus Cincinnatus Lamar did not differ drastically from other men in all sections of the country. His background did, however, set certain limits upon his potential achievement. He was born at a time when southern influence in national councils was great, and this continued to be so into his early manhood. As the son of an important planter family, he easily made his way into governmental circles, first on the state level and then, at the age of thirty-two, on the national level as a member of Congress. There was no reason to doubt that national politics might have thrust even greater distinction upon such a person.

The sectional crisis and the emergence of the Northeast as the dominant national force altered southerners' prospects. The pinnacle of planter leadership also marked the beginning of its decline. A career begun auspiciously enough tumbled with defeat in the Civil War. Thereafter, such a man as Lamar might rise to national office and influence, but he must always address himself primarily to southern questions. The opportunity to direct the thrust of America's destiny would not come again for southern leaders during the nineteenth century. The commitment to leadership did not disappear, but the area in which that talent might be exercised had been largely circumscribed. Accepting these limitations, Lamar emerged as a spokesman for the "New South." A framework for judging his career is thus suggested.[2]

1. Three genealogical studies treat the family history: Harold Dihel LeMar, *History of the Lamar or Lemar Family in America* (Omaha, 1941); William Harmong Lamar, "Thomas Lamar of the Province of Maryland and a Part of His Descendants," *Publications of the Southern History Association*, I (July, 1897), 203–10; and Edward Mayes, *Genealogy and History of Lamar and Related Families* (Hattiesburg, Miss., 1935).

2. This biography appeared in an earlier form as "L. Q. C. Lamar: Pragmatic Patriot" (Ph.D. dissertation, Louisiana State University, 1968).

The Georgia Background

Members of the Lamar family first arrived in Georgia about 1759. They had been substantial landowners for generations in Maryland and sold that property to acquire grants in other areas to the south. John Lamar and his brothers, grandsons of Thomas the immigrant, recorded the sale of several land tracts in January, 1755. Taking his share, John moved to South Carolina where in 1757 he held a grant of three hundred acres. Two years later he established a plantation in Georgia.

John Lamar had five sons. The eldest fathered a son whom he called John. The youngest fathered a daughter, Rebecca. John Lamar and Rebecca Lamar, first cousins, married and were the grandparents of L. Q. C. Lamar.[1]

Little is known about the grandparents, John and Rebecca Lamar. It is claimed that they were wealthy, cultured, and owned many slaves. Their nine-hundred-acre plantation on Little River in Putnam County, Georgia, provided the traditional "home-place" for several generations, and it was here that L. Q. C. Lamar was born in 1825.[2] Since his father was not a planter, the "homeplace" provided Lamar with an aura of the plantation South and an important sense of belonging to the cotton culture.

1. Mayes, *Genealogy and History*, 20, 25, 31.
2. Wirt Armistead Cate, *Lucius Q. C. Lamar: Secession and Reunion* (Chapel Hill, 1935), 15, 21; Edward Mayes, *Lucius Q. C. Lamar: His Life, Times, and Speeches* (Nashville, 1896), 15, 27. John Lamar died intestate. The bond posted by his administrator indicated an estate of some $13,000. J. Clayton Hargrove, Ordinary of Putnam County, Georgia, to author, March 14, 1967.

Two of John and Rebecca Lamar's children achieved prominence. Mirabeau Buonaparte Lamar was their most illustrious son. After migrating westward he participated in the Texas Revolution and emerged a military hero and a founding father. In consequence of his service, Lamar succeeded Sam Houston as president of the Republic of Texas. After annexation by the United States, which he at first opposed, Mirabeau Lamar served as United States minister to the Argentine Republic and to Costa Rica and Nicaragua.[3] Though there is no evidence of direct influence upon L. Q. C. Lamar, the family's pride must have welled up and taken substance from these romantic achievements.

John and Rebecca Lamar's second son of note was Lucius Quintus Cincinnatus Lamar, Sr., who achieved distinction as a lawyer and state judge. In pursuing a legal career in Milledgeville, Georgia, Lucius Lamar, Sr., initially met with a number of personal and professional difficulties. In the judgment of a contemporary, he lacked the practical bent necessary to material success. And more importantly, he suffered certain temperamental shortcomings. Nevertheless, through the help of his partner he overcame his lack of "address" and prospered. The young lawyer's competence led to a commission for the compilation of the *Georgia Statutes* for 1810–1820; and in 1830 the legislature elected him to the judgeship of his circuit—a top place in the legal system since the state had no supreme court.[4]

A mental breakdown ended Lamar's life at a tragically young age. After suffering periods of incapacitating depression and distraction, the thirty-seven-year-old judge (his son Lucius was nine) committed suicide—just one year after the death of his parents, John and Rebecca Lamar. Judge Joel Crawford, La-

3. "Mirabeau Buonaparte Lamar," *Dictionary of American Biography*, X, 553–54, hereinafter cited as *DAB*; *Appleton's Cyclopedia of American Biography*, III, 598–99.

4. Joel Crawford, Lamar's law partner, provided a sketch for Stephen F. Miller, *The Bench and Bar of Georgia* (Philadelphia, 1858), 136–40. Miller added material to the sketch and incorporated it in toto. This is the basis for all subsequent writing on Judge Lamar. See also W. H. Sparks, *The Memories of Fifty Years* (Philadelphia, 1882), 173.

mar's partner, sought to explain the suicide from his own knowledge of the circumstances and concluded that *"insanity,* resulting from accidental derangement of the cerebral organism," was "probably the true and only cause." [5] Another contemporary account maintained that Judge Lamar had suffered severe dyspepsia with high fever, from which he never completely recovered, and that he had killed himself in a moment of delirium.[6] These somewhat speculative descriptions seem noteworthy since L. Q. C. Lamar, Jr., had something of his father's bent toward despondency and distractedness. Such traits would obviously play a large role in Lamar's response to life—especially since his life was tinged with tragedy.

There is no way to measure precisely the traumatic impact which the father's suicide must have had upon nine-year-old Lucius. He does not seem to have dwelt upon the memory in his later life, but that in itself tells nothing. The violent death of his father and the subsequent adolescent years under female influence (Mrs. Lamar did not remarry until much later) must have marked Lucius' character. Several personality traits stand out as possible effects. For one thing, his correspondence throughout life had an effeminate ring in its unguarded expressions of devotion and fondness, and in the self-pity which was so conspicuous. It is also possible that Lamar later compensated for his loss through devotion to older and more influential men. Augustus Baldwin Longstreet, his teacher and father-in-law, furnishes the best example of these strong ties. The parallels in their lives were by no means ordinary; and the emergence of Longstreet as a father image seems quite likely.

Fortunately for Lucius and the other four children[7] their mother was financially secure and temperamentally strong

5. Crawford, in Miller, *The Bench and Bar of Georgia,* 137–39; Mayes, *Genealogy and History,* 29, 31, 40.

6. *Appleton's Cyclopedia,* III, 598.

7. There were five living children of eight births: Rebecca, born 1819; Lucius, born 1825; Thompson Bird, born 1828; Mary Ann Washburn, born 1832; and Jefferson Mirabeau, born after his father's death in 1835. LeMar, *Lamar Family,* 107–11, lists these children with sketches of their lives and lists of their offspring.

enough to bear heavy responsibilities. With the help of her brother-in-law, Jefferson Lamar, who managed the property, she provided a comfortable if not luxurious livelihood for her family.[8]

Soon after her husband's death, Mrs. Lamar moved from Milledgeville to Covington, Georgia, to place her three sons in the new Manual Labor School operated there by the Methodist Church. Lucius entered the new school prepared by a brief period of instruction in the Milledgeville schools and by learning at home. He later especially recalled reading classics from his father's library such as Franklin's *Autobiography*, Plutarch's *Lives*, and Marshall's *Washington*, and the writings of Lord Byron, John Locke, and others.[9]

Young Lamar prospered under the school's system of combined mental and physical training. The rigorous schedule began each day with chapel at six-thirty in the morning and continued until nine o'clock in the evening with classes, study, and about three hours of farm labor. Although he disliked the labor, it provided an important corrective for a child whose experience was largely limited to town environment and whose life lacked male direction. Also, since his health was not robust and he suffered from "dyspepsia," the work "strengthened up and toned up" his "whole system." [10]

This phase of Lamar's education continued from 1837 until 1840, when the Manual Labor School consolidated with the newly established Emory College in nearby Oxford, Georgia. Mrs. Lamar responded to this opportunity by moving with her children to Oxford. She was joined there by Lucius' uncle, Harmong Lamar, who had also lived with his sons in Covington. Although the distance was but one and a half miles, the serious-

8. Undated letter from Calvin M. Simpson, Ordinary, Baldwin County, Georgia, to author states that the estate was valued at $7,873.12.

9. Mayes, *Lamar*, 28.

10. Henry Morton Bullock states that though the Manual Labor School was new and the first of its kind in Georgia, educational systems combining manual and intellectual training were in vogue at this time. The curriculum resembled that of most established schools of the day. See Henry Morton Bullock, *A History of Emory University* (Nashville, 1936), 34–39; Mayes, *Lamar*, 28–31.

ness with which the mother and uncle treated the matter must have impressed the children.[11]

Actually the move from preparatory school to college and from Covington to Oxford involved only a slight adjustment. The Methodist Conference operated the newly organized college just as it had the Manual Labor School. Trustees and faculty consisted for the most part of the same individuals; likewise, most of the students transferred from Covington to Oxford. In short, Emory College was, and was intended to be, an extension of the Manual Labor School with the addition of a college curriculum.[12]

The atmosphere in which Lamar earned his degree was austere even for the nineteenth century. Besides the physical labor principle which remained in effect for a time, the community's religious orientation had a sobering effect. The village of Oxford where he lived was actually a part of the campus. Residential lots were cut from school property and leased to professors or to families like Lamar's. The houseowners, including Lucius' mother, provided room and board to nonresident students. The governing body, including town commissioner Harmong Lamar, used this arrangement to prohibit intoxicants and "games of hazard." To further reinforce this puritanical setting, the trustees chose a faculty made up entirely of Methodist ministers and provided for compulsory worship services.[13]

11. Several documents in the Emory University Library provide information. See Record Book of the Treasurer of Emory College: 1836–1839, p. 158, for Lamar's account at the Manual Labor School. A file containing "Title bonds for lots in Oxford, 1837–1839, 1849" includes a deed conveying property originally owned by Allen Turner to Sarah Lamar. Mrs. Lamar paid $1,800—including $600 cash and her Covington house—for the Oxford property. See also Mayes, *Lamar*, 32.

12. Catalogue of the Officers & Students in Emory College, Ga., and the Report of the Board of the Trustees to the General Conference, 1839 (Emory University Library); Bullock, *A History of Emory University*, 50–56, 62.

13. Catalogue of the Officers & Students in Emory College, Ga., and the Report of the Board of the Trustees to the General Conference, 1839; The Statutes of Emory College and the Bye-laws of the Faculty, 1839; Catalogue of the Officers and Students of Emory College, 1845; Catalogue of the Officers and Students of Emory College, 1846 (Emory University Library); Bullock, *A History of Emory University*, 57–58, 61, 75, 79. According to the catalogs of 1845–46, Mrs. Lamar boarded three students including her two sons of college age the first year and a kinsman's son in 1846 along with two other students.

His mind conditioned by such religious and academic influences, and his inner nature deeply affected by his father's
peculiar personality and death, it is not surprising that young
Lamar appeared thoughtful and intense. He did not mix well
with his classmates and seemed to prefer solitude to society; his
distraction became at times so great that it was mistaken for
moroseness—a charge levied against him all his life.[14]

Hypersensitive toward life's seriousness, Lamar launched into
a four-year course most notable for its comprehensiveness and
classical orientation. Study in Latin and Greek, including history
and the Scriptures, continued for the entire four years. The
English curriculum included grammar and composition with
periodic declamations and "Forensic Disputations." Religious
instruction encompassed the English Bible and "Evidences of
Natural and Revealed Religion." Scientific courses surveyed
geography, chemistry, mineralogy, geology, and natural philosophy. Senior year students also studied history, philosophy, moral
philosophy, intellectual philosophy (psychology and logic), political economy, and applied mathematics.[15]

Young Lamar did not excel as a scholar despite his serious
bent of mind. He did well enough with the classics, which were
his favorites, but fared poorly in mathematics.

Besides formal studies, however, Lamar devoted a good part
of his time and energy to campus debating activities. Stimulated
by innumerable sermons and orations, students joined competing
literary societies in which they attacked questions of the day.
Combined with the forensic requirements of formal courses and
with faculty orations, these speaking activities constituted a
major emphasis.[16]

Lamar not only gained experience in oratory—that most
serious of nineteenth-century pastimes—but in the process was
obliged to study the most compelling issues of his time. The debates often came much closer to real life than anything offered in

14. Mayes, *Lamar,* 29–30.
15. The Statutes of Emory College, 1839 (Emory University Library).
16. Mayes, *Lamar,* 33; Bullock, *A History of Emory University,* 116–19.

the classroom. Here current and vital questions came under the direct scrutiny of enthusiastic would-be political leaders. At Emory, Lamar learned both the art of forceful public speaking and its relationship to practical political questions.[17]

Debating and political discussion at Emory were profoundly affected by Augustus Baldwin Longstreet, president of the college. Speaking with the high authority of minister, college president, and professor, Longstreet unrelentingly espoused a particular religious and political philosophy, and he subordinated all aspects of education to that point of view.

Longstreet argued most vociferously on the slavery question. During the early 1840s he led a movement which culminated with the division of the national Methodist Church, an ominous symptom of growing sectional conflict. While Emory students debated the validity of slavery as an institution before God and mammon, their president fought the effort to make abolitionism an official Church policy. In characteristic language he declared: "Abolition among Churchmen is a mania, a fanatical monster, an insatiable polyphemus, which will tear to pieces and devour everything sacred and all political and religious institutions." [18]

The dispute reached a final crisis in 1844, the year before Lamar's graduation. The General Conference of the Methodist Church attempted to force Bishop James O. Andrew's resignation because he owned slaves. At the time Bishop Andrew also served as president of the Emory College trustees and resided in Oxford. Smarting from a blow struck so close to home, Longstreet led the withdrawal of the Southern Methodists.[19] This highly emotional and dramatic breakdown of a hallowed institution cannot have failed to affect serious minded students.

During this period at Emory, Lamar also began a profoundly

17. For a discussion of Lamar's early development as a public speaker, see Dallas C. Dickey and Donald C. Streeter, "Lucius Q. C. Lamar," in Marie K. Hochmuth (ed.), *A History and Criticism of American Public Addresses* (New York, 1955), III, 183–89

18. John Donald Wade, *Augustus Baldwin Longstreet: A Study of the Development of Culture in the South* (New York, 1924), 267–68, 280; Clement Eaton, *The Freedom of Thought Struggle in the Old South* (New York, 1964), 228.

19. Bullock, *A History of Emory University*, 86; Wade, *Longstreet*, 271–76.

important relationship with Longstreet's daughter Virginia. The courtship culminated with the couple's marriage in July, 1847, two years after Lamar left the college. Lamar joined the family, already so important in his life, and was now assured that his former mentor would continue the role that he had at first played as a teacher. Within a short time Lucius and Virginia Lamar would follow the patriarch to Mississippi to live. There the relationship would immediately provide a status not usually granted to a young and unproven man in a strange community.

For most of the remaining years of Longstreet's life, the two families lived in the same town and frequently even under the same roof. As Lamar's affection for the older man grew, he proclaimed in what is both a tribute to Longstreet and a key to Lamar's personality:

> I am indebted to you for ennobling influences from my boyhood up to middle age. I have doubtless often pained you, but for many years I have loved you as few sons love a father. And many a time in moments of temptation your influence, the desire of your love and approbation, have served me when my virtue might have failed. No applause of the public delights me so much as your declaration that I am unspeakably dear to you.[20]

As Lamar's letter suggests, it is likely that Longstreet reciprocated this affection. The death of Longstreet's own son had deeply saddened him and perhaps brought him closer to Lamar.[21]

---

20. Lamar to A. B. Longstreet, 1859, quoted in Mayes, *Lamar,* 40.

21. Wade, *Longstreet,* 245, 302. Coincidental to Longstreet's father-role, it is interesting to note that he studied law in Litchfield, Connecticut, just a few years before L. Q. C. Lamar, Sr., studied there. And Longstreet preceded the senior Lamar as judge of the Ocmulgee circuit. It is also interesting that Longstreet did preparatory work at the academy in Wilmington, South Carolina, John Calhoun's alma mater, under Moses Waddell. Both Lamar and Longstreet accepted Calhoun as their political mentor. Also, Lamar and Longstreet later taught at the University of Mississippi with John Waddell, son of Moses. Thus a web of influence was spun. See Wade, *Longstreet,* 39, 123–24; Mayes, *Lamar,* 17–18, 38; and Eaton, *Freedom of Thought Struggle,* 229.

Mississippi and Back

Within two years of graduation from Emory in 1845, Lamar made a number of important decisions, several of which affected his entire life. The first decision was to commit himself to a legal career as his father had done. A few months before his twentieth birthday, Lamar moved to Macon, Georgia, to read law in the office of his uncle, A. H. Chappell. The training he received there proved permanently useful. Although Lamar practiced law only intermittently thereafter, his various pursuits required legal knowledge to one degree or another.

Lamar studied two years and then entered into a partnership with Chappell, but the arrangement lasted only a short time. Probably because of sentimental attachment to his childhood home and the nearness of Emory and the Longstreets, Lamar moved to Covington to open his own practice. There he and his wife, Virginia Longstreet, set up housekeeping. Remaining documents do not permit a close assessment of Virginia Longstreet Lamar's influence on her husband's professional and political principles, but apparently she was affectionate and helpful to him especially in times of trouble. The move to Covington also demonstrated Lamar's inclination to stay close to the entire Longstreet family and to be influenced by Virginia's strong-willed father.[1]

1. Mayes, *Lamar*, 37. Little is known of Lamar's efforts in Covington. The tax digest for Newton County (Georgia State Department of Archives and History, Atlanta), shows ownership of five slaves and $3,800 at interest in 1848. In 1849 he reported twelve slaves, eleven acres of land, and $1,010 at interest.

In Covington, Lamar made his second important decision and immediately began a lifetime of partisan political activity. He had useful family connections of his own in this part of Georgia, and the Longstreet influence was at his disposal. A promising political career obviously lay before him if he wanted it. Newton County showed its willingness to encourage whatever ambitions Lamar might cherish by sending him as a delegate to the state Democratic convention in Milledgeville in 1847 and again in 1849. There he mingled with Georgia political stalwarts including Howell Cobb (who had married Lamar's cousin), Joseph E. Brown, and Hershel V. Johnson. In this stimulating company Lamar was confronted by the hottest political issue of the day—the Wilmot Proviso, which if adopted by Congress would forever exclude slavery from territory acquired from Mexico. The conventions of 1847 and 1849 passed strong resolutions against the Wilmot Proviso and other acts which might seek the same objective. Lamar participated wholeheartedly in the impassioned response of the state party. He had embraced politics and had taken an adamantly proslavery position. His attitude did not substantially change during the antebellum period.[2]

Lamar had hardly begun to make his own way politically and professionally when he and his wife decided to move with their infant daughter to Oxford, Mississippi. Ultimate responsibility for this crucial relocation rested with A. B. Longstreet, who had left Georgia to become president of the University of Mississippi in September, 1849. Since Longstreet's other daughter[3] and her husband, Henry Branham, followed the next year, the entire family cast its fate with the relatively young state of Mississippi.[4]

Lamar planned to turn the new situation to his benefit by combining a law practice with university employment. He was licensed as a lawyer in June, 1850, and forthwith presented his

2. Macon *Georgia Telegraph*, July 6, 1847, July 17, 1849; Willie D. Halsell, "Prelude to a Career: L. Q. C. Lamar Tries Politics," *Journal of Mississippi History* VII (April, 1945), 76.

3. Mrs. Frances Branham. Branham was a physician and sometime lawyer.

4. Wade, *Longstreet*, 300; Mayes, *Lamar*, 45.

business card in the local paper.[5] During the next month university trustees elected him assistant professor of mathematics at
an annual salary of eight hundred dollars, and an additional payment of one half the fees he received.[6]

The teacher-lawyer also found enough political excitement to
claim a part of his attention. The compelling issues that he left
behind in Georgia had risen to crisis proportions in Mississippi.
Debate centered on slavery problems, especially the Wilmot Proviso and the question of statehood for California. In October,
1849, before Lamar's arrival, a state convention had met to oppose efforts to halt the spread of slavery and openly threatened
secession. Fiery resolutions protested against northern efforts to
enact the Wilmot Proviso and called for a southern assembly in
Nashville "with a view and hope of arresting the course of aggression." If necessary, they resolved, southern states might establish "a compact of union that would afford protection to their
liberties and rights." [7]

In the interval between the states' rights convention of October, 1849, and the Nashville convention of June, 1850, Lamar
entered Mississippi politics. He addressed a Lafayette County
convention at the Oxford courthouse in May, 1850, in support of
the October resolutions and declared his opposition to California
statehood "with her present constitution" which excluded slavery. The anxious young Mississippian closed with praise for his
adopted state as the first to call a southern convention to counter
the antislavery threat.[8]

The Mississippi states' rights advocates of 1850 were not to
have their way; their solutions proved too extreme at the time for

5. Oxford (Miss.) *Organizer*, July 6, 1850.
6. Florence E. Campbell (transc.), "Journal of the Minutes of the Board of
Trustees of the University of Mississippi, 1845–1860" (M.A. thesis, University of
Mississippi, 1939), 123–24, 128. See also John N. Waddell, *Memorials of Academic
Life* (Richmond, 1891), 458.
7. James W. Garner, "The First Struggle over Secession in Mississippi," *Publications of the Mississippi Historical Society*, IV (1901), 91. Cleo Hearon reprints
the resolutions in "Mississippi and the Compromise of 1850," *Publications of the
Mississippi Historical Society*, XIV (1914), 63–68.
8. Oxford (Miss.) *Organizer*, May 4, 1850.

a majority of the state's population. Long before the Nashville convention, moderates throughout Mississippi and the South began rallying against the threat of secession. Although radical leaders stood fast, compromise was clearly the commanding sentiment. Delegates met and dutifully denounced the conciliatory Compromise of 1850 as well as northern policy. But more importantly, the convention avoided forcing the issue of disunion.[9]

The June crisis passed and the Compromise became law in September, but still unionists and radicals acted out their drama. The struggle in Mississippi hardened when the Congress of the United States voted on the Compromise: Senator Jefferson Davis and the entire Mississippi delegation in the House of Representatives opposed the measure. Senator Henry Foote, on the other hand, ignored the state legislature's instructions and supported the admission of California. When Congress adjourned, the battle continued as a struggle for control of the state. Braving legislative censure, Foote organized the Union party, based upon acceptance of the Compromise, and thus threw down the gauntlet to his antagonists.[10]

Both sides appealed to the people. Lamar joined with Congressman Jacob Thompson[11] and other prominents and toured the county in opposition to Foote. The local campaign climaxed with a bipartisan county convention in Oxford. Lamar answered the Unionists and came down hard on the Unionist rhetoric of the *"stars and stripes, glorious Union, bones of our ancestors, trophies of victory."* [12]

The struggle in Mississippi between resisters and compromisers continued through the winter of 1850–1851. Men of La-

9. Avery Craven, *The Coming of the Civil War* (Chicago, 1966), 259–64, *passim*; Holman Hamilton, *Prologue to Conflict: The Crisis and Compromise of 1850* (New York, 1966), 102.

10. Henry S. Foote, *Casket of Reminiscences* (Washington, 1874), 355–56; John F. H. Claiborne, *Life and Correspondence of John A. Quitman* (New York, 1860), II, 37; Garner, "Struggle over Secession," 93–96.

11. Thompson served in Congress from 1839–51, until defeated by the Union movement. He was later secretary of the interior under President James Buchanan. See "Jacob Thompson," *DAB*, XVIII, 459–60.

12. Oxford (Miss.) *Organizer*, November 2, 9, 16, 1850.

mar's convictions organized as the Southern Rights party (later Democratic States Rights party) which included most of the old Democratic party and a few states' rights Whigs. The opposition took the name Union party and absorbed most of the Whigs and those Democrats who preferred the Compromise to resistance.[13]

Lamar participated actively in the local organization of the Southern Rights party at Oxford in March, 1851, which promptly came out in favor of extremist John A. Quitman as gubernatorial candidate. Presumably Lamar did not object to the nomination, although he could have supported a more moderate candidate such as Jefferson Davis who considered secession a last alternative. The group then chose Lamar, Jacob Thompson, and four others as representatives to the statewide Southern Rights convention in Jackson. As expected, Quitman won the nomination.[14]

A drastic setback, however, forced the Southern Rights party to reorder its strategy. Only a month before the gubernatorial election, delegates were chosen for a state convention on state-federal relations. Moderates won a stunning 7,000 vote majority over extremists, and Quitman felt compelled to resign his candidacy. Jefferson Davis, who denied ever having favored disunion, became the Southern Rights candidate for governor. Secession, Davis believed, constituted the ultimate, but not the immediate, solution. The party then tried to save itself by opposing antislavery encroachments while playing down the secession threat.[15]

When Foote, the Union party nominee, carried his campaign

13. Garner, "Struggle over Secession," 99.
14. Oxford (Miss.) *Constitution*, March 22, May 17, 1851; and Columbus (Miss.) *Democrat*, January 11, 1851, cited in Halsell, "Lamar Tries Politics," 82. See also Memphis *Daily Appeal*, March 12, 1851; and Oxford (Miss.) *Constitution*, April 5, 1851.
15. Hearon, "Mississippi and the Compromise of 1850," 211–12; Garner, "Struggle over Secession," 99–102. Davis wrote letters on November 19, 1850, and on August 22, 1852, denying that he had favored disunion in 1850–51. These may be found, respectively, in *Congressional Globe*, 32nd Cong., 1st Sess., App. 171; and Varina Howell Davis, *Jefferson Davis . . . A Memoir by His Wife* (New York, 1890), I, 471–73. Hearon maintains that only Quitman and a few others favored secession. Davis, A. G. Brown, and Thompson would have supported secession only if by several states and actually believed that the threat of secession would be sufficient.

to northern Mississippi, Lamar faced him as spokesman for the Democratic States Rights party. Davis' poor health severely restricted his canvass, but no record remains to explain why a better known spokesman than Lamar did not appear. Whatever the explanation, the debate provided Lamar with his first political opportunity beyond the county level.[16]

Ignoring the apparent majority in favor of the Compromise, Lamar fastened upon Foote's infidelity to legislative instructions during the recent debate on California and charged that the senator had deserted southern friends and principles. Lamar denied that the election raised the question of union or disunion and charged Foote with forcing that issue. He insisted that "the miscalled compromise questions" constituted the heart of the matter. Lamar's speech was reportedly a devastating success: his students thought so at least and bore him away on their shoulders.[17]

Despite these efforts Lafayette County voted Union in the November election, and Henry S. Foote became governor of the state. The minority with which Lamar had identified had not given up the field, however. They simply acquiesced for the time.[18]

In 1851 L. Q. C. Lamar had made his first political commitment in Mississippi and had found only disappointment. He also grew experienced and made long-term gains in the acquisition of a nascent following. The Oxford *Democratic Flag* felt that he might even be sent to Congress. Unfortunately, this prediction ignored the Union victory over Southern Rights congressman Jacob Thompson in the election just passed.[19] Still it was true that Lamar had made friends with several of the state's most powerful figures. In days to come these men would favor his

16. Garner, "Struggle over Secession," 102; Hearon, "Mississippi and the Compromise of 1850," 215; Mayes, *Lamar*, 51.

17. Mayes, *Lamar*, 51–55. The only extant version of Lamar's speech is quoted, *ibid.*, 51–54.

18. Hearon, "Mississippi and the Compromise of 1850," 226–27.

19. Oxford (Miss.) *Democratic Flag*, May 5, 1852; The *Democratic Flag* article contains Lamar's public letter stating continued devotion to states' rights and the right of secession. See also "Jacob Thompson," *DAB*, XVIII, 459–60.

ambitions. Jacob Thompson, congressman and university trustee, never forgot Lamar's efforts, and Jefferson Davis had every reason to think kindly of him. A future alliance was not unlikely.

While the Compromise crisis rose and ebbed in Mississippi, Lamar contemplated a decisive move in his career. His beginning in Lafayette County was auspicious enough; but almost since his arrival in the state he had been dissatisfied. In letters to Robert Harper, an Emory classmate, Lamar confessed his unhappiness and spoke of his dislike for teaching and of his homesickness for Georgia and his friends. Lamar's attitude toward the classroom is not surprising since the job served principally to supplement his income as a lawyer. Furthermore, he was required to teach mathematics, and as he wrote Harper only a few months after the school term began: "you need have no apprehension of my ever becoming enamoured of Mathematics." In Lamar's judgment of the discipline, "All that is required for its complete mastery is close, *minute* & sustained study; and this *anyone* can give. I have very serious doubts about the beneficial effects upon the mind which its advocates claim for it." And "in my opinion if Newton's THOUGHTS had been compelled to go through the process which is now employed in the *demonstration* of his 'binomial theorem' the world would never have heard of the discovery." [20]

Such sentiments do not seem strange from the moody, distracted lawyer whose chief pleasures in school emanated from the classics and the literary society. That frame of mind never changed; Lamar could never have cheerfully given the "close, *minute* & sustained study" required in an exact science. Nor could he have departed sufficiently from the real world of politics to treat mathematics seriously.

20. Lamar to Robert Harper, December 20, 1850, in Lamar-Harper Letters, Lunsford Collection, Georgia State Department of Archives and History. It may be remembered that mathematics was his poorest subject at Emory. As to his competence, it should be noted that the University of Mississippi required only arithmetic for admission. See *Historical Catalogue of the University of Mississippi, 1849–1909* (Nashville, 1910), 16, hereinafter cited as *Historical Catalogue*.

There were other good reasons for his frustration at the university. The students proved a most unruly group and required constant policing. On November 12, 1850, for instance, a faculty meeting considered action against a student who had thrown a rock at President Longstreet. And on June 9, 1851, Lamar and the others worried over a brawl between two students. It was an interesting case. One student was clearly the aggressor; but, on the other hand, both were guilty of carrying weapons and therefore were deserving of punishment.[21]

Student raucousness could not have made the atmosphere altogether disagreeable. In many respects the university resembled Emory College, which Lamar had left only five years before. Both were religious in orientation. Despite state ownership, the university's faculty included two Christian ministers, Longstreet and John Waddell, and a theologian, A. T. Bledsoe, who also taught mathematics.[22] As at Emory, the curriculum was rigidly defined and easily taught by the 5-man faculty.[23]

Lamar profited from his association with several distinguished members of the Mississippi faculty, and in the last analysis that may have been the most important result of his teaching experience. The significance of Longstreet and trustee Jacob Thompson has been noted already. His colleague, Professor A. T. Bledsoe, would also be a lifelong friend. Although the two did not share a love for mathematics, they had many interests in common; and in many ways their careers were parallel. Lamar and John Waddell would work together again, though in a different

21. Record Book of the Faculty of the University of the State of Mississippi (University of Mississippi Library), 11, 32, hereinafter cited as Faculty Record Book; James A. Cabaniss, *A History of the University of Mississippi* (University, Mississippi, 1949), 25–26; Waddell, *Memorials of Academic Life,* 276.
22. *Historical Catalogue,* 7; Cabaniss, *A History of the University of Mississippi,* 32; "Albert Taylor Bledsoe," *DAB,* II, 364–65.
23. *Historical Catalogue,* 12. President Longstreet taught Mental and Moral Philosophy, Logic, Belles-Lettres, Political Economy, and International Law. A. T. Bledsoe—Mathematics; John Millington—Natural Sciences; John Waddell—Languages. See *ibid.,* 7–9; and Cabaniss, *A History of the University of Mississippi,* 8–10.

relationship, after the Civil War. It was an unusual group of men for a provincial college faculty of five.[24]

The fullness of the Lamar-Longstreet family life in Oxford also figured as an important consideration for Lamar when he thought of leaving the state. He and his wife seemed happy living close to the Longstreets and the Branhams, and there is no record of domestic friction. His brother, Jefferson Mirabeau Lamar, had joined them in Oxford to further enlarge the family circle.[25] Still, Lamar longed for his boyhood home and friends.

Lamar had been in Mississippi only a little over a year when he wrote his friend Robert Harper about "our little scheme" to become law partners in Georgia. Even while he participated in the political struggle over the Compromise of 1850, he was laying plans for his future elsewhere. In March, 1851, he remarked: "Well, my return to Georgia you may now regard as a *fixed fact.*" But the date remained indefinite. Almost a year later, in February, 1852, he wrote: "I have not heard from the Board of Trustees yet. You cannot be more anxious than I am that my return to Georgia should be a speedy one, for I fully appreciate the importance of my being at once in the profession; and I lament that I am not master of my own actions." [26]

In the same letter Lamar explained that he simply had no ambition for achievements in Mississippi whatever their nature. He claimed that he could make his fortune or, if he chose, win a place in Congress. But, he said, "all my patriotism and ambition (these are synonymous words now, are they not?) is [sic] in Georgia."

24. Bledsoe served as a Confederate military officer and then diplomatic agent to Europe. After the war the two men corresponded, but their points of view diverged sharply. Bledsoe edited the important *Southern Review* from 1867–77, making that journal a mouthpiece for the unreconstructed element in the South. Longstreet went on to serve as president of South Carolina College. Waddell was president of the University of Mississippi when Lamar returned there in 1867.

25. *Historical Catalogue,* 117. Jefferson Mirabeau attended the university and graduated in 1853 with honors.

26. Lamar to Robert Harper, December 20, 1850, March 8, 1851, February 8, 1852, in Lamar-Harper Letters. He referred to trouble with the university and to his wife, who was reluctant to leave her family.

Finally Lamar broke from the university, and temporarily leaving his wife with the Longstreets he returned to Georgia during the summer of 1852. In Covington, he and Robert Harper entered into their long-planned partnership. The arrangement was a fortunate one, and the young lawyers prospered. For Lamar circumstances were especially kind since he joined an already established practice in a community where he was well known from former times.[27]

The partnership and friendship transcended fundamental political differences between the two men. Harper had been a Whig, but became a Constitutional Unionist and had run on that ticket for the Georgia legislature in 1851, when the Compromise of 1850 was at issue. The Union party had defeated the Southern Rights party, as it had in Mississippi, and Harper had gone into office with Unionist Governor Howell Cobb.[28] Although Lamar remained loyal to the Democratic party, he was at the time disgusted with it. As he wrote Harper from Mississippi shortly before he left: "My party has quit its principles & is begging to get admission into a National party which we denounced as thoroughly corrupted on the slavery question." In his displeasure Lamar even pledged not to resist the Union party if it "will make amends for its past conduct by repudiating all partys [sic] that will not repudiate free-soilers." [29]

After 1851 the political climate changed sharply in Georgia. The passing of the great crisis allowed union and states' rights partisans to return to their former allegiances. The old Whig group kept the Union party label but could not dissuade the Democratic unionists from departing for their traditional party home. The consequent realignment resulted in the 1853 election

27. Herbert Fielder, *Life, Times and Speeches of Joseph E. Brown* (Springfield, 1883), 67; Mayes, *Lamar*, 56–57.

28. *Journal of the House of Representatives of the State of Georgia, 1851–1852*, p. 5, hereinafter cited as *Georgia House Journal*; U. B. Phillips, *Georgia and State Rights* (Washington, 1902), 166.

29. Lamar to Robert Harper, February 8 [or 5?], 1852, in Lamar-Harper Letters. Lamar put friendship before party when he offered to support Harper for the state senate in August 1852. See Lamar to Harper, August 2, 1853, *ibid.*

of Democrat Hershel V. Johnson as successor to Howell Cobb over the Union candidate, Charles J. Jenkins.[30]

The political tide which had gone against Lamar in Mississippi now flowed in his favor in Georgia. Sensing an opportunity, Lamar considered running for Congress in 1853, but finally decided against it. He explained to one who had counseled him not to make the race that: "Had I been worth $5000 more than I am now worth, I presume I would have yielded to the importunities of friends and the impulses of ambition." [31] These considerations did not apply to the state legislature, however, and Lamar decided to test his political strength on that level. Since Newton County (Covington) traditionally favored the Whig party and had voted Union in 1851,[32] the contest promised a real challenge.

The rugged campaign which followed combined several forms of political exercise indigenous to the time and place. Lamar baited and debated his opponent, and before election time the contest degenerated to a physical level. On one speaking occasion Lamar challenged his hapless rival to quote a disputed portion of the Constitution; and receiving the negative response desired, recited the document from beginning to end.[33] Another time, feeling ran so high that Lamar fought in a manner reminiscent of the frontier tales of A. B. Longstreet's *Georgia Scenes*. As he later recounted, he was knocked down in the Covington courthouse by Frank Nelms, "a big, six-foot country fellow." Three days later Newt Skelton knocked him down again and beat him until "I should have 'hollered' if my Democratic friends had not 'took him off.' " But then Lamar's gentlemanly veneer gave way, and "The next night (in the dark) in the courthouse

30. Phillips, *Georgia and State Rights*, 168–69; I. W. Avery, *The History of the State of Georgia from 1850 to 1881* (New York, 1881), 24–25.

31. Lamar to Bainbridge Troutman, June 26, 1853, in Lamar Letters, Miscellaneous Collection, Emory University Library. Troutman married Lamar's widowed mother in 1851.

32. Richard Harrison Shryock, *Georgia and the Union in 1850* (Durham, 1926), 320, 354.

33. Halsell, "Lamar Tries Politics," 86, citing the New Orleans *Picayune*, October 13, 1894. Considering the date, the story could be apocryphal.

square I whipped Newt. like a sack; but the boys had no idea that I had a small pair of iron tongs in my hands just as the fight started." [34]

Such aggressive response proved remarkably effective. Lamar won election in a county which sent a Whig as his colleague in the legislature and returned a heavy majority for the Whig gubernatorial candidate, Charles J. Jenkins. Statewide, however, Democrats did better. They elected the governor and a majority of the House. This happy circumstance gave Newton County's freshman legislator more influence, especially on committees, than would have been the case in a Whig victory.[35]

Georgia's state-owned railroad, the Western and Atlantic, immediately stimulated conflict in the 1853–1854 session. Outgoing Governor Howell Cobb opened the term with a plea for executive authority to appoint the road's superintendent. Enemies of his proposal, including Lamar, insisted upon legislative prerogative. Cobb's supporters tied up the attempted passage so successfully, however, that the legislature finally conceded.[36]

The state was also under pressure to sell the Western and Atlantic or to charter a private company which could lease the road.[37] Again Lamar sided with the minority and favored leasing the railroad, thereby removing the government from the transportation business.[38] In this attitude he differed from most Democrats. The *Federal Union*, administration organ, opposed

34. Lamar to a friend, May, 1879, quoted in Mayes, *Lamar*, 392. Another account of the fight is given by Halsell, "Lamar Tries Politics," 86, in which Lamar beat Newt with a piece of "waffle-iron" while still in the store.

35. Milledgeville (Ga.) *Federal Union*, October 18, November 22, 29, 1853; *Georgia House Journal, 1853–1854*, pp. 53, 99. Lamar served as chairman of the Committee on the State of the Republic and as member of the Committees on Agriculture and Internal Improvements, Judiciary, and Public Printing. He also chaired a special committee to deal with new counties and served on another to examine the state's inferior courts.

36. *Georgia House Journal, 1853–1854*, pp. 19, 41–43, 48, 66–68, 267–68, 288–89; James Houston Johnston (comp.), *Western and Atlantic Railroad in the State of Georgia* (Atlanta, 1931), 43; Milledgeville (Ga.) *Federal Union*, December 27, 1853.

37. Milledgeville (Ga.) *Federal Union*, December 13, 1853, claimed that this was the big issue of the session. See also U. B. Phillips, *A History of Transportation in the Eastern Cotton Belt to 1860* (New York, 1908), 322–23.

38. *Georgia House Journal, 1853–1854*, pp. 407–408, 559, 591, 602–603.

release of such an economically vital system to a private corporation, but Lamar voted with the Whigs who favored the lease.[39]

In electing a United States senator, the Democrat-dominated legislature dealt with a problem of an entirely different nature. Highly complex party factionalism made the choice difficult and foretold a bitter fight. Since the crisis of 1850–1851, when Union Democrats left the regular organization, there had been considerable confusion. Union Democratic leader Howell Cobb attempted to reconcile the factions in 1853, but with limited success. In the interest of unity Cobb supported states' rights Democrat, Hershel V. Johnson, for the governorship and asked a *quid pro quo* for his own wing of the party. When extreme states' rights men refused to yield the senatorship as a concession, a great struggle ensued.[40]

Lamar's position in this controversy developed from considerations more personal than ideological. In view of his opposition to Foote and the Compromise of 1850 in Mississippi, he might logically have supported a states' rights candidate. Instead he vacillated between two Union men and finally backed Howell Cobb "to the last." Significantly, both Cobb and A. H. Chappell, the other Union contestant, were relatives of the Lamar family. Either Lamar mellowed in his theoretical stance after 1850, or family ties and new political considerations proved more compelling.[41]

Lamar had not been directly involved in the bitter Georgia struggle of 1850–1851, and perhaps his distance from the scene

39. Milledgeville (Ga.) *Federal Union*, December 13, 1853; Phillips, *Transportation*, 322–23; *Georgia House Journal, 1853–1854*, p. 591.

40. Helene Greene, "Politics in Georgia, 1853–54: The Ordeal of Howell Cobb," *Georgia Historical Quarterly*, XXX (September, 1946), 197–98; Horace Montgomery, *Cracker Parties* (Baton Rouge, 1950), 95–101, 109, 116.

41. Lamar to Howell Cobb, September 21, 1853, in Howell Cobb Papers, University of Georgia Library; Lamar to Cobb, December 17, 1856, in U. B. Phillips (ed.), *The Correspondence of Robert Toombs, Alexander H. Stephens, and Howell Cobb*, American Historical Association, *Annual Report, 1911* (Washington, 1913), II, 385; Greene, "Ordeal of Howell Cobb," 200–201; John T. Grant to Howell Cobb, October 28, 1853, in Robert P. Brooks (ed.), "Howell Cobb Papers," *Georgia Historical Quarterly*, VI (March, 1922), 49–50. Phillips, 335–36, includes the letter of September 21, 1853.

made the acceptance of a moderate Union man more palatable. Furthermore, Cobb's cause offered Lamar an opportunity to establish a political importance in the state which his experience had not necessarily earned. Even after the party caucus had repudiated Cobb for a states' rights man, Lamar and other rebellious young Democrats offered continued efforts in behalf of the Cobb faction: "I have put to work here, agencies that will make you the acknowledged & honored leader of the Democracy. I thank God I have some influence here now, & you will see the evidence of it in the next Columbus Sentinel and the Telegraph." This "body of active & earnest young men" had chosen Cobb as its leader and Lamar "insisted on that, as the sine-qua-non." Strange talk for the opponent of Foote! The states' rights advocates won the struggle, however, and Cobb and Lamar ultimately supported the party candidate.[42]

Aside from party politics, the railroad, and the senatorship, Lamar mostly considered the miscellaneous bills which came before his committees. Later in the session, however, routine legislative business was ominously shunted aside while the House unanimously approved a resolution supporting United States Senator Stephen A. Douglas' Nebraska bill.[43] This measure would greatly inflame the sectional debate and would, when passed, repeal the Missouri Compromise and permit slavery in the northern area of the Louisiana Purchase. The issue of slavery in the territories, prominent in all political meetings thus far attended by Lamar, would come up again and again to plague him and the nation.

When the 1853–1854 session ended, Lamar had little cause for dissatisfaction. If the experience was not an especially remarkable one, he had at least completed his legislative indoctrination with dignity and reasonable success. He could expect to be re-

42. Lamar to Howell Cobb, December 3, 1853, in Howell Cobb Papers, University of Georgia Library. See also Lamar to Cobb, December 14, 1853, *ibid.*; Montgomery, *Cracker Parties*, 119–21; *Georgia House Journal, 1853–1854*, pp. 471–72, 476–78.
43. Milledgeville (Ga.) *Federal Union*, February 21, 1854.

turned in the next election or perhaps even aspire to some higher ambition. But Lamar was discontented. Early in the session, on December 3, 1853, he complained that he had accomplished little, and even then he was contemplating a move to some other location.[44]

Several factors contributed to Lamar's state of mind and to his decision to make an important change. Virginia Longstreet Lamar was in Mississippi awaiting the birth of their second child, and loneliness must have contributed to Lamar's dissatisfaction. Prospects were all the more gloomy because of uncertain financial involvements and the approaching end to his law partnership. Lamar had come to Georgia specifically to practice with Harper, an intimate friend, and Harper had become desperately ill. No wonder Lamar considered several possibilities for a new start including removal to Macon or to Columbus, Georgia, or possibly even to Texas.[45]

The legislative term ended in February, 1854, and the following summer Lamar moved to Macon where he opened a law office. The problem of location settled, he traveled to Mississippi in the fall to visit his wife and children (Fannie and the infant Lucius Q. C., Jr.), and transported a number of his slaves to Longstreet, who he felt might engage them more profitably.[46]

Despite these adjustments Lamar's legal career languished, and, as he later recalled, "The year that I lived in Macon I was more straitened in my circumstances than ever before or since, for I got a very small practice." [47]

Financial problems notwithstanding, Lamar launched into the political life of his new district. With support from his relative, former congressman A. H. Chappell, he soon became a strong

44. Lamar to Robert Harper, December 3, 1853, in Lamar-Harper Letters.
45. *Ibid.* Lamar apparently remained uncertain about moving since he asked Harper to see to the building of a new chimney on his house in Covington.
46. Mayes, *Lamar*, 58–59. Lamar to Robert Harper, February 8 [or 5?], 1852, in Lamar-Harper Letters, states that he owned fifteen slaves at that time. Circumstances surrounding the acquisition of these slaves are in doubt. Lamar reported ownership of five slaves on his tax return in 1848 (see note 1).
47. Lamar to John C. Butler, July, 1874, quoted in Mayes, *Lamar*, 200. John C. Butler was Lamar's cousin.

contender for the Democratic nomination for Congress.[48] By the spring of 1855 he felt certain of sufficient support to win the nomination unless some other aspirant packed the convention. On March 7, 1855, he wrote Longstreet for his advice: "Now what do you think? Stick to my profession and try to make something, or go to Congress if I can and be in the fight against the free-soilers? The next Congress will be an exciting one, you know." [49]

In considering the candidacy, Lamar and his friends had relied upon reports that the incumbent, David J. Bailey, would not seek renomination. When this information proved erroneous, Lamar asked that he not be considered. At the nominating convention held on May 22, 1855, in Forsyth, Georgia, Bailey deadlocked for three ballots with a challenger, a Mr. Ramsey. At that point Ramsey withdrew and Lamar's name was put forward, and he in turn deadlocked with Bailey for ten ballots. It appeared that Lamar might win, since at one time he received two thirds of the vote cast. The convention decided, however, that the two-thirds rule referred not to the number voting but to the number of delegates. Finally, on the seventeenth ballot a compromise candidate, James M. Smith, received the nomination.[50]

Lamar was disappointed, but he dutifully campaigned for the Democratic ticket in the fall election. The district, nevertheless, voted for the American candidate, Robert P. Trippe, and sent him to Congress to replace Bailey. Again the political tide had turned from Lamar. The third district Democrats had every

48. Chappell had some claim to political influence since he was a former member of the Georgia house and senate and the national House. See *Biographical Directory of the American Congress* (Washington, 1961), 683. Lamar had supported Chappell for the United States senatorship before finally backing Howell Cobb. Lamar had many other contacts in Macon including relatives John T. Lamar, a wealthy merchant, and John B. Lamar, a planter. G. B. Lamar owned a bank in Macon. See William T. Jenkins, "Ante Bellum Macon and Bibb County, Georgia" (Ph.D. dissertation, University of Georgia, 1966), 198, 205–206, 233.

49. Lamar to A. B. Longstreet, March 7, 1855, quoted in Mayes, *Lamar*, 58. Longstreet's answer is unknown.

50. Macon *Georgia Journal and Messenger*, May 30, 1855; Macon *Georgia Telegraph*, May 22, 1855. Lamar represented Bibb County at the Democratic state convention that year. See Macon *Georgia Telegraph*, June 12, 1855.

reason to be distressed by this particular defeat, since their state organization had retained the governorship and had won six of the eight congressional seats.[51]

Almost immediately after the election Lamar left Georgia for Mississippi, this time to stay. His decision to leave Macon after only one year there marked a milestone in his career. The circumstances which caused this decision seem clear. Political disappointment certainly played a part; and it will be recalled that his departure from Mississippi in 1852 and his move from Covington in 1854 had political overtones. His finances were in a poor condition and his law practice small. His wife, children, and slaves were all with Longstreet. In sum, there were many reasons for going to Mississippi and few for remaining in Georgia. An indifferent success in politics and law at age thirty, Lamar gave up his native state for the last time and headed back to the family which represented security and stability.

51. Macon *Georgia Journal and Messenger*, October 10, 1855; Halsell, "Lamar Tries Politics," 89–90; Montgomery, *Cracker Parties*, 152–53. See also Jenkins, "Ante Bellum Macon," 310.

Congress: Sowing the Bitter Fruit

The move to Mississippi began a new career. Rather than return to Oxford, Lamar established Solitude plantation twelve miles north of town on the Tallahatchie River. Lamar's retirement to the country also paralleled the relocation of his wife's family. Longstreet, who speculated in land in addition to his educational endeavors, sold Lamar the land on credit, and Longstreet himself moved to the hamlet of Abbeville, just two miles from the plantation. The Branhams (Longstreet's other daughter and her husband) joined the Lamars at Solitude.[1]

For a time Lamar participated directly in the plantation tradition. Although his flirtation with the southern idyll was brief, and only nominal after 1857, the interlude still has some significance. It enhanced Lamar's association with a tradition which previously had been his only by implication. Identification with the symbol which most accurately expressed the southern ideal

1. Complications surround the ownership of the plantation. Lands were deeded to Lamar and M. M. McEachin by Longstreet four years later in 1860. Apparently some less formal arrangement sufficed until then. See A. B. Longstreet to Lamar and McEachin, September 21, 1860, in Deed Book I, 594, Lafayette County Courthouse, Oxford, Mississippi; and L. Q. C. and Virginia Lamar to McEachin, December 1, 1860, *ibid.*, 596. These deeds suggest that Lamar became only half owner of a 984-acre tract in 1860, and that the Lamar-McEachin partnership underwent several alterations thereafter. Lamar finally reconveyed his share in Lamar to A. B. Longstreet, January 19, 1866, in Deed Book K, 367, *ibid.*, in satisfaction of his part of the original $5,000 debt on the 984 acres. Mayes, *Lamar*, 60, states that Dr. Branham was interested in the farm with Lamar, but no evidence has been discovered to confirm this. Lamar reported the land as his own in the census of 1860. On Longstreet's retirement from the university and his move see Wade, *Longstreet*, 310–13.

was no small asset, and it did not diminish as the actual experience receded into the past. Years later, Lamar's son-in-law, Edward Mayes, described life at Solitude in terms few would have
challenged: "It was the life of the Southern farmer of the highest type." Lamar was "surrounded by his slaves, to whom he was
at once master, guardian, and friend, loved and petted by his
women folk and his children, visited by cultivated and attractive
friends." [2]

While Mayes's description is somewhat romantic, Solitude did
place Lamar among Lafayette County's leading citizens. The
plantation consisted of about one thousand acres, large enough
to rank Lamar among the 11 percent who owned almost half the
county's land. The 26 slaves he owned in 1857 also qualified
Lamar as an aristocrat. The census returns of 1860 show that of
the 605 slaveowners in the county only 42 fell within Lamar's
class (15–30 slaves) while 50 owned more than 30 slaves each,
and 5 owned between 100 and 200.[3]

Since Lamar actively directed his plantation for only a short
period of time, its potential was never fully realized. The slaves
must have been employed primarily in land improvement and
in making the plantation self-sufficient. Lamar's success is difficult to gauge, but certainly he never became one of Lafayette
County's important producers, and Lafayette was not one of the
state's richer counties. By 1860, only two hundred acres had been
cleared; his slaves harvested only one thousand bushels of Indian corn and forty-three bales of cotton in addition to lesser
staples for home consumption.[4] Moreover, Lamar never came

2. Mayes, *Lamar*, 60.
3. Production of Agriculture in the County of Lafayette, from the "Original
Census Returns, 1860," in Lamar Subject File, Mississippi State Department of Archives and History, Jackson, Mississippi, hereinafter cited as MDAH; Personal Tax
Rolls, Lafayette County, Mississippi, 1857, MDAH; John Cooper Hathorn, "A Period
Study of Lafayette County from 1836 to 1860" (M.A. thesis, University of Mississippi, 1939), 85–86, 107–109.
4. Production of Agriculture in the County of Lafayette, from the "Original
Census Returns, 1860," in Lamar Subject File, MDAH. Hathorn, "Lafayette County,"
lists Lamar's acreage and production in Appendix B, 216.

close to retiring the debt on his property.[5] These facts indicate that he held a tenuous status as an antebellum planter.

The management of Solitude did not fully occupy Lamar, and he found sufficient time to practice law in nearby Holly Springs, seat of Marshall County. He joined two locally prominent lawyers to establish the firm of Lamar, Mott, and Autrey, an arrangement which proved durable until the outbreak of the Civil War. The association offered Lamar the possibility of political as well as pecuniary gain. C. M. Mott had served in the state legislature in 1850, and then as probate judge. James L. Autrey was a member of the state house of representatives during the years 1854–1859, and had been speaker of the house.[6]

Lamar doubtless had politics on his mind. The presidential campaign of 1856 revolved around the crucial question of slavery expansion into the United States territories. The newly formed and exclusively northern Republican party strenuously advocated congressional rather than popular control over the fate of slavery in the territories, while the Democrats disputed this contention. This national issue had radically changed circumstances in Mississippi and Lamar knew it. The states' rights philosophy which had been decisively rejected in 1850–1851 had again gained credence throughout the state. When Lamar emerged from the obscurity of Solitude, his political past proved a definite asset, not a handicap. Wrong in the Foote-Davis campaign was politically right by 1856. As he wrote Howell Cobb: "I made four or five speeches during the campaign [1856] and they took well. I think I shall be able to get pretty much what I please from the people out here." [7]

5. Lamar to "Jimmy" [James G. Paine], [1866?], in L. Q. C. Lamar Letters, Southern Historical Collection, University of North Carolina Library. Lamar wrote: "I owed Judge Longstreet for my land on which he had been paid 30 bales of cotton at 10 cts (he saved 13 of them getting 22½ cents for them) but the interest during the war ate that payment up & restored the debt to its original amount." Lamar reconveyed the land after the war.

6. For a sketch on Autrey, see Dunbar Rowland (ed.), *Mississippi: Comprising Sketches of Counties, Towns, Events, Institutions, and Persons, Arranged in Cyclopedic Form* (Atlanta, 1907), I, 176. On Mott, see *ibid.*, II, 284.

7. Lamar to Howell Cobb, December 17, 1856, in Phillips (ed.), *Correspondence*

Improvement of Democratic prospects in Lamar's congressional district[8] was in fact only a return to the prevailing norm. As early as 1840 Mississippi had taken on fairly permanent party divisions based largely on economic and geographic determinants. While the Black Belt area became unequivocally attached to the Whig party and its political descendants, the less wealthy and predominantly white eastern half of the state aligned with the Democratic party. This numerically unequal division insured statewide Democratic political power.[9]

The crisis born victory of the Constitutional Union party in 1851 quickly dissipated, and the old alignment again characterized Mississippi politics. As a result of the Compromise of 1850, Democrats had publicly accepted the principle of Union and backed away from secession. This maneuver undercut the Union coalition. Even before the debates over slavery in Kansas raised a furor, the Compromise leaders lost control. The Kansas-Nebraska issue destroyed the Whig party, and old Whigs in flight from ruin joined the impotent Know-Nothing organization.[10]

The 1856 presidential election showed how completely the Whig–Know-Nothings had been displaced in Mississippi and throughout the South. James Buchanan carried Mississippi by a majority of 11,265 votes (59 percent) while losing only the Mississippi–Yazoo River Black Belt counties to Millard Fill-

---

of Toombs, Stephens, and Cobb, 385. On Lamar's rather limited speaking schedule see Oxford (Miss.) Signal, September 11, 1856.

8. At this time the first district included: Tishomingo, Tippah, Marshall, Desoto, Tunica, Coahoma, Panola, Lafayette. These counties stretched entirely across northern Mississippi and were representative of an area graduating from Black Belt delta counties to the hilly, predominantly white northeast. See James E. Baxter, "Congressional Redistricting in Mississippi from 1817 to 1938" (M.A. thesis, Duke University, 1938), 53.

9. Percy L. Rainwater, Mississippi, Storm Center of Secession, 1856–1861 (Baton Rouge, 1938), 3–15. Between 1840 and 1860 Lamar's district voted Democratic with the single exception of the Compromise election of 1851. Lafayette County (Oxford) never voted Whig or American in a presidential election after 1840.

10. In the Mississippi gubernatorial election of 1853 the Democrats easily returned to power. See returns provided by Inter-University Consortium for Political Research (Ann Arbor, Michigan), hereinafter cited as Political Research Consortium.

more.[11] The continued emphasis on the slavery issue convinced the majority that the Democratic party alone offered a reliable defense of southern rights. Slavery had by that time become more sacred than party.

Under these circumstances it was by no means a small matter when Democratic Congressman Daniel Wright of the first district decided not to run for renomination in 1857. The vacancy created the opportunity that caused Lamar to turn away from the life of planter-lawyer and to reject the professorial seat which the university again made available. He decided to try for the nomination.[12]

The vacuum created by Wright's withdrawal left the Democratic organization in a turmoil. As early as March 15, 1857, the Memphis *Daily Appeal* mentioned Lamar as a possible candidate. Then in June his political stock rose as Lafayette County Democrats nominated him for the state legislature. When the congressional nominating convention met at Holly Springs on July 6 and 7, however, Lamar's name did not appear until the eighteenth ballot. Little support materialized and he withdrew four rounds later. After fifty-six indecisive ballots he was again offered to the convention, but received only six votes. Then in the face of what seemed an interminable deadlock, the leading contenders withdrew, the count was completed, and Lamar was chosen.[13]

The political considerations involved in Lamar's nomination are by no means clear. From preconvention accounts in the Memphis *Daily Appeal*, it appears that objections were made to Lamar from the beginning on the grounds that Lafayette County had had more than its share of congressmen. Although the newspapers did not say so, the fact that Lamar had recently returned from an abortive try at Georgia politics may also have disturbed

11. Figures provided by Political Research Consortium.
12. Memphis *Daily Appeal*, April 14, 1857; Mayes, *Lamar*, 63.
13. Memphis *Daily Appeal*, March 15, 20, April 14, 18, 23, July 18, 1857; Mayes, *Lamar*, 70–71. Lamar's early support came from the *Daily Appeal* which probably had a larger circulation in northern Mississippi than any other paper. Lamar was always a great favorite of that journal from 1857 onward.

some. According to his son-in-law, however, the chief objection lay elsewhere. Mayes was at least partially correct in maintaining that the crucial factor was Lamar's kinship with Howell Cobb of Georgia.[14] Lamar had been a political friend of Cobb's and had supported him for the United States Senate despite Cobb's leadership of the Union movement during the controversy over the Compromise of 1850. Many Southern Rights men opposed Buchanan's decision to include Cobb in his cabinet and blamed Cobb for the president's failure to immediately secure the admission of Kansas as a slave state. Lamar felt the effect of his relationship to Cobb and seemed defensive when he wrote him in July, 1857, only a week after the Mississippi convention had chosen its candidate. "The cloud," he said, "which obscures *your* prospects will ever cast its shadow over mine." [15]

Lamar's nomination appears, then, to have resulted only from a deadlock and to have occurred in spite of his serious political shortcomings. Although the full story is unknown, Lamar later credited his old friend and former congressman Jacob Thompson with having much to do with the nomination.[16] From these peculiar and not especially flattering circumstances Lamar had his first real chance at a political career.

Nomination in hand, Lamar took to the stump in his district to campaign against his Whig opponent, James Lusk Alcorn. The two men, who were on friendly terms, conducted a joint canvass with almost daily speeches distinguished by the enthusiastic oratory for which both were known. Alcorn stressed the danger of foreign suffrage in the United States and opposed the Kansas-Nebraska bill. Lamar linked Alcorn with the Know-Nothing party (with which he never actually professed affilia-

14. Mayes, *Lamar*, 70.
15. Lamar to Howell Cobb, July 17, 1857, in Howell Cobb Papers. The letter is published in Phillips (ed.), *Correspondence of Toombs, Stephens, and Cobb*, 405–406.
16. Lamar to Mrs. Annie Crawford, April 1, 1885, in Letterbook I, Lamar-Mayes Papers, MDAH. Thompson's death inspired the letter. Cate, *Lamar*, 51–52, gives a highly romantic story of Thompson's naming of Lamar as his choice and the spontaneous approval which followed; but this seems highly unlikely in view of the large number of ballots required.

ation) and spoke strongly in favor of the Kansas-Nebraska bill.[17]

In 1857 the Democratic hold on Mississippi was such that the election results were never in question. Alcorn fully realized this when he undertook the campaign as a Whig and claimed that he only ran as a means of keeping his career alive until a better day.[18] The Democrats carried the governorship and all the congressional seats. Lamar's majority in the first district was a comfortable one.[19]

This victory launched Lamar's political career. He would be secure as long as sectional politics prevented a Whig revival; and that, of course, proved to be the case until Mississippi seceded in 1861. In 1859, Lamar won his party's renomination without challenge; the opposition did not trouble to enter a candidate against him in the election.[20]

The move to Washington and into the vortex of political life must have been an exciting one for Lamar and his family. There he enjoyed his first taste of society outside a small southern town. And for the first time Lamar was really a man among men—a person of importance by the standards of the South and of the Lamar heritage. Contemporaries thought Lamar imposing enough for his new role. A newspaper vignette described him as "a rather tall and full figure . . . with a large high forehead bulging out over his face, long, sleek and plentiful brown hair, combed back behind his ears, a reddish-brown beard only

17. Memphis *Daily Appeal*, August 12, September 10, 13, 15, 1857; Lillian A. Pereyra, *James Lusk Alcorn: Persistent Whig* (Baton Rouge, 1966), 34–36. Pereyra, 36, observes that the most notable difference between the two men revolved around their dissimilar appeal. Alcorn's demeanor was that of the aristocrat; while Lamar appeared in homespun jeans and a wrinkled shirt driving a mule and cart. There is no other evidence that Lamar's appeal was geared to this level.

18. James Lusk Alcorn to Amelia Alcorn, September 9, 1857, quoted in Pereyra, *James Lusk Alcorn*, 35.

19. Returns are available for all counties in the district except Tishomingo; the vote for the other seven counties gave Lamar 3,705 to Alcorn's 2,888. The Democrats carried the governorship 27,377 to 14,095 and easily won all congressional seats. Figures provided by Political Research Consortium.

20. Memphis *Daily Appeal*, June 21, October 11, 1859.

shaved on the upper lip, blue eyes with a red tinge in them." [21] And his past connections in Georgia and Mississippi assured that he would be welcomed upon the scene by some of the most influential men in Washington, including Howell Cobb and Jacob Thompson, both of the cabinet, and his kinsman John A. Campbell of the Supreme Court.[22]

Lamar and his wife joined several notables and their wives in residence at Brown's Hotel. The group included Congressmen Orr and Chesnut of South Carolina; Fitzpatrick, Shorter, Dowdell, Clopton, Curry, and Clay of Alabama; Taylor and Sandrige of Louisiana; and Pugh of Ohio.[23] In these surroundings Lamar built a reputation as champion of the drawing room. One of the wives, Mrs. C. C. Clay, observed "that no member of our pleasant circle was more generally valued than the most lovable of men, Lucius Q. C. Lamar, 'Moody Lamar,' as he was sometimes called; for he was . . . full of dreams and ideals and big, warm impulses, with a capacity for the most enduring and strongest friendships, and a tenderness rarely displayed by men so strong as was he. Mr. Lamar was full of quaint and caressing ways even with his fellow-men. . . . I have seen him walk softly up behind Mr. Clay . . . touch him lightly on the shoulder, and as my husband turned quickly to see what was wanted 'Lushe' . . . would kiss him suddenly and lightly on the forehead." [24]

Perhaps the effeminate sensitivity described by Mrs. Clay had unfortunate consequences for Lamar. When his wife was not in Washington he felt lonely for his family and frustrated by the seeming insolubility of vital sectional problems. In his unhappiness Lamar applied to Chancellor F. A. P. Barnard of the University of Mississippi for a faculty position. He promptly received an offer but for some unexplained reason did not accept it until

21. New York *Times*, December 26, 1859.
22. Lamar's relationship with Cobb, however, appears to have been strained temporarily because of the Kansas question. See Lamar to Howell Cobb, July 17, 1857, in Howell Cobb Papers.
23. Mrs. Clement C. Clay, *A Belle of the Fifties* (New York, 1889), 43–45.
24. *Ibid.*, 48.

1860. Meantime he went his way as freshman congressman and fledgling spokesman for the southern point of view.[25]

The role of southern advocate dominated Lamar's antebellum congressional career. In his initial address to the House, Lamar proclaimed his commitment to southern rights, and thereafter he remained constant. Obviously considering his singlemindedness to be a virtue he declared: "Others may boast of their . . . comprehensive love of this Union. With me, I confess that the promotion of Southern interests is second in importance only to the preservation of Southern honor." [26] He meant it too. The line between North and South had been in the drawing since before Lamar's birth, and objective examination of sectional issues had ceased before he reached manhood. Defense of the South required a simple extension of his education and experience into the halls of Congress.

During the Thirty-fifth and Thirty-sixth Congresses Lamar made seven speeches, four on explicitly sectional questions. The three speeches not directly related to sectionalism comprised a major address on the tariff,[27] brief comments on an antipolygamy bill,[28] and lengthy remarks on the disputed election of C. L. Vallandigham of Ohio.[29] Except for the Vallandigham debate, even these topics had sectional overtones for Lamar. He believed that the tariff should continue to be low. Although this viewpoint reflected party principle, in Lamar's application any effort at upward revision became a conspiracy of manufacturers

25. Lamar to Mrs. A. B. Longstreet, May 4, 1858, quoted in Mayes, *Lamar,* 76; Lamar to Mrs. Lamar, [about May, 1858], quoted *ibid.*; F. A. P. Barnard to Lamar, March 25, 1858, quoted *ibid.*, 77–78. The Longstreet family at this time lived in Columbia, South Carolina, where Longstreet was president of South Carolina College.

26. *Congressional Globe,* 35th Cong., 1st Sess., 279–81. *Ibid.*, App., 49–53, reprints the entire speech.

27. *Congressional Globe,* 35th Cong., 2nd Sess., App., 199–203.

28. New York *Times,* April 4, 1860; New York *Tribune,* April 4, 1860. *Congressional Globe,* 36th Cong., 1st Sess., 1515, indicates that Lamar was to record his speech in the appendix after revision, although apparently he failed to do so.

29. *Congressional Globe,* 35th Cong., 1st Sess., 2331–36. Lamar was a member of the Committee on Elections. This accounts for his special interest in Vallandigham at this time.

against the farmer and planter. Straining his sectionalism somewhat, Lamar linked the slavery issue to a bill to suppress Mormon polygamy. He admitted that Congress possessed full power
to prevent polygamy or any other felony in the territories, but
warned Republicans against using this interpretation to inter-
fere with slavery.

Lamar's voting record in the House suggests the same preoccupation with sectional and party considerations as his speeches. Increasing identification of the Republican party with the North
and the Democratic party with the South meant that sectional
interest and party regularity became one and the same thing.
Although conspicuously derelict in answering roll calls, Lamar
voted often enough to establish a record of strong party regularity.[30] His propensity for regularity, however, did not indicate
any special lack of party independence. In fact, he departed from
party and sectional norms more frequently than many of his
colleagues, though the departures were not significant.[31]

According to Lamar's value system and that of many others,
the question of the expansion of slavery into the territories
eclipsed all current issues because of the immediate challenge
to southern status. The issue of Kansas statehood epitomized the
conflict. The controversy raged all during the summer preceding Lamar's election in the fall of 1857. During his campaign
he had opposed the actions of Robert Walker as territorial governor because Walker made clear his opinion that slavery could
not thrive in Kansas and that its protection in the proposed state
constitution was not of great importance. Lamar's reaction was

30. A sampling of 180 votes shows that Lamar was absent or abstained on
seventy-three questions. He departed from party discipline only eight times in
the 107 sample votes, seven times in the 35th Congress and once in the 36th Congress. These figures and conclusions are derived by checking Lamar's vote in the
House Journal against the sample roll calls given in Thomas B. Alexander, *Sectional Stress and Party Strength* (Nashville, 1967), 243–47, 256–58.

31. Alexander, *Sectional Stress and Party Strength*, 102, 106, provides scalograms
which make it possible to locate Lamar's relative position by comparing the
vote of his own and other sections. The reliability of the comparison is somewhat
mitigated by Lamar's failure to answer many roll calls. In Alexander to author,
October 6, 1967, Lamar is reported to hold scale position 1 on both of the
scalograms.

similar to that of Jefferson Davis, Jacob Thompson, and members of the Mississippi state convention, all of whom condemned Walker's plan to submit a constitution to the people for ratification. The outcome, they realized, might well be unfavorable.[32]

In December, 1857, after Buchanan arbitrarily decided to support a proslavery constitution, Walker quit his office. The southern element in Kansas then obtained ratification (with free-state people abstaining) of the Lecompton constitution guaranteeing slavery as a basis for admission to statehood. Lamar strongly supported admission with the controversial constitution, and in long speeches before the House and before Mississippi audiences he attacked Republicans and anti-Lecompton Democrats in the North for their recalcitrance. The Kansas issue, he claimed, was inseparably tied to the general history of slavery in the territories. Opposition to the Lecompton constitution "is but an offshoot of that damnable policy which has been preying upon the vitals of the South for the last forty years." [33] A piecemeal surrender by the South in the territories would not, in his opinion, bring lasting peace. The lesson of time was clear enough: the Missouri Compromise had served only as an interlude before the same issue arose in relation to the Mexican cession. The South had given way again and admitted California as a free state. That surrender marked for Mississippians a line beyond which they would not submit to free-soil aggression.[34]

Speaking before the House on January 13, Lamar went far beyond this historical argument. He tediously dealt with technical and legal questions surrounding admission to statehood and concluded that popular ratification of the Lecompton constitution as demanded by antislavery forces was unnecessary. Claiming an analogy between the convention at Lecompton and that

---

32. Lamar to Howell Cobb, July 17, 1857, in Howell Cobb Papers; Memphis *Daily Appeal*, September 15, 1857; Pereyra, *James Lusk Alcorn*, 34–35; R. F. Nichols, *The Disruption of American Democracy* (New York, 1962), 122–23.

33. *Congressional Globe*, 35th Cong., 1st Sess., 279–81, App., 49–53, contains a much longer version of the speech.

34. Speech given by Lamar to the Mississippi legislature, November 3, 1858, quoted in Mayes, *Lamar*, 618–20.

which drew up the United States constitution of 1787, he declared that "the authority of the people is fully recognized, the popular sovereignty, as a principle, is fully enforced, when an opportunity is afforded to the legal voters to deposit their vote for delegates to a constitutional convention." Lamar's legalistic evasion of the fact that a majority in Kansas actually favored free-state status also carried a barb, and he ominously warned Congress: "You may reject her application if you will, but it will be at your own peril." [35]

About two weeks after Lamar's speech and after much pressure had been brought by southern Democrats the president decided to force congressional acceptance of Kansas statehood with slavery. Although opposed by anti-Lecompton Democrats as well as by Republicans, Buchanan determined to drive the bill through at all costs and thus, he believed, to remove the issue from politics before the next presidential election.[36]

A mighty struggle followed between supporters and opponents of the bill. Taking advantage of a temporary majority in the closely divided House, anti-Lecompton forces pushed for a vote. Lamar and the advocates of admission with the Lecompton constitution countered by filibustering. The resulting standoff continued throughout the night of February 5, until adjournment after six o'clock on the morning of February 6, 1858.[37]

Respite must have been welcomed by the weary participants. Nerves and composure had completely broken at about two o'clock on the morning of February 6, when Galusha Grow of Pennsylvania testily objected to a proposition offered by John Quitman of Mississippi. This precipitated a fist fight which quickly turned into a general melee. Lamar paired off with Owen Lovejoy of Illinois. Some accounts state that the two men fought with gusto; others report that they "were pawing each

35. *Congressional Globe*, 35th Cong., 1st Sess., 279–81, App., 49–53. On Lamar's opposition to popular ratification see also Lamar to Howell Cobb, July 17, 1857, in Howell Cobb Papers.

36. Nichols, *The Disruption of American Democracy*, 163–64.

37. *Journal of the House of Representatives of the United States* (hereinafter cited as *House Journal*), 35th Cong., 1st Sess., 306–40.

other at one point—each probably trying to persuade the other to be still." [38] Another Mississippian, William Barksdale, went to the aid of Lamar and Quitman and became the only real casualty. When a Republican grabbed Barksdale's hair to set him up for a blow, the Mississippian's hair piece came off. Since few knew that Barksdale wore a wig, this occurrence put the House into a better mood. According to one account, the wig was thrown into the crowd and trampled while the poor man struggled to get it back. Another story says that Barksdale got his wig back, but in his frustration put it on wrong side out. [39]

Despite the delay, House administration leaders ultimately lost control of the bill. Lamar, for his part, voted for admission with the Lecompton constitution and a guarantee of the state's right to amend it at some later date. Assurances for the future proved inadequate and the effort failed. Lamar then opposed a move to submit the question to a new popular referendum and again he voted with the minority. Anticipating the House decision to require popular ratification in Kansas, the administration planned to rely upon a friendly House-Senate conference committee, which would reconcile the House bill with the pro-Lecompton senate version. Lamar supported the move to send the measure on to the committee. [40]

By this time Buchanan realized that Kansas could not be admitted without submitting the constitution to the people. Consequently a compromise measure—the English bill—emerged, allowing the president and southerners to save face while giving the substance of victory to the opposition. The English bill, named for William English, a moderate Indiana Democrat, would not allow the people of Kansas to vote on the provisions protecting slavery, but they could accept or reject the constitution as a whole. If they rejected it, admission to the

---

38. New York *Times*, February 8, 1858; New York *Tribune*, February 8, 1858.

39. See New York *Times*, February 8, 1858; New York *Tribune*, February 8, 1858; and Nichols, *The Disruption of American Democracy*, 165.

40. *House Journal*, 35th Cong., 1st Sess., 573–81, 618–20; Nichols, *The Disruption of American Democracy*, 167, 169, 173.

Union would be postponed without further congressional action for the time. Pushed hard by cabinet members, especially
Lamar's friends Cobb and Thompson, the Democrats accepted
the bill. Lamar himself acquiesced in the compromise and assisted in the crucial fight against delaying tactics. Defection was
limited to the staunchest Douglas supporters and extreme southern fire-eaters, including Lamar's colleague Quitman of Mississippi, who refused to compromise. Lamar at this point stayed
away from the radical position and voted for the conference
measure.[41]

Lamar's unwillingness to push the Kansas fight further actually demonstrated only slight flexibility on the slavery issue.
When the Kansas issue was most critical, very few southern
Democrats voted more consistently than Lamar for the proslavery position. His acceptance of the administration's policy probably reflected cabinet pressure coupled with dread of the dire
consequences threatened by Quitman.[42]

This mildly compromising attitude also showed in Lamar's
position toward foreign territorial acquisitions in areas where
chattel slavery might prosper. Though sympathetic with the impulse toward expansion into Mexico, Central America, and the
Caribbean, he nevertheless opposed filibustering activities and
supported enforcement of neutrality laws. Lamar would gladly
see "American liberty, with Southern institutions, upon every
inch of American soil," but he believed that expansion should
await final settlement of the slavery question in the United
States.[43] On the related question of reopening foreign slave
trade, Lamar stopped short of an extreme position favoring the

41. *House Journal*, 35th Cong., 1st Sess., 693–94, 719–21.
42. For a profile of the vote on slavery issues in the 35th Congress, 1st session,
see Alexander, *Sectional Stress and Party Strength*, 101. In Alexander to author,
October 6, 1967, Lamar is reported to hold scale position 1 on the scalogram.
43. *Congressional Globe*, 35th Cong., 1st Sess., 279–81. See also an address of
November 11, 1859, before the Mississippi legislature as reported in the Vicksburg
Whig, and quoted in Mayes, *Lamar*, 80. Lamar nevertheless voted to condemn
the arrest of filibusterer William Walker. See *House Journal*, 35th Cong., 2nd
Sess., 169–70.

trade but condemned northern meddling as part of the scheme to destroy slavery.[44]

It is significant that Lamar's treatment of domestic and foreign expansion dwelt upon the right rather than the likelihood of taking slaves beyond established confines of the plantation economy. In this respect his approach was an essentially negative one. He made no contribution to the vision of a great slave empire in South America nor to that of renewed southern domination in national affairs. His position was defensive, and he fell back ultimately on the threat that the South would secede rather than retreat further.[45]

The aggressiveness of the North's attack on slavery drove southern politicians to justify their "peculiar institution." Debate therefore sometimes transcended the purely economic and political issues at stake in Kansas and entered the more ethereal realms of philosophy and morality. Lamar clearly understood that majority opinion in the nation despised slavery in these terms, and the realization forced him again into an essentially negative kind of rhetoric. On February 21, 1860, in his only defense of slavery as an institution, he sadly admitted that "a moral sentiment thus diffused among the majority . . . will work itself out into practical action, and the law . . . must yield before it or be overborne by it." [46] Such a completely fatalistic appraisal meant that Lamar himself assumed that his arguments would do little to resolve the issues. Still he felt compelled to speak.

To the charge that slavery was incompatible with revered Revolutionary principles, Lamar replied, rather lamely, that men are not created equal. His lengthy catalog of groups inferior to

44. *Congressional Globe*, 36th Cong., 1st Sess., 228–29. Because of the sectional overtones of the question he voted with the South against expanding the prohibitive acts. See *House Journal*, 36th Cong., 1st Sess., 1008–1009.

45. Henry Nash Smith suggests that of all symbols developed by the South to express the ideal ends of slavery the only one with real depth revolved around the development of a Caribbean slave empire. Lamar exploited this symbol to only a slight degree, if at all. See Henry Nash Smith, *Virgin Land: The American West as Symbol and Myth* (New York, 1950), 165–76.

46. *Congressional Globe*, 36th Cong., 1st Sess., App., 113–17.

freemen included felons, minors, and women. The subordinate status of children and criminals was obvious enough; and he included woman because of her "consecration to those high and noble responsibilities which unfit her for the exercise of political rights." So, as Lamar argued by inference, the principle of natural equality was specious and inapplicable to the uncivilized Negro. Since his answer depended more on logic than on philosophy, such tactics merely underscored the fact that Lamar was essentially an orator and a propagandist rather than an original thinker.

Lamar's apology also fell back on the greatest authority known to the South—the Christian Church and its Bible. The use of spiritual authority added nothing new, but his approach was mildly ingenious in its irony. Instead of citing the biblical text, Lamar gave his antagonists "the language of a learned Northern divine . . . whose book on moral science is the textbook of your Northern colleges, academies, and schools." In quoting Dr. Francis Wayland's *The Elements of Moral Science* as proof that the Bible justified slavery, Lamar acted as a polemicist rather than as a scholar. Wayland had, in fact, concluded that while slavery could be justified by scriptural evidence, Providence had nonetheless intended it as a temporary expedient.

Lamar's argument contained positive claims for the South in addition to his refutation of northern positions. Quoting from Hegel's *Philosophy of History*, he demonstrated that Hegel excluded the Negro from his definition of civilized humanity. The African, Hegel maintained, "exhibits the natural man in his completely wild and untamed state." And then, to show that slavery was benign rather than barbarous, Lamar cited Hegel's estimation of chattel slavery as a positive good since "*slavery is itself a phase of advance.*" [47]

Having taken his text from Hegel, Lamar gave the usual southern comparison of the "natural condition" of the African

47. For the context of Lamar's quotations see G. W. F. Hegel, *The Philosophy of History*, trans. J. Sibree, with prefaces by Charles Hegel and J. Sibree (New York, 1944), 93, 95, 98–99.

to that of the slave. "The negro in the Southern states," he maintained, "has reached a moral and intellectual development superior to his race in any other position in which he has been placed." This progress notwithstanding, slavery must continue for a naturally backward people. In this concept, the black race was forever unfit for freedom, and slavery therefore was a positive good.[48]

Lamar sometimes showed little patience for those who would loose the barbarous African upon the land. When angered he could be "extremely fiery, and inclined to raise his voice" as the New York *Times* reported. At such times his rhetoric ran without restraint, as it did in his House reply to the antislavery threats of William H. Seward whose "pale, thin face, furrowed by the lines of thought and evil passions, kindled with malignant triumph, and his eye glowed and glared . . . as though the fires of hell were burning in his heart." [49]

As for the abolitionists' complaint that the presence of slavery somehow degraded free labor, Lamar replied: "There is no class among whom negro slavery secures such widespread blessings as the nonslaveholders of the South." And "God's sun does not shine on a nobler, prouder, happier, more prosperous and elevated class of people than the nonslaveholders of the South." The truly free system of labor was that of the southern farmer who allowed "neither monster, capitalist, nor employer to have any participation in its profits." This had little basis in truth, but it answered critics who presumed the superiority of northern society.[50]

48. In employing Hegel, Lamar departed from the usual argument of southern apologists. Although he did not abuse the source in a strict sense, *The Philosophy of History* is nonetheless a specious authority since the author was discussing the native African and addressed himself quite incidentally to European and American slavery.

49. New York *Times,* December 26, 1859; *Congressional Globe,* 36th Cong., 1st Sess., 228.

50. All the foregoing on defense of slavery is based upon Lamar's speech in the House of Representatives. See *Congressional Globe,* 36th Cong., 1st Sess., App., 113–17. For a general treatment of the arguments here attributed to Lamar see William Sumner Jenkins, *Pro-Slavery Thought in the Old South* (Chapel Hill, 1935), *passim.*

In his commitment to chattel slavery Lamar sought concessions and guarantees necessary to the South's security. He well
understood the danger that the antislavery North might over-
whelm the South. And because he foretold disaster in the failure
to preserve a sectional balance in Congress, Lamar turned to
constitutionalism as a solution to the South's imperiled existence.

For this southern spokesman, the federal Constitution presented the only real hope for a minority whose interests con-
flicted with the majority section. Pursued to the last extremity,
the South must fall back upon the provisions specifically recog-
nizing slavery and build from that foundation a defensive system which might stand against the onslaught.[51]

This defense was derived largely from more experienced and
profound political thinkers, especially John C. Calhoun. Lamar was a good student and effective in his oratory, and at a
time when his section rewarded ingenuity rather than original-
ity he served with some distinction as a spokesman for southern
orthodoxy.

In a speech on December 7, 1859, during a controversy over
Hinton Helper's bitterly antislavery *Impending Crisis*, Lamar
made his most comprehensive statement on the Constitution.
He reminded the House that the founding fathers had made the
slave "an institution of property and of society and of government" and that they had provided support for the system. Northerners, however, had violated the spirit of the Constitution:
"Being a majority, and looking upon it as an instrument of restraint upon your power, [you] have taken issue with the constitution and are attempting to throw off its restrictions. That
is the fight between us, and we are ready to meet it here." [52]

On other occasions Lamar's search for a policy caused him
to broaden his strict constructionist approach. By ascribing implied meanings to the Constitution, he stoutly advocated the

---

51. For a general treatment of the constitutional positions here attributed to
Lamar see Jesse T. Carpenter, *The South as a Conscious Minority* (New York, 1930),
passim.

52. *Congressional Globe*, 36th Cong., 1st Sess., 44–46.

principle of sectional balance in government. If the Constitution presumed a union of equal sections (the concurrent majority) as well as one of confederate states, then the South's weakness in the House of Representatives could be overcome. No less an authority than James Madison, he said, had claimed that "every peculiar interest" ought to be provided with a means of defense.[53]

Lamar's argument in favor of a strict checks and balances system and representational rather than direct government sometimes assumed an antidemocratic bias. In opposing a popular referendum on the Kansas constitution in 1858, for example, he came out squarely against direct democracy and concluded "that nearly all writers on governmental and social science, representing every class of opinion (except a few run-mad red Republicans of Germany and France) unite in condemning this theory of direct appeal to the people." [54]

If authorities were not sufficient—and he specifically cited Montesquieu and Rousseau—historical examples of the plebiscite provided an additional warning. The French constitution of 1799, for instance, was approved by the people and resulted in the transformation of France "into one moral and political volcano." All this he contrasted to the republican government envisioned by American founding fathers and embodied in the Lecompton constitution.[55]

Carrying his argument for the concurrent majority to its logical conclusion, Lamar rejected majoritarian democracy in favor of a republican form called "representative liberty," which allowed all interests to participate in government without reference to numbers. Thus sections might "counteract the tendency of any one part to usurp the sovereignty of the whole." When any section gains control over the common government, the "result is not liberty; it is tyranny unmixed." [56]

53. *Ibid.*, App., 113–17.
54. *Ibid.*, 35th Cong., 1st Sess., 279–81, App., 49–53.
55. *Ibid.*
56. Lamar to P. F. Liddell, December 10, 1860, quoted in Mayes, *Lamar*, 633–39. Lamar was writing after Lincoln's election, and by this time he had given up on constitutional defense.

Although Lamar did not advocate secession at any time before Lincoln's election, that alternative never left his mind. He feared that unless constitutional protection could be made absolute, the abolitionists' view would prevail, and the majority opinion would have its way despite laws to the contrary. The South would take no untoward action while the Constitution guaranteed its autonomy, but after that it would cease to rely upon legalisms. On December 7, 1859, in one of his more extreme outbursts, Lamar shouted his warning to Congress: "That constitution is the life and soul of this great government [and] when it is violated, persistently violated, when its spirit is no longer observed upon this floor, I war upon your government, I am against it. I raise then the banner of secession, and I will fight under it as long as the blood flows and ebbs in my veins." [57]

Although Lamar's theories of representative democracy did not require control of the executive branch of government by the South, it became apparent after Lincoln's election that this condition was implicit. The 1860 election gave the "fanatical majority section" control of both legislative and executive branches of the government. Lamar was unwilling to depend upon northern Democrats or the federal judiciary for the South's defense. Loss of the presidency marked an end to the South's ability to check the majority section's advance in a "revolution which has never gone backward, and whose very law is progression." [58] Lamar ignored Lincoln's commitment to protect slavery where it already existed, and believed that the Constitution had ceased to function as a protective device. His reasoning came close to Calhoun's conclusion that only a dual executive could protect southern interests.

These political setbacks came as no surprise. As early as March 8, 1858, during the Kansas debates, Lamar had viewed the sectional dispute with pessimism. He saw the struggle as one in which the South already held an isolated position, and envisioned the South's defeat in the perversion of the constitutional

57. *Congressional Globe*, 36th Cong., 1st Sess., 44–46.
58. Lamar to P. F. Liddell, December 10, 1860, quoted in Mayes, *Lamar*, 633–39.

relationship between sections. In terms suggesting a dark conspiracy Lamar informed a constituent that New England's ambition had always been to subdue nonmanufacturing areas and
that the South would not again concede. He realized the implications of his position but would not retreat: "I may deprecate,
but would not prevent, the fearful consequences. Dissolution
cannot take place quietly; the vast and complicated machinery
of this government cannot be divided without general tumult
and, it may be, ruin. When the sun of the Union sets it will go
down in blood." [59]

---

59. Lamar to B. S. Rozell, March 8, 1858, quoted in Mayes, *Lamar*, 73–74.

Secession: Toward a New Nation

L. Q. C. Lamar's role in the South's secession was by no means decisive.[1] Still, his influence was not altogether negligible within the context of Mississippi politics, and in many respects he spoke for men of his social class in both point of view and degree of emotional involvement.

After three years in Congress as prophet of crisis, Lamar could at least figuratively represent his section in that most ominous gathering, the Democratic national convention in April, 1860. Although not an official delegate, he went to Charleston where he observed and, to an extent, participated in an irrevocable step toward fulfillment of the nation's nightmare.[2]

Lamar appeared in Charleston as an emissary for his friend Jefferson Davis, conveying the message that Davis "did not wish the Southern delegates to secede on the platform, because he knew that we could achieve a more solid and enduring triumph by remaining in and defeating [Stephen A.] Douglas." [3] Lamar relayed the message and personally emphasized the importance of blocking the northern Democrats' efforts to attain the nomination. His appeal had little effect: the Mississippi delegation

1. Histories of the secession crisis virtually ignore Lamar. Perhaps the dearth of personal correspondence during this period is partially responsible.
2. William B. Hesseltine (ed.), *Three Against Lincoln: Murat Halstead Reports the Caucuses of 1860* (Baton Rouge, 1960), App. A, 284, lists the delegates. Lamar likewise was not an official delegate to the Baltimore or "Seceders" conventions. See *ibid.*, App. B, 290, and App. D, 301, for lists of the delegates. Cf. Cate, *Lamar*, 68; and Mayes, *Lamar*, 83, who treat him as a delegate.
3. Lamar to C. H. Mott, May 29, 1860, quoted in Mayes, *Lamar*, 83.

left the hall in disgust before either platform or nominee could be chosen.[4]

Strangely, Davis' chosen spokesman seemed less than completely dedicated to the view that the South should accept a compromise platform even if control of the nomination did prove possible. Indeed, Lamar harangued a mass meeting of southern sympathizers for an hour and a half on the very night of the withdrawal. He denounced Douglas' position permitting exclusion of slavery from the territories until he had him "in the fanged jaws of his logic and fact." [5] Then he announced that the Democratic party had been split and could not be mended. Following the address the crowd was treated to a speech by that most radical of southerners, William Lowndes Yancey.[6]

Lamar believed that he had done his best to carry out Davis' wishes, but he could not be sure that seceders from the convention were wrong in what they had done; and he felt that his own lot was cast with them. Somewhat confused, Lamar remained inconsistent in his feelings about what had happened at Charleston. Not long after the convention, he wrote his more temperate relative, Supreme Court Justice John A. Campbell, a "penitential" letter for his actions at the convention. Campbell accepted the younger man's explanation, but with considerable displeasure.[7]

Despite these ambivalent feelings, Lamar publicly supported Jefferson Davis' efforts to delay formation of a southern party. He, Davis, and other leaders, signed an address urging southern states to participate in the national Democratic convention reconvening in Baltimore. The southern convention scheduled to meet in Richmond should, the address declared, be deferred

4. *Ibid.*
5. Hesseltine (ed.), *Three Against Lincoln*, 86.
6. *Ibid.*; Henry Wilson, *History of the Rise and Fall of the Slave Power* (Boston, 1875–77), II, 682; Joseph Hodgson, *The Cradle of the Confederacy: or the Times of Troup, Quitman and Yancey* (Mobile, 1876), 417.
7. Lamar to C. H. Mott, May 29, 1860, quoted in Mayes, *Lamar*, 83; Lamar to John Campbell, June 7, 1860, cited, *ibid.*, 84; Campbell to Lamar, June 12, 1860, quoted, *ibid.*, 84.

until efforts at agreement with the Douglas Democrats proved futile.[8]

Davis and Lamar stood alone among Mississippi Democratic leaders in urging caution; the other members of the state's congressional delegation declined to sign the appeal. Again, Lamar seems to have been moved by loyalty to Davis rather than by firm conviction. As he wrote C. H. Mott, his law partner, "Davis had signed it, and I was determined that his name should not go unsupported by any of the [Mississippi] delegation." [9]

For a time the counsel of Davis and Lamar prevailed, and Mississippi's delegates did in fact attend the Baltimore convention. Getting no satisfaction there, however, the southerners again withdrew. Nomination of John C. Breckinridge followed as a reaction to the Douglas ticket named by the northern wing of the party.[10]

Once the nominations were past, Lamar made an extraordinary move for a man whose life had been so politically oriented, and he did so despite the rapidly gathering clouds of political crisis. He accepted the professorship of mental and moral philosophy at the University of Mississippi and made plans for retirement from Congress at the session's end. In a public letter to his constituents, Congressman Lamar announced that he would not run again because of pressing private matters and suggested that his claim on the congressional position had been a limited one. His original nomination for the office, the letter explained, had resulted from an impasse in the convention and a compromise. For that reason he had desired to retire after one term, but had been convinced by friends that vindication of his course in Washington required reelection. That having been achieved, Lamar would not run again.[11]

Lamar's judgment must also have been affected by the general

8. Oxford (Miss.) *Intelligencer*, June 6, 1860.
9. Lamar to C. H. Mott, May 29, 1860, quoted in Mayes, *Lamar*, 83.
10. Nichols, *The Disruption of American Democracy*, 311–18.
11. Campbell (transc.), "Journal of the Minutes of the Board of Trustees," 426, 428; Oxford (Miss.) *Intelligencer*, July 4, 11, 1860.

dissatisfaction and frustration which pervaded Washington. As the situation worsened during the winter of 1860, he grew more and more restless and desirous of returning to his family.[12]

Practically speaking, however, acceptance of the professorship had no effect on Lamar's political activity. Immediately afterwards, he entered into the presidential campaign, speaking in a number of northern Mississippi towns and in Memphis. To these audiences he emphasized the well-worn story of northern hostility since the Compromise of 1850 and urged the South to unite without regard to party. Ominously, he cited John Brown's raid as justification for purchase of arms.[13]

Despite Lamar's efforts and the unification of Mississippi Democrats behind Breckinridge, the vital question of union or disunion remained open. Supporters of John Bell's Constitutional Union party, who claimed that slavery could be preserved only within the Union, won heavy support in river counties where Whigs and Unionists had prevailed in crises past. Nevertheless, opinion had now swung to the Democrats, and their candidate succeeded.[14]

Breckinridge's success in Mississippi paled before Lincoln's national victory. Southern Democrats believed themselves driven before the alternatives of submission and secession. Mississippi's Governor John J. Pettus called a strategy meeting with the congressional delegation for November 22, 1860, in preparation for the special session of the legislature to convene on the twenty-sixth. The governor wanted advice: the question was whether to recommend a policy of immediate and separate secession to the legislature or to advise cooperative secession with other southern states.

12. Lamar to A. B. Longstreet, November 13, December 11, 1860, quoted in Mayes, *Lamar*, 86, 89.

13. Oxford (Miss.) *Intelligencer*, August 22, 29, September 12, 1860; Memphis *Daily Appeal*, September 5, 1860.

14. Lamar's first congressional district voted 6,962 for Breckinridge; 5,920 for Bell; and 1,607 for Douglas. Lafayette County (Oxford) gave 1,034 for Breckinridge; 686 for Bell; and 144 for Douglas. Figures provided by Political Research Consortium.

The party's leadership divided as it had at Charleston. Lamar joined Senators Davis and Albert Gallatin Brown in favoring cooperative secession. Governor Pettus voted with Congressmen O. R. Singleton, Reuben Davis, and William Barksdale to reject a policy of cooperation and called for immediate secession instead.[15] A second resolution answered South Carolina's request for an opinion as to whether she should secede immediately or delay until March 4, and again the impatient Pettus cast the deciding ballot. Having been outvoted, Lamar, Davis, and Brown made the resolutions unanimous.[16]

In favoring cooperative secession, Lamar's position showed some signs of ambivalence. As late as May, 1860, he believed a united South "could secure all her rights," [17] but Lincoln's election caused him to despair. Thereafter he considered secession a necessary policy, but seemed undecided about its application. On November 13, 1860, he described himself to his secessionist father-in-law as "anxious and dejected" but still sanguine enough to hope that "if South Carolina will only have the courage to go out, all will be well. We will have a Southern Republic, or an amended Federal Constitution." [18] Either he was unable to decide between separate state action and a cooperative approach or he willfully dissembled to satisfy both Longstreet and Davis. Within ten days time he voted with Davis against encouraging South Carolina and wrote Longstreet advocating that state's independent secession.[19]

After the conference with the governor and the passage of the immediate secession resolutions, Mississippi's leaders closed

15. Congressman John J. McRae did not attend the meeting.

16. Reuben Davis, *Recollections of Mississippi and Mississippians* (Boston, 1891), 390–92; James B. Ranck, *Albert Gallatin Brown: Radical Southern Nationalist* (New York, 1937), 284–85; Halsell, "Friendship of Lamar and Davis," 135.

17. Lamar to C. H. Mott, May 29, 1860, quoted in Mayes, *Lamar*, 83.

18. Lamar to A. B. Longstreet, November 13, 1860, quoted in Mayes, *Lamar*, 86.

19. It is peculiar that Jefferson Davis' account of secession in *Rise and Fall of the Confederate Government* (New York, 1881) does not mention Lamar. An opinion describing Lamar as relatively moderate may be found in Mrs. Jacob Thompson to Mrs. Howell Cobb, December 15, 1860, in Phillips (ed.), *Correspondence of Toombs, Stephens, and Cobb*, 522–24.

ranks and Lamar never again mentioned the realization of southern rights within the Union. Circumstances had at last committed him to a final solution; the vicissitudes and inconsistencies seemed to disappear.

At a mass meeting in Brandon, Mississippi, the day after the governor's conference, Lamar indicated his firm support of secession. More importantly, he described a plan for the formation of a confederacy. That proposal, considered original by his contemporaries, would be presented to the legislature convening on November 26, and on several other occasions.[20]

Lamar believed his plan had the peculiar virtue of allowing an orderly transition from the Union into a new political alliance. The "evils of provisional governments" might be avoided since the states would adopt the constitution, laws, court decisions, and treaties of the United States, unless and until altered by the new government. He proposed that the coming Mississippi convention should adopt ordinances leading to this end. First, the convention should repeal its 1817 ordinance consenting to join the federal Union. Then it should authorize formation of a new federal union including all slave states, the territory of New Mexico, and the Indian territory. Legal regulations of the United States applicable to Mississippi would remain in effect, and all United States offices within Mississippi would continue to function. Pending formation of the new central government, Mississippi's governor would perform the duties of the president of the United States. Following acceptance of the government by nine states, the governor would order an election of congressional representatives and electors for executive offices as under the laws of the United States.

Lamar perhaps betrayed naïveté in supposing that a transferral of sovereignty could take place easily and with little disrup-

20. Davis, *Recollections of Mississippi and Mississippians*, 392; Mayes, *Lamar*, 87–88; Lamar to P. F. Liddell, December 10, 1860, quoted in Mayes, *Lamar*, 633–39; and Wiley P. Harris, "Autobiography," in Dunbar Rowland (ed.), *Courts, Judges, and Lawyers of Mississippi, 1798–1935* (Jackson, 1935), 322; Oxford (Miss.) *Intelligencer*, December 5, 1860.

tion of institutions. Still, the possibility of preserving "our old glorious constitution . . . safe in the affections of our people from the attacks of fanaticism" was an attractive one. Continuation under the Constitution would supply southerners with an instrument of government and would enable them to defend the legality of their action. As Lamar put it: "In a word, it gives us the Union and constitution as the fathers made them, and separates us from the enemies to both, who themselves have seceded from the constitution, and are indeed rebels and traitors." [21]

Lamar presented his scheme to a caucus of southern leaders in Washington when Congress convened in December. While hope for compromise dwindled, it offered a possibility for coordinated action. The political mood which prevented southern agreement on any program, however, excluded Lamar's plan from any real chance of adoption. Its practical significance therefore would await application in Mississippi when the secession convention organized in January. Lamar returned home to run for election to the convention.[22]

Lamar's election did not commit Lafayette County irrevocably to any given position in the convention. He and the other delegate, T. D. Isom, ran against only nominal opposition and received no instructions from their constituency; nor did they promise in advance what course of action might be followed. Isom and Lamar, as Lafayette County knew, did not agree in their attitudes toward secession. Lamar had become an avowed secessionist, whereas Isom condoned secession only if the Lincoln government failed to offer guarantees, and even then he believed that Mississippi ought to secede only in concert with other southern states. Sentiment in the county had been divided in

21. Lamar to P. F. Liddell, December 10, 1860, quoted in Mayes, *Lamar*, 633–39; E. Merton Coulter, *The Confederate States of America, 1861–1865* (Baton Rouge, 1950), 20.

22. T. William Compton to Alonzo Snyder, December 23, 1860, in Alonzo Snyder Papers, Louisiana State University Library; Nichols, *The Disruption of American Democracy*, 395–98; Oxford (Miss.) *Intelligencer*, December 5, 1860; Rainwater, *Mississippi, Storm Center of Secession*, 198. This issue of the *Intelligencer* also announced the formation of the "Lamar Rifles" in his honor.

the November presidential election when the Union and northern Democratic parties had polled 44.5 percent of the vote; and
the "coalition ticket" of Isom and Lamar suggested that while
the people had generally come to accept the likelihood of secession, they still had not caught up with the state's more extreme
leaders.[23]

Judging by a letter from Supreme Court Justice Campbell,
Lamar himself felt that a division of opinion in the state continued to cloud the issue. In answer to a letter of December 25,
Campbell wrote: "I think it to be obvious from your own statement that secession is not desired by the people of Mississippi.
They want peace." [24] Even if Campbell exaggerated Lamar's
meaning, the recognition of persistent unionism in Mississippi
is striking. In another communication, however, Lamar declared
himself pleased with the candidates elected. He wrote Jefferson
Davis, who was still in Washington: "The friends of Southern
independence, of firm and bonafide resistance, won an overwhelming victory" and "Upon the whole, you have great cause
for gratification in the action of your state." Lamar's rather flattering letter presumed that Davis would lead Mississippi: "That
God may preserve you to us, and that your mind may retain all
its vigor to carry us through these perilous times, is my most
fervent aspiration." [25]

The delegates convened on January 7, 1861. On that same day
Lamar set the tone of the convention by moving to establish a
committee to prepare a secession ordinance and to propose a new
confederacy. Thereafter things happened quickly. The following day, January 8, he was appointed chairman of such a com-

23. Political Research Consortium; Rainwater, *Mississippi, Storm Center of Secession*, 177–79, 196–98. Rainwater does a great deal with the geographic and economic factors in the secession movement. Lafayette County occupied an inter-mediate location between the strongest prounion and the strongest prosecession areas.

24. J. A. Campbell to Lamar, January 5, 1861, New York Historical Society Papers, New York Historical Society, New York City. The Lamar letter of Decem-ber 25, 1860, has not been located.

25. Lamar to Jefferson Davis, December 24, 1860, quoted in New York *Times*, August 15, 1863.

mittee. The third day of the convention, January 9, the committee reported an ordinance of secession.[26]

It appears that Lamar had prepared the secession ordinance prior to the convention and simply presented it to the committee at that time. He had maintained close touch with southern leaders including Davis, Jacob Thompson, and John A. Campbell during late December and early January. Thompson and Campbell, at least, had offered him advice on the construction of a secession document.[27] Lamar's own prescription for withdrawal and formation of a new confederacy had been in circulation since early December and presumably served as a basis for discussion. The final document differed little from Lamar's original plan.

The ordinance of secession did not pass the convention uncontested; and there is even some reason to believe that supporters feared its repudiation if tested in a statewide popular vote. Opponents offered a series of emasculating amendments, but without success. Lamar joined the three-fourths majority in defeating the "Yerger Amendment," offered by Union Whig James Shall Yerger, which sought constitutional guarantees within the Union. Another amendment, proposed by James Lusk Alcorn, would have postponed action until Alabama, Georgia, Florida, and Louisiana also withdrew from the United States. It suffered the same fate. A final effort required submission of the ordinance to the people for ratification. The delegates would brook no such appeal to popular sentiment; nor would they tolerate further delay. By a vote of 70 to 29, the popular ratification amendment was defeated, and the ordinance, as presented, passed 84 to 15 on January 9, 1861.[28]

26. *Journal of the State Convention and Ordinances and Resolutions Adopted in January 1861* (Jackson, 1861), 9, 11–14, hereinafter cited as *Journal of the State Convention.*

27. Jacob Thompson to Lamar, January 6, 1861, Record Group No. 109, National Archives; J. A. Campbell to Lamar, January 5, 1861, New York Historical Society Papers; Lamar to Jefferson Davis, December 24, 1860, in New York *Times,* August 15, 1863; Rainwater, *Mississippi, Storm Center of Secession,* 209.

28. *Journal of the State Convention,* 14–16. Rainwater, *Mississippi, Storm Center of Secession,* 207–208, believes that the old-line Whigs provided the backbone of the Union faction. A contemporary account, Horace S. Fulkerson, *A Civilian's*

Lamar then sought to promote his larger plan through the Committee on a Southern Confederacy to which he was appointed on January 10, 1861. He successfully introduced resolutions declaring Mississippi's sympathy with South Carolina's secession and accepting an invitation to meet with seceding states to form a confederacy. On the floor, the majority fought off efforts to require that the constitution, to be drawn up at Montgomery, be submitted for popular ratification. An amendment then passed which allowed the Mississippi convention already in session to ratify the southern constitution for the state. In this form the ordinance providing for representation at Montgomery passed, and the way opened for membership in a new union.[29]

When the business of secession and confederation was finished, a committee which included Lamar drew up a declaration of causes in much the same fashion as the American colonies had done.[30] The convention then turned to the practical details of the new order. The state constitution and legal codes were amended so as to implement Mississippi's newly independent status. A postal system was set up and the state's defense provided for. Having created a republic, the convention adjourned to await results from the assembly in Montgomery.

If Lamar had been chosen as a delegate to Montgomery, that might well have predetermined a career in the legislative branch of the Confederate government. The Mississippi convention briefly considered him for the job, but he was not elected. The convention decided to distinguish between representation to the Montgomery convention and the permanent Mississippi congressional delegation. Senators and representatives who had served in the United States Congress of 1861 would constitute the permanent delegation until the regular election time came around. In

Recollections of the War Between the States, ed. P. L. Rainwater (Baton Rouge, 1939), 5–6, held that the fifteen nay votes to the ordinance represented more than one half of the state's property. The amendments were offered by delta Whigs: James Shall Yerger of Natchez, Alcorn of Coahoma County, and Walker Brooke of Vicksburg.
29. *Journal of the State Convention*, 17, 39–40, 48–50.
30. *Ibid.*, 86–88.

the course of events, however, the temporary delegation assumed permanent duties in the provisional Confederate congress; Lamar never became a member.[31]

Lamar had already, while still in Mississippi, resigned his seat in the United States Congress on January 12, 1861.[32] Two months later, in March, he joined the convention when it reconvened to consider the results of the Montgomery provisional congress. At once the dispute over ratification of the confederation constitution again burst forth. A majority report from the committee favored immediate ratification by the convention. The opposition offered an amendment requiring a popular referendum; but the majority, including Lamar, defeated it. Another amendment required a special ratification convention. The result was the same. Finally, on March 29, 1861, the majority report passed 78 to 7, and the constitution was accepted. Its historic work finished, the convention adjourned the next day *sine die*.[33]

Despite their magnitude, these events must in many ways have been anticlimactic for L. Q. C. Lamar. He had pondered the South's uncertain relationship to the Union since the tenuous beginnings of his political career in 1850–1851. And he had actually been educated around that one issue at Emory College under Longstreet. By March 29, 1861, the central question of his life had been resolved, and he had helped lead the South to its destiny. Now at age thirty-five, he must have felt concerned self-importance as he envisioned an end to the fundamental antagonism of his era.

A politician without a job, Lamar presided over classes in mental and moral philosophy at the University of Mississippi during the remaining months of peace. Whether he expected to continue this relatively unexciting livelihood is not known, but it seems unlikely. Within two weeks of the convention's adjournment, his students had begun leaving for Confederate military

31. *Ibid.*, 51–58, 73–75, 43.
32. *Congressional Globe*, 36th Cong., 2nd Sess., 345. No correspondence exists for these months, so his thoughts and plans are unknown.
33. *Journal of the State Convention*, 24, 26, 32–36, 47.

service. The administration, supported by Lamar, attempted to
dissuade the "University Grays" from precipitant action but to
no avail. On April 29, 1861, the chancellor reported to the faculty that only five students were in regular attendance and that
these were expected to leave within hours. Two weeks later the
university suspended operations.[34]

After a summer vacation the faculty gathered again on September 18, 1861, to learn that only four students were present.
On October 1, the board of trustees accepted the resignation of
Lamar and most of his colleagues. Actually, this was recognition
after the fact. Lamar had already left Oxford.[35]

The events of the spring of 1861 which closed the university
also carried Lamar into active service in the Confederate army.
Although he never questioned the need to go, it must have been
a sobering prospect. He left a wife and three children[36] to the
uncertainties of the time and without adequate financial security. Neither his legal career nor the plantation were sufficiently
developed to endure a long period of neglect. And furthermore,
the Longstreets had moved to South Carolina and would not be
able to see after his interests.

Despite these considerations Lamar and his law partner C. H.
Mott organized the 19th Mississippi Regiment of volunteers with
Mott as colonel and Lamar as his second in command. The regiment reported to the Confederate War Department on May 14,
1861. After Lamar and Mott had been commissioned and their
command mustered, they left Montgomery for Richmond, the
new seat of the government.[37]

Lamar joined President Jefferson Davis in Richmond in time

34. Faculty Record Book, 175–78; F. A. P. Barnard, "Autobiographical Sketch
of Dr. F. A. P. Barnard," *Publications of the Mississippi Historical Society*, XII, 115.

35. Faculty Record Book, 182; Minutes of the Board of Trustees of the University of Mississippi (University of Mississippi Library), 442–45, hereinafter cited
as Board Minutes.

36. Francis, Lamar, Jr., and Augusta.

37. Oxford (Miss.) *Intelligencer*, May 22, 1861; "Journal of the Congress of the
Confederate States of America," *Senate Documents*, 58th Cong., 2nd Sess., No. 234,
XXV, 435, 501. L. Q. C. Lamar File, Record Group No. 109, indicates that Lamar's
commission was technically issued on June 11, 1861, and took effect that date.

to help celebrate the capital's transfer from Montgomery. At that moment history seemed to pause and the Confederacy's future appeared very bright. Davis' mere presence merited a serenade at his hotel. Lamar was known in the city, and after Davis and Governor Henry Wise spoke, he was called forth. With enthusiasm and platitudes befitting the occasion, he assured the people of the South's rectitude. Cloaked in the righteousness of its cause, the South would fight if necessary, and Virginia would play her accustomed role: "Grand, glorious old commonwealth! Proud, free empress! Mother of States, themselves free, standing here in robes of steel, raising a majestic arm to press back the foe that dare attempt to force her daughters into an unnatural and unwilling union!" [38]

38. Richmond *Daily Examiner*, June 3, 1861, quoted in Dickey and Streeter, "Lucius Q. C. Lamar," 176.

The Confederacy: Patriot at Large

Soldiering near Richmond seems not to have been too stringent during the summer of 1861. Lamar therefore forsook the encampment for the capital's social life. Old acquaintances from the Brown's Hotel clique were there, and Lamar joined drawing room festivities with enthusiasm. With rather striking levity he wrote Mrs. Lamar: "If I were well enough off, I should give up public life and devote myself to social duties." [1]

The wife of former United States Congressman James Chesnut remarked that Lamar called frequently and stayed late to talk of matters both light and serious. On one visit he said "he could only stay five minutes; he was obliged to go back at once to his camp. This was a little before eight o'clock; but at twelve he was still talking to us on that sofa." [2]

Another recollection by Mrs. Chesnut presented a view of Lamar never observed by the public. Perhaps he encouraged her to attribute her own prejudices to himself. She spoke of a "Mr. Lamar, who does not love slavery any more than Sumner does" and who said that "slavery is too heavy a load for us to carry" and a Lamar who looked ahead to "see all the risk, the loss of land, limb and life; of home, children and wife." [3]

1. Lamar to Mrs. Lamar, November 22, 1861, quoted in Mayes, *Lamar*, 97.
2. Mary B. Chesnut, *A Diary from Dixie*, ed. Ben Ames Williams (Boston, 1949), 67.
3. *Ibid.*, 70, 151. Although Lamar probably had his doubts, Mrs. Chesnut must have exaggerated. Cf. Henry Adams, *The Education of Henry Adams* (Boston, 1918), 246, who wrote that "Lamar used to say that he never entertained a

These drawing room forebodings of "limb and life" struck home almost immediately and in a peculiar way while Lamar camped at Richmond. Just before the 19th Mississippi moved to the front, Lamar suffered "a violent vertigo, something like apoplexy . . . followed by . . . paralysis of one side." [4] The illness, which sometimes affected even his speech, kept him bedridden for about two weeks, and then he got about only on crutches. In mid-July Lamar and his family left Richmond for Oxford, where he convalesced until November. His health continued to improve despite "frequent slight rushes of blood to the head" and prolonged lameness of the left leg. [5]

In the absence of complete medical data, there is no way to evaluate Lamar's "apoplexy." The loss of consciousness, the crippling effect, and the loss of speech all suggest the rupture or occlusion of an intracerebral artery. Whether this resulted from some congenital defect or from hypertension aggravated by an approaching military confrontation cannot be determined. Nor can it be said whether Lamar's life was actually in immediate danger or whether his long-term physical and mental ability was lessened. Whatever the medical facts, the attack must have diminished Lamar's concept of what he might personally achieve during the war. Possibly he even arrived at the painful assumption that his life would be a short one. Since Lamar's evaluation of this traumatic event is not known we can only surmise its effect upon his thinking. "Apoplexy" struck him several more times before he died. The pattern which emerged al-

---

doubt of the soundness of the Southern system until he found that slavery could not stand a war."

4. Mayes, *Lamar*, 96. Chesnut, *A Diary from Dixie*, 70, called it "paralysis, or some sort of stroke." She went on in the same paragraph: "Will men flatter and make eyes until their eyes close in death? Except that he was in bed, with some learned professor at his bedside, and that his wife has been telegraphed for, he was the same old Lamar of the drawing-room."

5. Chesnut, *A Diary from Dixie*, 81–82; Mayes, *Lamar*, 96–97; Walter B. Hill, "L. Q. C. Lamar," *The Green Bag*, V (April, 1893), 158. Hill wrote that Lamar had traveled to Paris in 1859 to consult physicians in reference to a cerebral disease from which he suffered. No other evidence supports the contention that there were attacks before 1861.

ways included the presence of great stress and tension resulting from physical or political danger. Whenever a great crisis arose Lamar's very life appeared to be in jeopardy.

Lamar gained strength during his convalescence in Oxford until he felt able to return to duty about November 1, 1861. He remained in Richmond most of November, devoting a limited amount of time to regimental business as his health permitted. Late in November he wrote his wife: "I hope I am nearly cured of my sickness. I can manage to get along with a stick, though my leg is quite weak and uncertain in its movements. My vertigo comes upon me very rarely, and then in a very modified form." [6]

Possibly because of this lameness, Davis sent his friend on a special mission to General Joseph E. Johnston's headquarters late in November to clear up "some wrong impressions" held by Johnston and his corps commander, James Longstreet.[7] An improvement in the strained personal relations between Johnston and Davis seemed to have come at about this time. Lamar may have effectively served as a mediator because of his intimacy with Davis, his relation to Longstreet, and his political reputation. But on the other hand, his sickness confined him to his room during much of the winter and may have negated his efforts. Details of the mission are lacking.[8]

Lamar returned to Richmond where he stayed in touch with Davis and apparently served him as an adviser. It was upon Lamar's recommendation that Davis employed a former University

6. Lamar to Mrs. Lamar, November 22, 1861, quoted in Mayes, *Lamar*, 97.

7. *Ibid.* See also Gilbert E. Govan and James W. Livingood, *The Haskell Memoirs: John Cheves Haskell* (New York, 1960), 13. Lamar File, Record Group No. 109, shows Lamar detached to Johnston during both November and December, but the letter to Mrs. Lamar indicated a shorter stay. Lamar's name is not mentioned in the correspondence surrounding this argument, and it is likely that he did not figure too prominently. See Dunbar Rowland (ed.), *Jefferson Davis, Constitutionalist: His Letters, Papers, and Speeches* (Jackson, 1923), V, 156, 164–66, 176–77.

8. Govan and Livingood, *The Haskell Memoirs*, 13. Haskell was Lamar's roommate at Johnston's camp. Later in the war, after Haskell had lost an arm, Lamar visited him and, according to Haskell, broke into tears and had to be taken from the room. It should be noted, however, that Haskell wrote forty years after the war ended. See *ibid.*, 13–14.

of Mississippi professor, Burton N. Harrison, as his personal secretary. The choice was an interesting one since Harrison had taught with Lamar just before the suspension of classes at Oxford and had wished to join Lamar's regiment. According to Harrison, Lamar had discouraged him from joining the army because of his dependent mother and sister. Harrison believed that Lamar had these considerations in mind when he talked to Davis.[9]

Lamar left Richmond for Oxford about February 7, 1862, on a thirty-day leave of absence. He missed a proposed meeting with Harrison in Atlanta and went home to rest. On returning to Virginia, Lamar would not reenter the Davis entourage. After being away from field duties for almost a year, he would again join with Mississippians who had committed themselves to serve the Confederacy by force of arms.[10]

In March, Lamar joined the 19th near Yorktown as a Federal drive up the peninsula to Richmond seemed certain. Lamar's troops, although on alert, saw no action through April except for "skirmishes of little importance and significant of nothing." [11] But then General Joseph Johnston ordered a retreat on May 3, 1862, in anticipation of an opening barrage by superior Federal artillery. General James Longstreet's Corps, including the 19th Mississippi, fell back to Williamsburg where they joined with three other divisions.

At Williamsburg, General George McClellan's Federal forces finally overtook Johnston. On the morning of May 5, the 19th Mississippi joined in a counterattack and Lamar experienced his first real fight. The initiation must have been a sobering one since the regiment suffered, by Lamar's calculation, 25 percent casualties. Colonel C. H. Mott fell in the charge, leaving Lamar

9. Lamar wired Burton N. Harrison: "You are Private Secretary to the President." See Fairfax Harrison (ed.), *Aris Souis Focisque . . . The Harrisons of Skimino* (n.p., 1910), 149–50; and Mrs. Burton Harrison, *Recollections, Grave and Gay* (New York, 1911), 69.

10. Lamar to Burton N. Harrison, March 1, 1862, in Mrs. Burton Harrison's Scrap Book: 1858–1909, Burton N. Harrison Papers, Manuscript Division, Library of Congress; Lamar File, Record Group No. 109.

11. Lamar, no date or addressee, quoted in Mayes, *Lamar*, 97.

to complete the engagement in command. At the end of the
battle, with the Union offensive temporarily checked, Johnston
withdrew his greatly outnumbered troops and retreated further
along the road to Richmond. Lamar, for his part, had acquitted
himself well enough to earn the usual commendations by his
superiors.[12]

McClellan's troops pushed on up the peninsula while Johnston continued his march westward. By the fifteenth Lamar had
reached the Chickahominy, and on that day the army crossed
the river toward Richmond to draw up a line of defense. There
his role in the martial drama ended. In the midst of preparation
for the next encounter, and intensely anxious about its outcome,
Lamar suffered another violent seizure—only eleven months after
the first illness. This time he quit the field for good. He was
physically and perhaps emotionally unfit for combat.[13]

Lamar was taken to Richmond while McClellan and the Confederates waited in a standoff. He convalesced there until June,
when he felt well enough to travel to Mississippi and Georgia
for an extended rest. Misfortune abounded during the following summer and fall of 1862. As if his own poor health and shat-
tered military career were not burden enough, word came in
September that his younger brother, Jefferson Mirabeau, and
his cousin, John B. Lamar, had died at Crampton's Gap in the
Antietam campaign. Sensitive and given to despair even in better
times, Lamar sought spiritual solace and committed himself to
God by joining the Methodist Church that July.[14]

The war had also taken a turn for the worse in Mississippi. On

12. For Lamar's report on the engagement see *The War of the Rebellion: A
Compilation of the Official Records of the Union and Confederate Armies* (Wash-
ington, 1880–1901), Ser. I, Vol. II, Pt. 1, 597–600, hereinafter cited as *Official
Records*. For other official reports see *ibid.*, 564–93, *passim*. See also Joseph E.
Johnston, *Narrative of Military Operations Directed During the Late War Be-
tween the States* (Bloomington, 1959), 116–26; Gilbert E. Govan and James W.
Livingood, *A Different Valor: The Story of General Joseph E. Johnston, C. S. A.*
(New York, 1956), 114–24; and G. Moxley Sorrel, *Recollections of a Confederate
Staff Officer*, ed. Bell Irvin Wiley (Jackson, Tenn., 1958), 58–59.
13. Johnston, *Narrative of Military Operations*, 126–28; Govan and Livingood,
General Joseph E. Johnston, 124–28; Mayes, *Lamar*, 101.
14. *Official Records*, Ser. I, Vol. XIX, 871; Mayes, *Lamar*, 101–102, 559–60.

November 13, 1862, A. B. Longstreet, again living in Oxford, wrote his son-in-law: "Your plantation will soon be a battle-field. We shall be whipped on it, and the Yankees will make a desert of it." Longstreet's pessimism offered no hope whatever: "It matters but little," he wrote, "whether it be made the camping-ground of our forces during the winter or fall into the hands of the enemy. . . . The prospect before us is awful." He indicated that Lamar's wife and children would be sent to Georgia.[15]

Longstreet's apprehension was not misplaced. Armies soon overran Holly Springs, where Lamar had practiced law; Oxford, where he had lived and taught; and the area along the Tallahatchie, where Solitude lay deserted.[16]

Lamar's health improved sufficiently to allow his return to staff service early in November. At first he was assigned to a place on the military court at Richmond. On November 19, 1862, however, Davis appointed Lamar commissioner to the Russian Imperial Government, with the proviso that upon recognition of the Confederacy he would continue as envoy extraordinary and minister plenipotentiary to the emperor.[17]

A diplomatic career must certainly have suited Lamar's disposition better than the battlefield, where he had achieved so little.[18] Still, the auspiciousness of the appointment paled in light of the circumstances. Davis and Secretary of War Judah P.

15. A. B. Longstreet to Lamar, November 13, 1862, quoted in Oscar Pen Fitzgerald, *Judge Longstreet, A Life Sketch* (Nashville, 1891), 198–99.

16. *Official Records*, Ser. I, Vol. XVII, 470, 477–78, 487–89, 491–96, 503, 514–16; John K. Bettersworth, *Confederate Mississippi: The People and Policies of a Cotton State in Wartime* (Baton Rouge, 1943), 280.

17. Lamar File, Record Group No. 109; J. P. Benjamin to Lamar, November 19, 1862, in Confederate States of America Papers (hereinafter cited as CSA Papers): State Department, Diplomatic and Consular, XIII, 1–6, 8–11, Manuscript Division, Library of Congress. Lamar had earlier predicted that he might receive such an appointment: "If we ever have peace, I expect I shall be sent as Minister to Spain or Sardinia." See Lamar to Mrs. Lamar, November 22, 1861, quoted in Mayes, *Lamar*, 97.

18. See Adams, *The Education of Henry Adams*, 185; and J. L. M. Curry, *Civil History of the Government of the Confederate States* (Richmond, 1900), 135, for contemporary appraisals of his suitability for the position. Both were highly flattering. Curry was a kinsman of Lamar.

Benjamin had not sent a representative to Russia previously, because recognition seemed so unlikely and for fear of "assuming
an attitude which could possibly be construed into a supplica-
tion for favor as inferiors." The later Confederate contention
that Russian recognition might be forthcoming since "we have
conquered our position by the sword" did not carry conviction.
Indeed, Lamar's instructions specifically provided that he might
postpone presentation of his credentials to the emperor should
circumstances in Europe require it.[19]

Optimism in diplomacy, however, was not completely vision-
ary early in 1862 when southern armies seemed invincible on the
battlefield. Then strong movements in favor of the South had
stirred England and France at least for a time. But Russia did
not hesitate even momentarily. Unlike England and France, she
categorically favored the Union. The establishment of a mission
to that country was an empty gesture.[20]

Commissioner Lamar did not arrive in England en route to
Russia until March 1, 1863, three and a half months after his
appointment. Either Lamar's uncertain health delayed his journey or the Confederacy was in absolutely no hurry to present its
minister to Russia. Because of the hazards of running the Union
naval blockade, Lamar eventually left the country via Matamoros, Mexico. But first he visited in Vicksburg, Mississippi, for
five days before taking steamboat passage on the Mississippi and
Red rivers to Alexandria, Louisiana. From the Red River he

19. J. P. Benjamin to Lamar, November 19, 1862, in CSA Papers: State Department, Diplomatic and Consular, XIII, 1–6, 8–11. Lamar's instructions are
contained in two letters from Benjamin of this same date. These two letters and
several accompanying documents may be found in Official Documents relating to
the Mission of L. Q. C. Lamar, Commissioner of the Confederate States of America
to Russia, MDAH. Some of this material is reprinted in James D. Richardson (ed.),
A Compilation of the Messages and Papers of the Confederacy Including the
Diplomatic Correspondence, 1861–1865 (Nashville, 1905), II, 364–68; and in Official Records of the Union and Confederate Navies in the War of the Rebellion
(Washington, 1894–1927), Ser. II, Vol. III, 137–38, 606–608, hereinafter cited as
Official Records, Navies.
20. Norman A. Graebner, "Northern Diplomacy and European Neutrality" in
David Donald (ed.), Why the North Won the Civil War (Baton Rouge, 1960), 57–
58, 68, 77.

traveled by land to the Sabine, to Houston by water and land, and then to Matamoros by way of San Antonio. Three weeks passed between his departure from San Antonio and his embarkment on the *Malabar*. After a stopover in Havana, where he was reported to be "feeble" but improving in health, the commissioner traveled to St. Thomas Island, and then across the Atlantic at last to England.[21]

Although Lamar safely evaded the blockade, the North did not fail to exploit his mission. Union propagandists intercepted the Confederate State Department's first dispatch to the commissioner to Russia. The circular, which explained that the Confederate Constitution prohibited foreign slave trading and thereby rendered unnecessary any treaty arrangements to that effect, was published under the suggestive title "The African Slave Trade, the Secret Purpose of the Insurgents to Revive It." With this gratuitous notoriety preceding him, Lamar entered London.[22]

As instructed, Lamar first set out to acquaint himself with European attitudes toward the Confederate States of America. After three weeks in England, he felt sufficiently informed to advise the State Department of his findings—or perhaps he simply wished to record his activities. Lamar believed both political parties to be sympathetic to the South. Only circumstances prevented their recognition of the Confederacy. For one thing, England greatly dreaded a war with the United States, and therefore was reluctant to antagonize her. Furthermore, he believed, the composition of Parliament worked against the South. Since

21. Mayes, *Lamar*, 106; Lamar to Mrs. Lamar, December 24, 1862, quoted, *ibid.*; Col. P. N. Luckett (Commander of Lower Rio Grande) to Maj. A. G. Dickinson, January 26, 1863, in *Official Records*, Ser. I, Vol. XV, 961; Ch. J. Helm (Confederate Agent in Havana) to J. P. Benjamin, February 14, 1863, in *Official Records, Navies*, Ser. II, Vol. III, 690–91; James Mason to J. P. Benjamin, March 30, 1863, *ibid.*, 732.

22. J. P. Benjamin to Lamar, Dispatch No. 1, January 15, 1863, in CSA Papers: State Department, Diplomatic and Consular, XIII, 11–16. See the same circular in J. P. Benjamin to James Mason, January 15, 1863, in *Official Records, Navies*, Ser. II, Vol. III, 651–53. The propaganda pamphlet is on file in the Boston Public Library.

neither party enjoyed a working majority, "this gives to the
Radicals, under Bright and others, the balance of power," and
"these men are the warm partisans of the United States." Lamar
saw little reason to expect an immediate change in this dilemma.
As for the Continent, he considered Prussia and Austria likely
areas for Confederate diplomacy. He did not despair of his own
assignment and reported: "There does not exist any feeling [in
Russia] of hostility towards the South." Lamar's first dispatch
closed with the news that the Confederate government's success
in attaining loan subscriptions constituted "financial recognition of the Confederacy." [23]

Lamar remained in England until mid-April measuring opinion and apparently enjoying London society. Having satisfied
himself on these accounts he traveled to Paris, where he intended
to occupy himself in much the same way. This visit to Paris, the
first of several, extended from mid-April to June 25, 1863. During the early part of his stay Lamar studied the diplomatic and
social maze surrounding the French court. In the process he
learned what he could about the prospects for Russian recognition through that government's representatives in Paris. Audiences with Louis Napoleon and his half brother, the Duc de
Morny, convinced Lamar that Napoleon favored the Confederate cause and that he would have taken some official action if
England or Russia had agreed to cooperate with him.[24]

23. Lamar to J. P. Benjamin, Dispatch No. 1, March 20, 1863, in CSA Papers:
Pickett Papers, Container 7. Also printed in Richardson (ed.), *Messages and Papers
of the Confederacy*, II, 453–56; and in *Official Records, Navies*, Ser. II, Vol. III,
716–18.

24. John Slidell to J. P. Benjamin, April 20, 1863, in *Official Records, Navies*,
Ser. II, Vol. III, 743; John Slidell to J. P. Benjamin, June 25, 1863, *ibid.*, 821;
Beckles Wilson, *John Slidell and the Confederates in Paris, 1862–1865* (New York,
1932), 69–71. Evidence of the interviews is contained in two statements made by
Lamar in 1887 and 1888. The first is quoted in Curry, *Civil History*, 135, and in
Mayes, *Lamar*, 108–109. The second is a recollection of a story told by Lamar
shortly after his appointment to the Supreme Court in 1888 contained in Augustus
C. Buell to Charles H. Cramp, September 12, 1901, in Balch Papers, I, 10 (The
Historical Society of Pennsylvania, Philadelphia). Lamar's views on the prosouthern
stance of Napoleon may be found in Lamar to Mrs. Clay, August 8, 1863, in C. C.
Clay Papers, Duke University Library; Clay, *A Belle of the Fifties*, 204; and Lamar's
speech of April 14, 1864, reprinted in Mayes, *Lamar*, 639–56. Cate, *Lamar*, 103,

Lamar also concluded that a journey to Russia would not improve that country's attitude toward the Confederacy. He reported to his government that until the Polish revolt could be settled, his efforts would be futile. The outbreak threatened to engulf all Europe, and the czar's government felt deeply grateful for Secretary of State Seward's refusal to condemn Russian efforts to stem the uprising. Relations between the two countries had, therefore, reached a new level of amity.[25]

Lamar much later gave a fuller account of his judgment of Russian-Confederate relations. In Paris, Emperor Napoleon III had impressed him with a telling analysis of Russian policy. Napoleon claimed that the Russians would naturally take a position antagonistic to their traditional enemies, the French and English. More importantly, Confederate efforts to win independence represented to Russia a doctrine of political separation, and that doctrine was especially odious while Russia was attempting to put down the Polish insurrection in her own dominion. Under these circumstances, Napoleon pointed out, efforts in Russia could only result in embarrassment for the Confederacy with adverse effects in other European courts.[26]

With no immediate prospects for continuing his mission, Lamar entered into the multifarious activities being conducted by Confederate agents in France. Neither his relationship to these men nor his authority within their spheres of operation was ever defined. In fact, Lamar received no written instructions whatsoever beyond the original orders accompanying his appoint-

---

quotes a "later" statement by Lamar to the effect that emancipation of the slaves would have gained recognition.

25. John Slidell to J. P. Benjamin, April 20, 1863, in *Official Records, Navies,* Ser. II, Vol. III, 743; Lamar to J. P. Benjamin, Dispatch No. 2, July 22, 1863, in CSA Papers: Pickett Papers, Container 7.

26. Lamar's account of Napoleon's advice is contained in Augustus C. Buell to Charles H. Cramp, September 12, 1901, in Balch Papers, I, 10. Lamar's assessment agrees generally with evaluations by historians. See Frank L. Owsley, *King Cotton Diplomacy* (Chicago, 1931), 464; Donaldson Jordan and Edwin J. Pratt, *Europe and the American Civil War* (Boston, 1931), 200; and Graebner, "Northern Diplomacy and European Neutrality," 57–58. According to Buell's account Napoleon was particularly well disposed toward Lamar because of assistance given him by the Lamar family in the 1840s during his exile in the United States.

ment. Fortunately for him, the diplomatic service proved highly absorbant of uninstructed and ill-classified Confederates away from home.

Lamar began working with and assisting John Slidell, commissioner to France.[27] Then, in early June, he and Slidell joined with James M. Mason, minister to England, to confer on several important matters. The three commissioners were especially concerned with fiscal difficulties and with problems involved in the procurement procedures of the Confederacy in Europe; they therefore brought in two key financial figures, Confederate General C. J. McRae and Emil Erlanger. McRae controlled the proceeds of a loan subscribed through the banking house of Emil Erlanger and Company, the Confederacy's most important source of revenue in Europe. Lacking directions from Richmond, and with the supply situation precarious, Lamar and his fellow representatives acted independently and upon their own responsibility. With their approval McRae prepared to pay out £22,000 necessary to release crucial materials and to maintain the Confederate government's credit.[28]

The conferences also considered the progress of Confederate naval construction which was beset by financial difficulties and by the English government's close enforcement of the neutrality laws. After contacting Commander James H. North, who was superintending the building of a great ram, the group at first decided to use the Erlanger loan to provide North with £30,000. But the potentially more dangerous question of seizure

27. John Slidell to J. P. Benjamin, May 15, 1863, in *Official Records, Navies,* Ser. II, Vol. III, 771, enclosed a draft by Lamar for a piece of legislation desired by Slidell which would allow the administration of the Confederate oath by persons in Europe.

28. James Mason to J. P. Benjamin, Dispatch No. 38, June 4, 1863, in *Official Records, Navies,* Ser. II, Vol. III, 782; John Slidell to J. P. Benjamin, Dispatch No. 37, June 12, 1863, *ibid.,* 806–807; William G. Crenshaw to James A. Seddon, June 6, 1863, in *Official Records,* Ser. IV, Vol. II, 587–88; William G. Crenshaw to James Mason, June 4, 1863, *ibid.,* 590; memorandum by J. M. Mason, John Slidell, L. Q. C. Lamar, C. D. McRae, June 4, 1863, contained in C. D. McRae to C. G. Memminger, Dispatch No. 2, June 19, 1863, in War Department Records, Record Group No. 109; Charles S. Davis, *Colin J. McRae: Confederate Financial Agent* (Tuscaloosa, 1961), 38–39.

by the British plagued them. The hardening of English policy, marked by the confiscation of the *Alexandria*, indicated that North should sell the ship unfinished "as the only sure means of saving the large amount expended upon it." They further suggested that the Russian government might be willing to assume the contract.[29]

North and Mason were not entirely convinced that the step needed to be taken. But as Union minister Charles Francis Adams continued to inveigh against construction of warships for the Confederacy, and as public opinion in England became more antagonistic, the commission's advice prevailed. Finally, in the spring of 1864, the Confederate Navy Department reluctantly sold the ship to Denmark.[30]

The business of the conferences completed, on June 25, 1863, Lamar crossed the Channel for England with the intention of continuing on to St. Petersburg. He was by no means confident that he would obtain recognition, and both he and Slidell considered Vienna to be a more likely diplomatic field.[31]

Their concern turned out to be purely academic. Unknown to Lamar, the Confederate Senate had refused to confirm his appointment; his service had officially terminated on June 11, 1863. According to Benjamin, the action resulted from a general revulsion against European nations. Throughout 1862 and early 1863, ill will had developed until, finally, Confederate diplomacy was admitted to be a failure. Angry with Europe's rejection

29. James H. North to C. J. McRae, May 28, 1863, in *Official Records, Navies,* Ser. II, Vol. II, 431; J. M. Mason to Captain North, June 5, 1863, *ibid.,* 432; L. Q. C. Lamar, John Slidell, and J. M. Mason to Commander James H. North, C. S. Navy, June 13, 1863, *ibid.,* 439–40; Mason to Capt. North, C. S. Navy, June 16, 1863, *ibid.,* 440.

30. J. M. Mason to Capt. James H. North, June 16, 1863, in *Official Records, Navies,* Ser. II, Vol. II, 440; S. R. Mallory, Sect. of Navy, to Commander James D. Bulloch, C. S. Navy, June 19, 1863, *ibid.,* 440–42; North to Mason, June 26, 1863, *ibid.,* 443; Mason to North, June 27, 1863, *ibid.,* 443; Mason to North, November 27, 1863, *ibid.,* 528; North to Mallory, February 18, 1864, *ibid.,* 587–88; Mallory to North, February 24, 1864, *ibid.,* 595; undated "Memorandum of meeting between Mssrs: Slidell, Mason, Barron, McRae, and North," *ibid.,* 326–29.

31. John Slidell to J. P. Benjamin, June 25, 1863, in *Official Records, Navies,* Ser. II, Vol. III, 820–21.

of the South's appeal for recognition and irritated by the anomalous presence of English consuls in the Confederacy, the Senate Committee on Foreign Affairs squelched Lamar's mission.[32]

Probably because of the growing frustration of European relations, Davis had delayed submitting Lamar's papers for four months until March 16, 1863. Three days later the Committee on Foreign Affairs returned a resolution deeming it "inexpedient at this time to send a commissioner to Russia." At the same time the committee resolved against receiving nominations for James Mason and John Slidell until the Confederacy's independence had been recognized.[33]

The Senate did not trouble to take up the committee's recommendations until April 10, 1863. The resolution on the inexpediency of sending a commissioner to Russia was then brought up and amended so that it called for an explanation from the president. Jefferson Davis complied on April 20. The Senate took no specific action on Davis' statement but passed a resolution opposing the sending of "envoys extraordinary and ministers plenipotentiary" before the recognition of the Confederate States of America. The administration ignored the Senate's rebuff until June 11, 1863, when Secretary of State Benjamin finally notified Lamar.[34]

The uncertainties of transatlantic diplomatic correspondence delayed Lamar's recall still more. Five weeks later he finally replied to Benjamin, graciously accepting the Senate's reasoning

32. J. P. Benjamin to Lamar, Dispatch No. 2, June 11, 1863, in CSA Papers: State Department, Diplomatic and Consular, XIII, 17–18; also printed in Richardson (ed.), *Messages and Papers of the Confederacy*, II, 505–506; and in *Official Records, Navies*, Ser. II, Vol. III, 796.

33. "Journal of the Congress of the Confederate States of America," *Senate Documents*, 58th Cong., 2nd Sess., No. 234, XXVII, 172, 174, 180–81; Burton N. Harrison to Secretary of State, June 1, 1863, in CSA Papers: State Department, LXI, at end of volume and out of order.

34. "Journal of the Congress of the Confederate States of America," *Senate Documents*, 58th Cong., 2nd Sess., No. 234, XXVII, 276, 289–90, 320, 348; Burton N. Harrison to Secretary of State, June 1, 1863, in CSA Papers: State Department, LXI, at end of volume and out of order; J. P. Benjamin to Lamar, Dispatch No. 2, June 11, 1863, in CSA Papers: State Department, Diplomatic and Consular, XIII, 17–18.

as very similar to his own. Lamar had almost determined independently, he said, to ask that he be given new instructions or be recalled. The influence of France, which he had counted on, had dwindled with that country's support of the Polish insurrection. Lamar did hope, however, "that the principle which has governed this decision will not be extended to the withdrawal of diplomatic representatives at London and Paris"; and he maintained that "the presence of these gentlemen at their respective posts is imperiously demanded by the exigencies of [the] public service." [35] Having given that advice, which was not followed, Lamar accepted his government's judgment.

Lamar remained in Europe without official status for more than three months after his letter to Benjamin. Although frequently incapacitated by poor health, he performed various services for the Confederacy, both in England and on the Continent. Part of this time he assisted Henry Hotze, propagandist and editor of the Confederate government's organ, the *Index*. Soon after Hotze learned of Lamar's recall, he wrote Secretary Benjamin of his disappointment since "the suggestions of his [Lamar's] fruitful intellect were an invaluable advantage to me." Three months and some days later Hotze took credit for keeping Lamar in Europe and expressed "regret at losing his counsel and assistance." [36]

During this period of association with Hotze, Lamar's health may have caused an extension of his stay. On August 1, 1863, Lamar wrote his wife of his intention to leave England on September 1, 1863, despite delicate health.[37] A week later he wrote

35. Lamar to J. P. Benjamin, Dispatch No. 2, July 22, 1863, in CSA Papers: Pickett Papers, Container 7; also printed in *Official Records, Navies*, Ser. II, Vol. III, 848–49.

36. Henry Hotze to J. P. Benjamin, Dispatch No. 26, July 23, 1863, in *Official Records, Navies*, Ser. II, Vol. III, 849–51; Henry Hotze to J. P. Benjamin, Dispatch No. 31, October 31, 1863, *ibid.*, 944–48. As Grover Cleveland's secretary of the interior, Lamar later offered Hotze employment for the department in Germany. See Lamar to Henry Hotze, June 2, 1885, in Letterbook I, Lamar–Mayes Papers. According to Cate, *Lamar*, 101–102, he also wrote for the London *Times and Telegraph*.

37. Lamar to Mrs. Lamar, August 1, 1863, quoted in Mayes, *Lamar*, 110. This complaint may have been exaggerated for a wife's sympathetic ear since he con-

much the same to Mrs. C. C. Clay, saying he expected to be well enough to start home soon.[38]

For some reason Lamar did not leave as planned. In early October he returned to Paris, where he conferred with Mason, Slidell, and C. J. McRae. Again the Erlanger agent reported fiscal difficulties. The loan's balance was dreadfully reduced, and the Confederacy's uncertain credit made additional funds unattainable. Lamar's part in this conference is not clear; but McRae wrote Secretary of Treasury Memminger that Lamar had offered to deliver a dispatch and to confer with him in Richmond on his return.[39]

On October 16, 1863, Lamar was back in England presenting the Confederate cause to an agricultural society in a speech which Hotze's *Index* praised. After at least one additional public appearance, and three weeks after his planned departure with McRae's dispatch, Lamar at last made ready to leave England. This time there was no change in plans. He departed about November 1 from Liverpool aboard the *Asia* for Halifax.[40]

From Halifax Lamar sailed to Bermuda and boarded a British blockade runner, the *Ceres*, bound for Wilmington. The ill-fated steamer ran aground at the mouth of the Cape Fear River, but passengers and crew managed to get away in boats before the vessel was seized by Federal troops as a prize of war. For one year and some days Lamar had wandered about in a strangely unreal role. Now he had, at last, returned to the South.[41]

---

tinued in somewhat maudlin tones: "If I should be captured by the Federals, do not be alarmed. They will only place me in confinement, if they do that. Well, I can stand anything that they can inflict. *They can't break my spirit*, and I will be restored to you sometime or other."

38. Lamar to Mrs. Clay, August 8, 1863, in C. C. Clay Papers.

39. C. J. McRae to C. G. Memminger, October 2, 1863, in *Official Records*, Ser. IV, Vol. II, 980–81; C. J. McRae to C. G. Memminger, October 7, 1863, *ibid.*, 982–85.

40. *The Index, A Weekly Journal of Politics, Literature and News*, III (October 22, 1863), 405, 408–409; *ibid.*, III (October 29, 1863), 423. The speech of October 16 appears to be the same speech given in Mayes, *Lamar*, 112–13; and described in Cate, *Lamar*, 102–103.

41. "Report of Acting Rear-Admiral Lee, U. S. Navy," December 17, 1863, in *Official Records, Navies*, Ser. I, Vol. IX, 337–38; Mayes, *Lamar*, 113; Clay, *A Belle of the Fifties*, 181; Dwight Franklin Henderson (ed.), *The Private Journal of*

Lamar spent some three weeks with his family. He then traveled to Richmond, arriving about January 1, 1864. He first consulted with Jefferson Davis and Judah P. Benjamin regarding the European situation and then turned to the numerous acquaintances whose company he doubtless had missed.[42]

Friends who welcomed him back to the social rounds of the capital city thought him somewhat the worse for wear. His old friend, General James Chesnut, claimed that he did not at first recognize Lamar. And Mrs. Chesnut, after asking the returned diplomat to a special dinner, only to have him come on the wrong night, believed him "more absent-minded and distrait than ever." Nevertheless, he played the same old drawing room role and fascinated his audience with tales of the Europeans. Try as he might to please listeners with his own adventures, Lamar related only hopelessness for the Confederate cause in Europe.[43]

Lamar worked briefly for the War Department in Richmond and then he again became an emissary for Jefferson Davis.[44] This time Davis' critics in Georgia were the object of Lamar's diplomacy. A dispute between Georgia and the central government had started during the summer of 1862, centering on the conscription acts, and by 1864 the question of authority had become crucial. On February 15, 1864, a law providing for suspension of the writ of habeas corpus caused resentment throughout the South, but the trouble again focused in Georgia. Alexander H.

Georgiana Gholson Walker, 1862–1865, With Selections from the Post-War Years, 1865–1876 (Tuscaloosa, 1963), 47, 54.

42. J. P. Benjamin to Henry Hotze, Dispatch No. 13, January 9, 1864, in *Official Records, Navies,* Ser. II, Vol. III, 993–96; Chesnut, *A Diary from Dixie,* 347. Mrs. Lamar spent Christmas in Georgia and presumably Lamar joined her there. See James I. Robertson, Jr. (ed.), *The Diary of Dolly Lunt Burge* (Athens, Georgia, 1962), 88. He reached Richmond in time to stand in the "visiting line" at a New Year's party given by Jefferson Davis. See Ishbel Ross, *First Lady of the South: The Life of Mrs. Jefferson Davis* (New York, 1958), 190.

43. Chesnut, *A Diary from Dixie,* 347, 360–61; Clay, *A Belle of the Fifties,* 181.

44. Lamar's brief service for the War Department in January and perhaps February, 1864, is suggested in the following War Department correspondence: Lamar to T. L. Merriweather, January 27, 1864; Lamar to J. A. Campbell, Assistant Secretary of War, February, n.d., 1864; and J. A. Campbell to Lamar, March 11, 1864, all found in Record Group No. 109.

Stephens, vice president of the Confederacy, his brother Linton, and Governor Joseph E. Brown organized a campaign of protest which included denunciation of Davis by the Georgia legislature and the passing of peace resolutions by that body. Ultimately, the Stephens-Brown clique intended to carry its protest beyond the state government into a popular movement against the president.[45]

Davis, who had good reason to expect trouble, countered with an organized effort to neutralize the opposition. Already well known in the state, Lamar joined Georgians Ben Hill, A. H. Kenan, and Howell Cobb to make a round of progovernment speeches.[46]

After preliminary exchanges between Davis' critics and defenders, the Georgia legislature convened on March 10, 1864, in special session to hear the governor's message and to consider his antiadministration resolutions. Comparing Davis' government to the English Star Chamber, Brown denounced its encroachments upon state sovereignty and charged that the suspension of the writ of habeas corpus was unconstitutional.[47] That same day Linton Stephens introduced resolutions condemning the suspension and urging that peace proposals be made after each major Confederate military victory. Vice President Alexander Stephens capped the effort by appealing to the legislature to pass the condemnatory measures.[48]

Later, Howell Cobb and A. H. Kenan responded with a series of speeches both to the public and to the legislature. During March and April Lamar spoke in the state house and to audiences in Milledgeville, Columbus, and Atlanta; and, as did Cobb

45. Albert Burton Moore, *Conscription and Conflict in the Confederacy* (New York, 1924), 255–58, 270, 273–74; T. Conn Bryan, *Confederate Georgia* (Athens, Ga., 1953), 95–96; Frank L. Owsley, *States' Rights in the Confederacy* (Gloucester, Mass., 1961), 183–90.

46. Bryan, *Confederate Georgia*, 95–96.

47. A. D. Candler (ed.), *The Confederate Records of the State of Georgia* (Atlanta, 1909–11), 587–665; Milledgeville (Ga.) *Confederate Union*, March 15, 1864.

48. *Georgia House Journal, 1863–64*, pp. 51–52, 68; Milledgeville (Ga.) *Confederate Union*, March 15, 1864.

and Kenan, he attacked the critics of the Davis administration.[49]
Lamar's "State of the Country" speech in Atlanta summarized
the European situation and then turned upon the "efforts to
excite opposition and dissatisfaction among the people." Armed
with British precedents and Confederate constitutional authority, Lamar described the circumstances which made the suspension of the habeas corpus act necessary. He denied any imputa-
tion of disloyalty but urged that "the best service that any one
can render at this time to the cause of States' rights is to sustain
and uphold the Government of these Confederate States." [50]

These efforts may not have been totally unsuccessful. Even
though the Georgia legislature passed resolutions condemning
the suspension, it also expressed confidence in President Davis—
to the chagrin of the antiadministration forces. The victory over
the central government was at best a qualified one.[51]

Although apparently without official position, Lamar remained in Georgia on the government's behalf. He continued
to make public speeches, and on May 28, 1864, he wrote Mrs.
Lamar explaining a delay in Macon: "I have some important
matters in the military line on my hands." The nature of these
important matters is not known. There was, however, a great
deal to do as northern Georgia faced the prospect of William T.
Sherman's drive from Chattanooga to Atlanta and then to the
sea. As the summer wore on and Atlanta fell, Davis himself

49. Louise Biles Hill, *Joseph E. Brown and the Confederacy* (Chapel Hill, 1939),
210; Milledgeville (Ga.) *Confederate Union*, March 22, 1864; Milledgeville (Ga.)
Southern Recorder, March 22, 1864; Atlanta *Southern Confederacy*, March 19,
April 29, 1864. Milledgevile (Ga.) *Southern Recorder*, May 17, 1864, reported that
Lamar's father-in-law, A. B. Longstreet, was publishing a number of articles in the
Columbus *Times* against "Stephens and Co."

50. Lucius Quintus Cincinnatus Lamar, *Speech of Hon. L. Q. C. Lamar, of
Miss., on the state of the country* (New York, 1972). Also printed as "Address
delivered at the Atheneum, Atlanta, Georgia, April 14, 1864," in Mayes, *Lamar*,
639–56. The speech was reported and summarized in Atlanta *Southern Confederacy*,
April 29, 1864. For Brown's reaction to this speech see Joseph E. Brown to A. H.
Stephens, April 19, 1864, in Phillips (ed.), *Correspondence of Toombs, Stephens,
and Cobb*, 641.

51. These resolutions are given in *Official Records*, Ser. IV, Vol. III, 234–37.

rushed to Georgia to rally again the waning resolve of that unhappy land. In September, Davis gave major addresses in Macon
and Augusta. Remembering Lamar's earlier role as a presidential spokesman, it seems reasonable to surmise that he contributed as before to the support of Davis' effort.[52]

Probably Lamar could not have made a more strenuous effort
during these months. He had returned from Europe physically
weak and had suffered further illness during the summer of
1864.[53] In addition, Lamar was overwhelmed with other personal cares. His sister died in May; then his surviving brother,
Thomas B. Lamar, fell in battle in June, 1864; and his daughter
was "quite sick." Furthermore, Lamar feared that Federal troops
might overrun Oxford, Georgia, where his wife was visiting, and
that she would be forced to flee in his absence. If she must flee,
he directed her to "take the gold and put it in my black carpet
bag and carry it with you." [54]

Understandably, this crisis atmosphere nurtured a special interest in religion. Although he had formally joined the Methodist Church in 1862, Lamar was still searching for the selfless
devotion and spiritual tranquility that he associated with the
Christian faith. In June he confessed to Mrs. Clay that to him
"religion is only a DUTY, not a joy." [55] Six months later, again in
Richmond, Lamar wrote his wife of his struggle: "I am still trying to subordinate all worldly things to the considerations associated with eternity . . . the favor of God, and the well-being of

52. Lamar to Mrs. Lamar, May 28, 1864, in Lamar Letters, University of North
Carolina Library; Lamar to Mrs. Clay, June 12, 1864, in C. C. Clay Papers. Lamar
dated the May letter in Macon. The June letter was written in Oxford and mentioned plans to go on to Athens. On Davis see William J. Cooper, "A Reassessment
of Jefferson Davis as War Leader: The Case from Atlanta to Nashville," *Journal of
Southern History*, XXXVI (May, 1970), 198–99.

53. Clay, *A Belle of the Fifties*, 204; unaddressed Lamar letter, filed September
21, 1864, in Jefferson Davis Papers, Record Group No. 109.

54. Lamar to Mrs. Lamar, May 28, 1864, in Lamar Letters, University of North
Carolina Library; Lamar to Mrs. Clay, June 12, 1864, in C. C. Clay Papers; Mayes,
Lamar, 114.

55. Lamar to Mrs. Clay, June 12, 1864, in C. C. Clay Papers.

my soul hereafter. . . . Pray to God, my darling, that we may all be his children." [56]

Lamar's difficulties at this time also included a misunderstanding with Jefferson Davis. The nature of the argument is unknown, but there is some reason to believe that the morbidly sensitive Davis found fault in remarks Lamar made regarding the strategy employed by Confederate forces and the roles of Beauregard, Johnston, and Bragg during the battle of Shiloh. At any rate Lamar pathetically pleaded with his friend Burton Harrison to intervene with Davis for him.[57] Despite this effort, Lamar's subsequent Confederate career did not reflect any special favor from Richmond. On December 3, 1864, he once again received a commission as colonel in the Confederate army with duty as judge advocate in the military court of A. P. Hill's 3rd Army Corps in Richmond.[58] According to his son-in-law, Lamar disliked the work and considered it "the most unpleasant duty I ever had to perform in my life." [59]

As a judge advocate Lamar found time to visit with his friends in the capital as they waited for what by this time must have been obvious to all—that the war was coming to an end. But there could have been little joy in society for an ill-fated soldier of a hopeless cause. In an intensely personal letter to Mrs. Clay, Lamar seemed to try to substitute religion for unkind destiny: "The reason why I withdrew more and more from the world, is that I find it more and more in my way as a Christian"; but agonizingly, "I have not yet felt that my nature has been regenerated. I have not realized the promises of pardon made to

56. Lamar to Mrs. Lamar, December 15, 1864, quoted in Mayes, *Lamar*, 560.

57. In an unaddressed letter, filed September 21, 1864, in Jefferson Davis Papers, Record Group No. 109, Lamar attempted to correct a mistaken representation of a conversation he had with Louis T. Wigfall and others about the battle at Shiloh. See also "Sister" to "Brother" [Burton N. Harrison], October 18, 1864, quoted in Halsell, "Friendship of Lamar and Davis," 137.

58. Lamar File, Record Group No. 109; "Journal of the Congress of the Confederate States of America," *Senate Documents*, 58th Cong., 2nd Sess., No. 234, XXVII, 320, 325.

59. Quoted in Mayes, *Lamar*, 115.

those who truly repent & believe." And for Mrs. Clay he recommended the same medicine as his own: "Oh my dear Mrs. Clay .... Become a Christian yourself." [60]

While Lamar thought on things spiritual, the Army of Northern Virginia began its evacuation of Petersburg on April 3, 1865, and moved toward the war's final act. When Lee admitted defeat at Appomattox Courthouse, Lamar was acting aide to General James Longstreet, though still commissioned as judge advocate. After the surrender he was paroled and released.[61] According to his perceptive but sometimes over romantic son-in-law, Lamar sadly committed himself from that moment to the future of the South, declaring: "I shall stay with my people, and share their fate. I feel it to be my duty to devote my life to the alleviation, so far as in my power lies, of the sufferings this day's disaster will entail upon them." [62]

60. Lamar to Mrs. Clay, February 11, 1865, in C. C. Clay Papers.
61. "Paroles of the Army of Northern Virginia," in *Southern Historical Society Papers*, XV (1887), 70.
62. Quoted in Mayes, *Lamar*, 115. Mayes gives no source for these words.

Early Reconstruction: Hiatus

After Appomattox, Lamar faced the problems of supporting his family and reconstructing some kind of career for himself. Following several weeks delay in Richmond, he started for Oxford, Mississippi, to face these responsibilities. There he would at long last be reunited with his wife, his children, and the Longstreets who had moved from South Carolina. However this prospect might please him, it was dampened by the realization that his two brothers and his law partners, Autrey and Mott, had not returned from the war.[1]

The deaths of Autrey and Mott certainly exacerbated the sense of dislocation and bewilderment which inevitably enveloped Lamar and other returning veterans. Perhaps no less important to his sense of well-being was the persistent possibility that the Federal government might not permit former secessionist and high ranking Confederates to remain at home unpunished or to keep their property. At this early date rules had simply not been established for the new order. And of course until the Federal government provided rules no one could know what the new order would be. This fear faded but slowly while the government vacillated in its treatment of the South.

Lamar did not immediately resume his antebellum employment, and indeed there was nothing to resume. To his way of thinking political office was out of the question since the old

1. Wade, *Longstreet*, 351; Mayes, *Lamar*, 117, 120; Rowland (ed.), *Mississippi Sketches*, I, 176; *ibid.*, II, 284.

leadership would only excite the suspicion of United States authorities. Reconstruction, he reasoned, could best be directed by individuals not identified with the Confederacy. And even if Lamar had been of a different mind about his political future, the war-chastened people of Mississippi were in no mood to again follow men who had fashioned secession and initiated the war against the Union whose power proved to be overwhelming.[2]

President Andrew Johnson's reconstruction policy gave little cause to doubt the wisdom of this judgment. Provisional Governor William L. Sharkey and the elected administration of Benjamin G. Humphreys were by no means radical and did not endanger the old economic and social order. Johnson's grant of amnesty to former Confederates did not include Lamar because of his military and diplomatic rank, but he seems not to have been otherwise inconvenienced; and there is no evidence that he applied for a special pardon.[3]

The university's reopening offered him no more than politics. There were only three professorships initially, and there is no indication that Lamar was offered a position.[4] Prospects in agriculture seemed dismal too. Though he had not lived at Solitude since his first election to Congress in 1857, the place represented virtually all his capital. The plantation had sustained physical damage, but this was dwarfed by the loss of his investment in slaves.[5] Furthermore, he had been unable to make payments on

2. Lamar to Burton N. Harrison, August 13, 1867, in Burton N. Harrison Papers. J. S. McNeily, "War and Reconstruction in Mississippi, 1863–1890," *Publications of the Mississippi Historical Society*, Centenary Series, II (1918), 313, holds this attitude to be typical. Charles Sallis, "The Color Line in Mississippi Politics, 1865–1915" (Ph.D. dissertation, University of Kentucky, 1967), 22; and William C. Harris, *Presidential Reconstruction in Mississippi* (Baton Rouge, 1967), 47–51, analyze the political inactivity of former secessionists.

3. James D. Richardson (ed.), *A Compilation of the Messages and Papers of the Presidents, 1789–1897* (Washington, 1894–1899), VI, 312.

4. Waddell, *Memorials of Academic Life*, 447. Board Minutes make no mention of Lamar.

5. In the last antebellum personal tax return made by Lamar in 1857, he paid taxes on twenty-six slaves. The census of 1860 shows land estimated at $11,000, and some seventy-five head of stock. In 1864 Lamar reported fifteen head of cattle and twenty slaves. See Personal Tax Rolls, Lafayette County, Mississippi, 1857 and 1864, MDAH; and Production of Agriculture in the County of Lafayette, from the "Original Census Returns, 1860," in Lamar Subject File, MDAH.

the property during the war, and the aggregating interest wiped out earlier installments. In January, 1866, Lamar finally deeded the place back to his father-in-law, from whom he had bought it on credit. This depressing event was enough to exasperate the former lord of Solitude even with Longstreet.[6]

A law practice provided the only remaining alternative. Here again Lamar's past caught up with him. He wrote a Georgia friend about the prospect of moving back to Georgia, since in Mississippi old Whigs had largely preempted the legal field during the antebellum period when they were excluded from public office. Even for Whig lawyers, northern Mississippi was forbidding in 1865. The area had suffered physical ruin from both military destruction and normal deterioration, and the war had ended too late in the year for spring plowing. Furthermore, it was believed that the Negro would not work outside the bonds of slavery. These conditions indicated a troubled future for an economy in which lawyers, merchants, and most others depended upon agricultural production.[7]

Considering these poor prospects, it is no wonder that "Moody Lamar," as Mrs. Clay had called him,[8] had to fight the despair which clouded this period of his life. According to his son-in-law, Lamar's unrest was such that "loving eyes . . . watched him narrowly then . . . for more than one anxious heart interpreted those volcanic moods, and trembled lest in some weaker hour a dreadful deed, born of fury and despair, should spring like a tiger from its lair, and ruin all." [9] An anxious family perhaps recalled Lamar's father and his tragic end.

6. Lamar to "Jimmy" [James G. Paine], [1866?], in Lamar Letters, University of North Carolina Library; Lamar to A. B. Longstreet, January 19, 1866, in Deed Book K, 367, Lafayette County Court House, Oxford, Mississippi. In Lamar to Mrs. Fanny Paine, April 20, 1869, in Lamar Letters, University of North Carolina Library, he remarked that Longstreet gave Mrs. Lamar some land and some stock but does not describe it except to say that it pays nothing.

7. Lamar to Judge James Jackson, May 30, 1870, quoted in Mayes, Lamar, 127–28; Ross H. Moore, "Economic and Social Conditions during Reconstruction in Mississippi" (Ph.D. dissertation, Duke University, 1937), 3–7; Harris, Presidential Reconstruction in Mississippi, 18–36.

8. Clay, A Belle of the Fifties, 48.

9. Mayes, Lamar, 167; George J. Leftwich, "Lucius Q. C. Lamar," The Methodist Review, XLIV (1896), 71.

Lamar rested at Longstreet's residence until September, 1865, when he entered a law partnership with his good friend and later political ally, General Edward C. Walthall, at Coffeeville, Mississippi, about thirty miles south of Oxford. Although Coffeeville was the seat of Yalobusha County and on the Mississippi Central Railroad line, it was still no more than a village. Lamar had for the time resigned himself to obscurity as a hamlet lawyer.[10]

In their practice the two veterans did fairly well by the standards of the day. Undoubtedly Lamar benefitted from Walthall's reputation as a foremost lawyer and former district attorney in Coffeeville. He felt this obligation to Walthall so deeply that in his sentimental way he later wrote: "Do you know that but for you I could not keep up? I would have given up long ago, and never made an effort." [11]

With this assistance Lamar made some headway in meeting his financial obligations and slowly paid off bills dating back to prewar times. So numerous were the collectors that he had "begun to think that I never paid for anything in my life." [12] By March, 1866, he felt heartened enough to make light of his situation. Mrs. Jefferson Davis wrote that "in Lamar's woeful account of his difficulties I forgot for a time my griefs, and laughed heartily." [13]

Time might have secured financial stability but for a recurrence of bad luck. Under pressures of overwork, or maybe nervous tension, Lamar's health "gave way," and the partnership with Walthall necessarily dissolved.[14] Fortunately, a less demand-

10. Lamar to "Jimmy," [1866?], in Lamar Letters, University of North Carolina Library; Mayes, *Lamar*, 120.

11. Lamar to Edward C. Walthall, n.d., 1861, quoted in Mayes, *Lamar*, 120; *ibid.*, 119–20; Lamar to "Jimmy," [1866?], in Lamar Letters, University of North Carolina Library.

12. Lamar to "Jimmy," [1866?], in Lamar Letters, University of North Carolina Library.

13. Mrs. Jefferson Davis to Jefferson Davis, March, n.d., 1866, in Hudson Strode (ed.), *Jefferson Davis: Private Letters, 1823–1889* (New York, 1966), 238.

14. Lamar to "Jimmy," [1866?], in Lamar Letters, University of North Carolina Library.

ing position at the university became available about this time. The rapid growth of the student body to nearly 250 prompted the board to add several new instructors. Chancellor Waddell, who had been a member of the antebellum faculty, asked Lamar to join his staff for the fall term of 1866.[15]

As professor of ethics and metaphysics, Lamar received the regular, if meagre, income of $2,000 a year plus student tuition payments which were made directly to teachers. This latter benefit, however, was partially cancelled because Lamar permitted and often invited poverty-stricken students to attend class without charge. The board also supplemented his salary by authorizing faculty housing on campus; and by boarding students in his home, Lamar enhanced this advantage.[16]

Lamar's relative security as a teacher found expression in the assistance he gave to those less fortunate than himself. Exhibiting an apparently sincere interest in the welfare of his former comrades in arms, he worried especially about Jefferson Davis, Burton N. Harrison, and Clement C. Clay, all imprisoned by Union authorities. When Clay was released in April, 1866, Lamar wrote asking him to live in the Lamar household. "Please come," he wrote. "I believe the sight of you will restore my health—at least if anything can." [17] When Davis left prison, Lamar suggested to students at the university that they make up a gift of appreciation for the ex-president. He collected some $460 and added $40 of his own money. Ironically, the bank where Lamar deposited the $500 failed three days later and he had to put up another $500 himself: "I got the money for Jeff & sent it to him," he wrote. "Poor fellow he dont know what the 500 cost." [18]

15. John N. Waddell to Lamar, June 2, 1866, in Lamar-Mayes Papers; Waddell, *Memorials of Academic Life*, 300, 456; Board Minutes, 89–90.
16. Board Minutes, 90; A. G. Brown to Lamar, January 2, 1867, in Lamar-Mayes Papers; Lamar to "Jimmy," August 11, 1868, in Lamar Letters, University of North Carolina Library; Lamar to Mrs. Fanny Paine, April 20, 1869, in Lamar Letters, *ibid.*; Daniel J. Meador, "Lamar and the Law at the University of Mississippi," *Mississippi Law Journal*, XXXIV (May, 1963), 237.
17. Lamar to C. C. Clay, April 24, 1866, in C. C. Clay Papers.
18. Lamar to "Jimmy," [1866?], in Lamar Letters, University of North Carolina Library; Lamar to Burton N. Harrison, August 13, 1867, in Burton N. Harrison Papers.

In assuming the chair of ethics and metaphysics, Lamar returned to the position he had held briefly in 1860–1861. After only one month, however, he assumed additional duties as professor of law. Lamar occupied the two positions until January, 1867, when the board elected him professor of governmental science and law and cancelled all other teaching responsibilities. Lamar in effect became the law department since he was its only professor.[19]

Lamar directed the law department for the duration of his stay at the university. Though he also practiced law privately and later dabbled in politics, he was in fact a full-time academician and presumably intended to remain one. Teaching was now a career for him rather than a supplementary position as it had been in his earlier relationships with the university.

As a professor of law Lamar drew directly from his own educational experience and antebellum background.[20] His legal training had been informal and probably had less impact than the more comprehensive instruction he received at Emory College and at the Manual Education School. These institutions were committed to a classical philosophy of education and his system for training lawyers naturally conformed to this approach. Lamar taught his two-year course within a broad framework which related law to the great public themes which concerned him most profoundly. As in his own practice, he eschewed details and trivialities. Further reflecting his Emory background, he considered the inculcation of ethical standards to be an integral part of a teacher's duty.[21]

19. Board Minutes, 93, 96–97; Faculty Record Book, 210–11; Jackson (Miss.) *Daily Clarion*, January 25, 1867.

20. Meador, "Lamar and the Law at the University of Mississippi," is an invaluable guide to this subject.

21. *Ibid.*, 235, 242–43; Sylvester J. Hemleben and Richard T. Bennett, "A Historical Sketch of the Early Law School of the University of Mississippi: A New Found Memoir," *Mississippi Law Journal*, XXXVII (December, 1965), 48. In a congressional speech Lamar later proudly recalled these efforts and claimed that "I have always endeavored to impress the belief that truth was better than falsehood, honesty better than policy, courage better than cowardice." See *Congressional Record*, 45th Cong., 2nd Sess., 1061.

To accompany his rather loose personal approach, Lamar prescribed a highly technical curriculum typical of university law schools of the day. Texts were the same standard works used in the antebellum law course at Mississippi, but Lamar added his own touch. Oral examinations played a regular part in his class, and he commonly designated students to summarize his lectures and to submit to questioning by classmates.[22] He developed the principle of student participation further by employing the moot court system. Lamar usually served as judge while his charges filled the court's other positions and acted out the hypothetical cases which he devised. Students were trained by this method in the actual workings of court machinery as well as in the application of legal opinions.[23]

Lamar's methods flourished in the university environment of that time. Enrollment was so small that he could give constant personal attention to his students. And happily, most were mature enough to profit from this relationship and willingly accepted the required discipline. A large number were veterans of the war and by no means as casual about their education as their antebellum predecessors.[24]

During his first two years at the university, Lamar devoted his time almost entirely to academic obligations. In 1867 he became a director of the Mississippi Central Railroad Company, but the

22. Meador, "Lamar and the Law at the University of Mississippi," 235–36, 240; Edward Mayes, *History of Education in Mississippi*, ed. Herbert B. Adams (Washington, 1899), 145.

23. Meador, "Lamar and the Law at the University of Mississippi," 240, maintains that Lamar originated the moot court system. This is denied by Hemleben and Bennett, "Early Law School of the University of Mississippi," 49. Cate, *Lamar*, 123, holds that Lamar introduced the case study system into American legal education, but this is questioned by Meador, 240, and by Hemleben and Bennett, 49n. There seems to be no conclusive evidence of innovation by Lamar as an educator, although he obviously showed imagination in his approach. A contemporary description of the law school is in the Oxford (Miss.) *Falcon*, August 17, 1867.

24. *Historical Catalogue*, 106–108; Waddell, *Memorials of Academic Life*, 447–48. Meador, "Lamar and the Law at the University of Mississippi," 242, 256, judges Lamar a successful teacher. *Historical Catalogue*, 61, refers to him as "that prince of teachers." Davidson College honored Lamar in 1867 with a Doctor of Laws degree. See Oxford (Miss.) *Falcon*, August 10, 1867. He also served as a trustee of Vanderbilt University in 1874. See Edwin Mims, *History of Vanderbilt University* (Nashville, 1946), 53–56.

position appears to have been only nominal in the beginning. Lamar's stock, apparently given to his wife by A. B. Longstreet, was not considered valuable.[25]

He had intended at first to combine private practice and teaching but did not do so until the spring of 1868, when he decided that he could not adequately support his family without supplementing his university salary.[26] His first opportunity to practice came in a federal court meeting in Oxford where he defended four clients against debt collections. At about the same time he served as defense attorney in at least one murder case, in which a white man was charged with killing a Negro woman.[27]

In the fall of 1868 Lamar attempted to improve his situation by entering into a partnership in Oxford with a young lawyer, E. D. Clark.[28] The two men became fast friends and their practice developed auspiciously. By September, Lamar's good friend E. C. Walthall could remark: "I understand you are getting some good cases. I have never had any doubt about your getting a hand in all the good cases in your region, when you get fairly to work." [29] In the next year Lamar repaired his fortunes well enough to be able to purchase a tract of land in Oxford and build a "humble but attractive cottage of six rooms." [30] Still,

25. *Annual Report of the President and Directors of the Mississippi Central Railroad Company* (1867), 1 (MDAH). Lamar to Mrs. Fanny Paine, April 20, 1869, in Lamar Letters, University of North Carolina Library, refers only to "stock" and land which "make no income at all."

26. Lamar to Mrs. A. B. Longstreet, July 26, 1866, quoted in Mayes, *Lamar*, 124; Meador, "Lamar and the Law at the University of Mississippi," 248. Lamar offered to handle a sick friend's cases in August, 1867, but apparently nothing came of it. See Lamar to Mrs. H. W. Walter, August 8, 1867, in Harvey Walter Papers, Southern Historical Collection, University of North Carolina Library.

27. Lamar to "Jimmy," August 11, 1868, in Lamar Letters, University of North Carolina Library; Meador, "Lamar and the Law at the University of Mississippi," 249; Lamar to C. C. Clay, July 14, 1869, in C. C. Clay Papers.

28. Lamar to E. D. Clark, July 16, 1868, in L. Q. C. Lamar Papers, University of Mississippi Library; Oxford (Miss.) *Falcon*, August 8, 1868. Clark previously practiced in Coffeeville as a partner of E. C. Walthall. He was a young man at the time without an established clientele.

29. E. C. Walthall to Lamar, September 21, 1868, in Lamar-Mayes Papers.

30. John Cullen to V. L. [Mrs. L. Q. C.] Lamar, June 18, 1868, in Deed Book L, 7, Lafayette County Court House, Oxford, Mississippi, shows $1,500 paid cash and a balance of $1,500 paid June 12, 1869. See also Mayes, *Lamar*, 126, 166. Mayes credits the house to the growing practice.

his legal fees barely supplemented his university salary of $2,000. He grossed only $500 in 1869, and presumably made even less in 1868, when he first resumed legal practice.[31]

In 1868, however, the Mississippi Central board of directors, including Lamar, leased the financially ailing railroad to the Southern Railroad Association controlled by Henry S. McComb, a railroad entrepreneur who had come south from Wilmington, Delaware. The new operator employed Lamar's legal services from time to time until 1872, when control of the road changed hands once again. The company's records show no payments to Lamar until 1870, but then he received sizable sums through 1872, the year the reorganization took place. His fees came to $3,194 in 1870, $1,500 in 1871, and $3,000 in 1872.[32]

In April, 1872, the Southern Railroad Association and the Mississippi Central joined with the New Orleans, Jackson, and Great Northern Railroad, and the Illinois Central Railroad to gain rail connections and financial assistance. A five million dollar debt and incomplete lines of the Mississippi Central made such an agreement desirable. As a consequence, the Illinois Central purchased eight million dollars worth of Mississippi Central bonds in return for a mortgage on the road's lines that were to be completed to the Ohio River. Then in 1874 the Mississippi Central consolidated with the New Orleans, Jackson, and Great

31. Personal Tax Rolls, Lafayette County, Mississippi, 1869, MDAH. Meador, "Lamar and the Law at the University of Mississippi," 249, lists only seven cases in federal court for Lamar during the period of two years when he practiced and taught. The Tax Roll shows income of $300 from land which was apparently that sold by Lamar, V. L. Lamar, H. R. Branham, and Francis Branham to Robert Hill, January 23, 1869, in Deed Book L, 218, Lafayette County Court House, Oxford, Mississippi, for $580. The land presumably was a gift from Longstreet to his daughters. See Lamar to Mrs. Fanny Paine, April 20, 1869, in Lamar Letters, University of North Carolina Library.

32. *Annual Report of the President and Directors of the Mississippi Central Railroad Company* (1868), 5–6, 8–9 (MDAH); Southern Railroad Association Ledger (Illinois Central Archives, Newberry Library, Chicago), II, 408; III, 434; IV, 476. On one point the Southern Railroad Association Ledger is unclear. Vol. II, 408, shows a debit entry on June 14, 1868, for $1,500 and a credit entry for the same amount dated June, n.d., 1870. The obvious (but not conclusive) deduction is that payment to Lamar was deferred for two years. There is no other entry prior to 1870.

Northern as the New Orleans, St. Louis, and Chicago. Completed track and running arrangements with the Illinois Central thus provided service from the Great Lakes to New Orleans.[33]

The consolidation apparently provided no position for Lamar. At any rate the road soon encountered fateful difficulties which led to its absorption by the expanding Illinois Central. In March, 1876, a receiver was appointed and a foreclosure sale followed in 1877. Whatever investment Lamar had retained was lost. His financial windfall as corporation lawyer was short-lived and there would be no repetition of this prosperity.[34] Many lawyer-politicians of the New South profited enormously from business connections as many had benefitted from the plantation system of antebellum times; but Lamar would remain after this a man of modest and even meagre means.

At about the same time that Lamar opened his Oxford law office in 1868, he also became active in political affairs once more. Prior to that time he had made only one known speech, and that for commencement exercises in June, 1866. Then after almost two years of public silence, he began to speak out again during 1868 and 1869. In addition to several political speeches he addressed a ladies' literary society, a four-county Confederate veterans' reunion, a county fair crowd, and the Female Institute in Jackson, Mississippi.[35]

Since Lamar presented himself as a practicing lawyer during these months, such appearances must have served as an advertising medium announcing his return from the ivory tower. Moreover, these activities bore important political implications should Lamar care to return to public life. This was most obvious dur-

33. Tripartite Agreement of April 11, 1872 (Illinois Central Archives); Mortgage of the Mississippi Central on May 1, 1872 (Illinois Central Archives); *Annual Report of the President and Directors of the Mississippi Central Raliroad Company* (1873), 5, 6, 12 (Illinois Central Archives).

34. *Chicago, St. Louis and New Orleans Railroad Company Laws and Documents* (1881), 87–89 (Illinois Central Archives).

35. Oxford (Miss.) *Falcon*, July 5, 1866, April 18, July 11, October 17, 1868, June 9, 1869.

ing a festive reception for Jacob Thompson, who returned from self-imposed exile in the spring of 1869. The celebrations, enthusiastically attended by the townspeople, ended with the two men being paraded through town. Lamar had apparently become a local favorite once again.[36]

Lamar was undoubtedly more concerned with political appearances in 1868–1869 than he had been when he first returned to Mississippi. With good reason he had felt it wise to remain in obscurity until the process of readjustment had run its course. In 1867–1868, however, the political situation changed. What had seemed a transitional subordination to the national government assumed more ominous tones. Civil control gave way to military administration, and the state government was relegated to a provisional capacity. Freedmen for the first time claimed the right of suffrage, and the proposed constitution of 1868 would strictly prohibit political participation for Confederate leaders. Under these circumstances passive men drastically changed their attitude toward nonparticipation. Since Congress specifically provided that a majority of the votes cast would ratify the constitution, the old leadership was forced to act or face permanent exclusion.

Though Lamar's part in the struggle was small, he did take a public stand against the pending "Mongrel Constitution" and the Republican party. Toward this end he appeared with Benjamin G. Humphreys, the conservative gubernatorial candidate, at mass meetings in Oxford and in Water Valley, a few miles to the south. Lamar must have been gratified when the victorious anticonstitution ticket led by Humphreys carried Lafayette County and the congressional district by a substantial margin against B. B. Eggleston, the radical candidate.[37]

Since the proposed constitution suffered defeat along with Eggleston, military government of the state continued until 1870. The future dimmed even more when Brevet Major Gen-

36. *Ibid.*, April 24, May 1, 1869; Cabaniss, *A History of the University of Mississippi*, 77.
37. Oxford (Miss.) *Falcon*, May 16, 1868; Political Research Consortium.

eral Adelbert Ames, acting civil governor, assumed command
of the military district in March, 1869. As both military commander and civil governor, and in the absence of a functioning
legislature, Ames's authority was virtually complete.[38]

The troops in Mississippi, however, numbered only about
a thousand, and none were stationed regularly at Oxford.
Nevertheless, several incidents occurred involving university students,[39] and Lamar heatedly wrote to a friend: "The truth is
our loves & friendships are the only things which the Yankee
sons-of-b_____ cannot confiscate. Let us hold on to it." [40]

No evidence has survived to prove that Lamar went beyond
this bitter resignation. But perhaps he did. A highly suggestive
letter of February 27, 1869, which left a great deal unsaid, informed him that "there will be an important conference . . . of
friends from different parts of the State. We are anxious for you
to meet us." [41] A meeting may or may not have taken place. If
Lamar participated in any political activities, clandestine or
otherwise, the records have since disappeared.

While Lamar smarted under Federal authority, President
Grant proclaimed that Mississippi should vote once more on
the constitution devised by the convention of 1868. To improve its chances of passage, Grant ordered that the most offensive clauses—those proscribing numerous Confederate leaders—
should be voted upon separately from the main body of the
constitution.

The proscriptive clauses were a divisive factor in the Mississippi Republican party. One faction which opposed the severity

38. James W. Garner, *Reconstruction in Mississippi* (New York, 1901), 229–30.
39. Waddell, *Memorials of Academic Life*, 456–57; Garner, *Reconstruction in Mississippi*, 230. Julia Kendel, "Reconstruction in Lafayette County," *Publications of the Mississippi Historical Society*, XIII (1913), tells a story of radical domination and troops garrisoned in Oxford. According to Kendel, 237, 240–41, a Negro militia unit was organized in 1870, but the Ku Klux Klan dispersed them. The account is so generally biased as to be of little help.
40. Lamar to "Jimmy," August 11, 1868, in Lamar Letters, University of North Carolina Library. This is the only profanity found in the existing Lamar papers.
41. W. Yerger, E. Barksdale, W. P. Harris to Lamar, February 27, 1869, in Lamar-Mayes Papers.

of the punitive provisions accused the other branch of going beyond the law's requirements. Calling themselves the National Union Republican party, they invited people of like mind, regardless of party or race, to join them in putting forth a ticket. The Democrats, with no prospects of victory, accepted the National Union Republican gubernatorial candidate, Louis Dent, brother-in-law to President Grant. Lamar approved the expediency of such an arrangement and even advised Dent on his campaign. He did not, however, take part in the canvass. Perhaps he feared that such a compromise might be costly in the future.[42]

James Lusk Alcorn, the regular Republican candidate, easily carried the state, including Lamar's home county. The constitution, ratified without the proscriptive clauses, entitled Mississippi to her first fully recognized government since the end of the war and permitted her to rejoin the Union.[43]

Alcorn's election and the inauguration of a Republican administration probably had a greater effect upon Lamar's career than any other event between 1866 and 1870. Either by design or chance, the university had been virtually untouched by the vicissitudes of reconstruction. Sharkey and Humphreys befriended the institution, and their policies were naturally acceptable to Lamar. General Ames also gave no reason for complaint: the board of trustees even favored Lamar with an honorary LL.D.[44]

Alcorn, on the other hand, provided immediate cause for alarm. Even before taking office he wrote his wife: "Chancellor Waddel [sic], Lamar, and others at the University at Oxford have sent overtures to me" and "Lamar thinks I will not turn him out as we have been personal friends." [45] In May, 1870, Alcorn appointed a new board of trustees dominated by men of his own political persuasion and presided over by himself. A fear that the

42. Garner, *Reconstruction in Mississippi*, 237–40; Mayes, *Lamar*, 164.

43. Alcorn won a majority of 38,089 from the entire state, a majority of 90 votes in Lafayette County, and a majority of 3,381 votes in the first district. Election data provided by Political Research Consortium.

44. Board Minutes, 183.

45. James Lusk Alcorn to Amelia Alcorn, December 27, 1869, quoted in Pereyra, *James Lusk Alcorn*, 123.

university would be "radicalized" spread instantly, and there was even talk of admitting Negro students.[46]

Lamar reacted in a partisan but predictable way and immediately resigned effective at the end of the term. Since the university continued its operation without great difficulty under the same chancellor and faculty, it is possible that he could have continued if he had so desired.[47] Perhaps the defeat galled Lamar's pride beyond endurance, or maybe he feared identification with the Republicans for political reasons. Whichever the case, he cloaked himself in martyrdom and took leave of the university for the third and final time. With characteristic eloquence and sentimentality he closed his academic career in a commencement address as pertinent to the speaker as to the audience: "And now, young gentlemen," he said, "as you go home I pray that you may have prosperity and happiness through life, with just enough of sorrow to remind you that this earth is not your home." [48]

Separation from the university evidently did not come easily. In this instance, as in others, Lamar's health furnished a fair gauge of his emotional state. Although he suffered no seizure, Lamar told a correspondent in late May, 1870, "I am so nervous that I cannot write with a pen." A few days later he wrote the same person, saying "it gives me great pain to write." [49] Lamar further displayed uneasiness when he considered moving to Georgia once again. Corresponding with a prospective law partner, Judge James Jackson in Macon, he spoke of the difficulty of practice in

46. Cabaniss, *A History of the University of Mississippi*, 80–81; Mayes, *History of Education in Mississippi*, 163–64; Waddell, *Memorials of Academic Life*, 465–68, 470.

47. Cabaniss, *A History of the University of Mississippi*, 81; Waddell, *Memorials of Academic Life*, 472–76; Memphis *Daily Appeal*, September 26, 1870; Oxford (Miss.) *Falcon*, August 20, September 3, 1870.

48. Mayes, *Lamar*, 127; Oxford (Miss.) *Falcon*, July 2, 1870.

49. Lamar to A. T. Bledsoe, May [25?], 30, 1870, in A. T. Bledsoe Papers, Manuscript Division, Library of Congress. Lamar's second letter began: "I wrote to you yesterday, but fearing that in my haste I misdirected my letter to some other place than Baltimore, I will . . . repeat the business part of the letter." On June 9, 1870, Lamar wrote to Bledsoe a third time without mention of his health. See Lamar to Bledsoe, June 9, 1870, in Hampton L. Carson Collection, Free Library of Philadelphia.

Mississippi and related his judgment that "I must take my property and family from the State." He indicated that he had discussed the problem with his old friend Jefferson Davis and that he "approves my purpose, and says he sees nothing but sorrow and wrongs for Mississippians in the future." [50] That sorrowful letter, however, preceded by several weeks the receipt of his first substantial legal fee from the Southern Railroad Association.

A. B. Longstreet also figured in Lamar's consideration of Georgia as a place to begin anew. In corresponding with Judge Jackson, Lamar proposed the establishment of a law school in Macon in conjunction with his practice and mentioned that Longstreet might be the chancellor. [51] By this time, however, Longstreet was in his eightieth year, and plans for a law school had to be abandoned when he died on July 9, 1870. A few days later, Lamar traveled to Georgia to deliver a commencement address at Emory College. According to Edward Mayes, he was at that time offered a professorship of belles lettres and history in the college; it came too late, however, for he had already determined to remain in his adopted state. [52]

A. B. Longstreet may or may not have instigated Lamar's aborted plan to move to Georgia. But the great influence that the old man always had upon his son-in-law, and the loss that Lamar felt at his death, doubtlessly figured into his deliberations at this time. There is also the possibility that Longstreet's death had another and more mundane effect, since he left an estate later estimated at about $50,000 in real estate and cash. Lamar's portion, combined with his income as railroad attorney, should have solved his immediate problems and may have made it easier to stay in Mississippi. [53]

Lamar's decision to remain in Oxford occasioned the forma-

50. Lamar to Judge James Jackson, May 30, 1870, quoted in Mayes, *Lamar*, 127–28.

51. *Ibid.*; Wade, *Longstreet*, 368–69.

52. Oxford (Miss.) *Falcon*, July 16, 1870; Mayes, *Lamar*, 33–34, 128–29. Mrs. Longstreet had died in October, 1868. See Wade, *Longstreet*, 356.

53. Wade, *Longstreet*, 303. No will is on file in the Lafayette County Court House. A number of deeds from Mrs. Lamar make it clear that she inherited land, but no estimate of the acreage can be made.

tion of a new law partnership with his brother-in-law, H. R. Branham.[54] He also continued to fulfill the public engagements which had begun in 1868. In the fall of 1870 he made several pronouncements of a semipolitical nature. On one occasion he addressed the Agricultural and Mechanical Association of Carroll and Choctaw counties on the merits of scientific farming as an adjustment to the free labor system. Lamar treated his listeners to blunt criticism of the North, but at the same time urged partial imitation of northern ideas on the relationship between the government and the economy.[55] In December, 1870, he engaged in another ostensibly nonpolitical but widely publicized act when he wrote a public letter eulogizing Robert E. Lee.[56] Except for these activities and two short speeches at the university, Lamar devoted the year and a half after Judge Longstreet's death to legal practice in Oxford.[57]

Lamar's life during this period was generally uneventful. On June 22, 1871, however, he became involved in an altercation reminiscent of the 1853 Georgia campaign. While attending federal court in Oxford, where several persons awaited trial under the Ku Klux Klan law, outlawing the Klan's "conspiracy," Lamar (who defended several accused Klansmen[58]) got into an argument with one of the government's witnesses. Lamar's de-

54. Oxford (Miss.) *Falcon*, July 30, 1870. Branham was better known as a physician.
55. Dunbar Rowland, *History of Mississippi: The Heart of the South* (Chicago, 1925), II, 525; Mayes, *Lamar*, 129–30. Agriculture was a subject which interested Lamar greatly. See Willie D. Halsell, "L. Q. C. Lamar's Taylor Farm: An Experiment in Diversified Farming," *Journal of Mississippi History*, V (October, 1943), 185–96; and Lamar to "Jeems" [Monroe], March 2, 1871, in Lamar Letters, University of North Carolina Library. See Mayes, *Lamar*, 120–21, for an excerpt from another address in the "latter part of 1870" in which he dealt with his separation from politics since 1865.
56. Lamar to Col. William H. McCardle, December 5, 1870, quoted in Oxford (Miss.) *Falcon*, March 4, 1871. The "Lee Letter" answered an invitation to speak on Lee's birthday. Though Lamar could not accept, he probably appreciated the value of being identified with Lee. Lamar also used the letter in his platonic wooing of Mrs. C. C. Clay: "I often thought of you when I was preparing it. And when the sublime subject seemed to rise . . . the thought, that your eyes would see what I might write, inspired me to try to say what was in my heart about Robert E. Lee." See Lamar to Mrs. Clay, March 13, 1871, in C. C. Clay Papers.
57. Oxford (Miss.) *Falcon*, June 23, July 7, 1871.
58. *Ibid.*, March 31, 1871.

fenders claimed that the disagreement began outside the courtroom when he upbraided the witness, a man by the name of Whistler, for his mistreatment of an old, drunk townsman. Inside the courtroom Lamar called upon the bench to arrest the malefactor. A great deal of confusion ensued, and Lamar threatened Whistler with a chair. In the uproar a United States marshal approached, and Lamar struck the officer in the face with his fist and knocked him down. Soldiers poured into the courtroom and restored order, but not before Lamar had made an inflammatory speech and threatened dire consequences if he should be arrested. Before further violence could occur, however, Lamar regained his composure and apologized to the court for his part in the fracas. Although the judge, a Republican, accepted the apology, he ordered Lamar's name stricken from the roll of the court's attorneys. This banishment, which could have been ruinous, continued only a few days and was then rescinded.[59]

The Oxford incident was not of great significance, at least not in any direct way. Lamar's practice was only briefly inconvenienced. His political opponents in later years revived the story to embarrass him, but with little effect. Lamar was in no way implicated with the Klan in the government reports, nor did anyone charge him with a connection. On the other hand, many people in Mississippi may have been favorably impressed and even enthusiastic about the thrashing of a United States official. Ironically the marshal, himself a carpetbagger, supported Lamar's subsequent election to Congress and opposed political exploitation of the incident.[60]

59. See "Testimony Taken by the Joint Select Committee to Inquire into the Condition of Affairs in the Late Insurrectionary States," Senate Reports, 42nd Cong., 2nd Sess., No. 41, Pts. 11 & 12, pp. 297–98, 348, 850, 857, 910–11, 1160–62, for testimony intended to be unfriendly to Lamar. For examples of "historical" but friendly accounts see Kendel, "Reconstruction in Lafayette County," 244–46; J. S. McNeily, "The Enforcement Act of 1871 and the Ku Klux Klan in Mississippi," Publications of the Mississippi Historical Society, IX (1906), 142–43; Mayes, Lamar, 131–35; and Cate, Lamar, 129–35. See also Oxford (Miss.) Falcon, June 30, July 14, 1871.

60. Unaddressed letter from J. H. Pierce (former U. S. marshal), December 31, 1887, in the Senate file relating to L. Q. C. Lamar's appointment to the Supreme Court, SEN50B–A3, Record Group No. 46, National Archives.

Nevertheless, Lamar's loss of self-control revealed something of his emotional state. This was the "violent mood" which his son-in-law believed threatened "a dreadful deed." [61] In a sense the event only dramatized the long pent up frustration Lamar felt during this period of forced retirement from public life. But even if the Republican government had been as oppressive as he believed, the futility of such physical violence, like the futility of his quitting the university, suggests that Lamar suffered profound mental anguish during these years. It also suggests once again that his delicate sensitivity to pressure could under certain circumstances incapacitate him for the task at hand.

61. Mayes, *Lamar*, 167.

Return to Politics and the
Sumner Eulogy

The state elections of 1868 and 1869 impressed upon Lamar an unforgettable lesson. The Democratic party in 1868 had defeated the Republican gubernatorial candidate and the constitution by a large majority, only to suffer a disastrous reversal in 1869. In the latter year the Democrats did not offer a candidate to oppose Alcorn, and their support of Louis Dent, a conservative carpet-bagger, was half-hearted. Nonparticipation by Democrats, including Lamar, had clearly contributed to the Republican victory. Future contests would also go by default unless Democrats fully reentered the state's political life.[1]

Lamar certainly had no reason to continue his self-imposed political exile after Mississippi's readmission to the union on February 23, 1870. On the other hand, a great deal could be gained if the state could be wrested from the Republican party. During his political retirement Lamar's greatest desire was to see an end to outside control of the state. "Our nominations and our platforms," he wrote in 1873, "were all made with a view to these Federal & external exigencies & relations." [2] Associated as

1. According to figures provided by the Political Research Consortium, Humphreys' majority in 1868 was 6,249 votes, while Alcorn won by 38,089 votes in 1869. Humphreys carried Lafayette County by 1,591 votes, while Alcorn won by 90 votes.
2. Lamar to E. D. Clark, October 14, 1873, in Lamar Papers, University of Mississippi Library. The letter concerned Lamar's support of the independent Republican ticket in 1873. Another version, unchanged in substance, is quoted in

he was with secession and war, his participation would have handicapped efforts to gain home rule. But these considerations changed with readmission to the union. Lamar looked to politics with renewed optimism.

The Republicans had anticipated a Democratic revival and, among other things, had designed the apportionment section of the 1868 constitution to entrench themselves in power. That document based legislative representation on total population distribution rather than on white population as had been the case previously. In this new order the plantation counties with their overwhelming Negro majorities became disproportionately powerful in the state.[3]

Despite this disadvantage, white Democrats fought hard to win the legislature in 1871. Lamar remained generally inactive in the campaign, but joined the debate on one occasion. He spoke then because Robert Lowry, a leading Democrat, fell ill just prior to a scheduled debate with Governor Alcorn at Holly Springs on October 9, 1871. Despite the hasty preparation, the Democratically biased Memphis *Appeal* felt that Lamar's effort "told with so much effect upon the Governor it was, indeed, pitiable to see the miserable subterfuges and shifts adopted by the gentleman." [4] The Oxford *Falcon* echoed these sentiments and urged Lamar out of retirement because "he is a man of the times . . . and is destined soon to take the lead in Southern politics." [5] Perhaps this return to the stump and a favorable reception from two of north Mississippi's most important papers stirred memories and a taste for political action.

In the voting which followed, Lamar received additional encouragement. Republicans won control of the legislature again,

---

Mayes, *Lamar*, 177–78. See also Lamar to Clark, October 16, 1873, in Lamar Papers, University of Mississippi Library.

3. Jackson (Miss.) *Daily Clarion*, June 10, 12, 1868; Vernon L. Wharton, *The Negro in Mississippi, 1865–1890* (Chapel Hill, 1947), 151.

4. Memphis *Daily Appeal*, October 11, 1871.

5. Oxford (Miss.) *Falcon*, October 13, 20, 1871. Alcorn disagreed with these judgments and wrote his wife, Amelia, October 11, 1871: "I think—and it was the judgment of every fair minded person, that I whaled both Lowery [*sic*] and Lamar badly—very badly indeed." See Pereyra, *James Lusk Alcorn*, 143.

but their majority was a small one; and many white counties went over to Democratic control.[6]

The startled Republican legislature hastened to consolidate its domination of the state's congressional representation. Republican candidates had carried all districts in 1869, but in several their small majorities appeared vulnerable. The legislature therefore reapportioned the states in 1872 so that five of the six districts were rendered absolutely secure while one was conceded to the Democrats. This was achieved by grouping the heavily white counties of northeast Mississippi into a single congressional district, thereby assuring Negro majorities in all the other districts.[7]

The reapportionment stratagem did indeed achieve the Republican objective, and its significance for L. Q. C. Lamar did not end there. Whereas under the old apportionment no Democrat from Lafayette County had even a slight chance of election, the Republicans now conceded that the first district should choose a Democratic congressman. This remarkable development placed the possibility of a public career squarely before Lamar, and he could not ignore it except at permanent peril to his political future. Furthermore, since only one Mississippi Democrat could become a congressman, Lamar had a unique opportunity to increase his status within the party. The antebellum ranking within the party leadership had been canceled out by war and reconstruction, and a new hierarchy might emerge with Lamar in a commanding role.[8]

6. Memphis *Daily Appeal*, November 8–9, 11, 13, 1871.

7. The 1872 population of the first district (including Alcorn, Benton, Calhoun, Itawamba, Lafayette, Lee, Pontotoc, Prentiss, Tippah, Tishomingo, Union, and Yalobusha counties) was 90,523 whites and 36,242 Negroes. The first district in 1860 (including Tishomingo, Tippah, Marshall, Desoto, Tunica, Coahoma, Panola, and Lafayette) had 72,720 whites and 67,029 Negroes. *Ninth Census of the United States, 1870*, I, 42–43, gives figures for 1860 and 1870.

8. A comparison of election figures provided by Political Research Consortium shows: (1) gubernatorial election of 1869: Alcorn won a majority of 3,381 in the first district. If the district had been constituted in 1869 as it was in 1872, Dent would have carried the district by 2,322 votes. Lafayette voted for Alcorn; (2) congressional election of 1869: the Republican candidate carried the district by 3,826 votes. If the district had been constituted in 1869 as it was in 1872, the conservative

A drive to put Lamar in Congress began as early as July, 1872. On the fifth of that month talk had become so general that he wrote John M. Stone, Democratic state senator and party leader, saying that the movement was not of his own doing and that his nomination would be legally complicated by the Fourteenth Amendment which banned many Confederates from holding office unless they first received a congressional pardon. In his disclaimer Lamar simply restated his fundamental postwar political belief: "I am *not* a candidate, but I am so convinced of the impropriety of nominating a man under disabilities, that I cannot see how it should be tendered." [9]

Lamar's insistence upon his unavailability continued through July. His misgivings, if misgivings rather than calculated timing, clearly did not preclude involvement in the rapidly changing local and national political scene. Early in May he had expressed enthusiasm for the anti-Grant Liberal-Republican movement within the Republican party and especially for the leadership of Carl Schurz.[10] Then in July he served as delegate to the Lafayette County primary convention. That same month Lamar was listed as a member of the state executive committee for Mississippi's Democratic-Conservative party. The party's convention, which Lamar presumably attended, adopted a platform favoring consolidation of all anti-Grant forces and opposing the nomination of a Democratic candidate in opposition to the Liberal-Republicans' presidential choice.[11]

Notwithstanding these advantageous developments, Lamar still held back from a commitment to seek public office. The Jackson *Clarion* listed candidates for the first congressional dis-

---

would have won by 1,894. Lafayette voted for the Republican; (3) complete statistics for the state election of 1871 are not available.

9. Lamar to John M. Stone, July 5, 1872, in John M. Stone Papers, MDAH.

10. Lamar to Charles Reemelin, May 6, 1872, quoted in Mayes, *Lamar*, 170. Reemelin corresponded with Lamar as early as 1870 and advised him to return to politics in 1872. He was a writer for the Cincinnati *Commoner*, and held various state offices in Ohio. See *Biographical Encyclopedia of Ohio of the Nineteenth Century* (Cincinnati, 1876), 560–61; and Mayes, *Lamar*, 130, 171.

11. Oxford (Miss.) *Falcon*, July 21, 1871; Jackson (Miss.) *Weekly Clarion*, July 4, 1872.

trict as late as July 11, 1872, without including him,[12] and four days later Lamar still denied that he had sought the congressional nomination: "I give it no encouragement. My aversion to reentering public life increases." But time was growing short and he hedged as a running politician hedges: "If there is a genuine and general desire of our people to have me go, I shall hardly know how to decline." [13]

As if by signal, the powerful Jackson *Clarion* and Memphis *Appeal* began on August 1 to urge that Lamar come out for the nomination before the district convention later that month. Both papers ridiculed the argument put by some that Lamar's disqualification under the Fourteenth Amendment would be prohibitive. This complication, they maintained, could easily be removed by Congress during the year before his term should begin.[14]

Meantime, Lamar met with the Democratic-Conservative executive committee to plan a statewide course of action. The group decided to communicate with the Liberal-Republicans of Mississippi and to invite their cooperation in choosing a single presidential electoral ticket.[15] Though not enthusiastic about Horace Greeley, whom he considered "unsound and pestilent," Lamar felt that the South had no choice but to combine its votes against Grant.[16]

A week later, Lamar decided to actively solicit support for nomination to Congress. Professing now to believe that his political disability could be removed, Lamar sought to convey that conviction to others. To local leader A. Y. Donaldson, Lamar wrote that Governor Alcorn, Republican representative in Congress, and other officials would support his case before Congress if he should be elected. He believed that the legal prece-

12. *Jackson* (Miss.) *Weekly Clarion*, July 11, 1872.

13. Lamar to Charles Reemelin, July 15, 1872, quoted in Mayes, *Lamar*, 170–72.

14. Jackson (Miss.) *Weekly Clarion*, August 1, 15, 1872; Memphis *Daily Appeal*, August 4, 5, 15, 1872.

15. Jackson (Miss.) *Weekly Clarion*, August 15, 1872. The consolidation took place as planned.

16. Lamar to Charles Reemelin, July 15, 1872, quoted in Mayes, *Lamar*, 170–72.

dents were on his side and that the runner-up in the election could not replace him if his disability were not removed. There was, Lamar felt sure, plenty of time to apply for relief in the coming session of Congress which would meet before his term commenced.[17]

Lamar apparently succeeded in rallying support, but neither this nor his rather enviable credentials assured an easy victory at the Tupelo meeting of Democrats on August 21. The fear expressed by the Memphis *Appeal* that the weaker candidates might combine to defeat him did not materialize, but fifteen ballots passed before he secured the nomination.[18]

Since nomination, in this case, was considered tantamount to election, Lamar emerged as an important political figure after eight years of almost complete retirement. Now he must have glimpsed a bright future; and at the same time he realized that so long as the state government remained in radical hands he would remain vulnerable to gerrymandering or other partisan tactics.

The Republican party chose R. W. Flournoy, a native white of Pontotoc County and an outspoken Radical, to oppose Lamar. While Flournoy's chances appeared nil at first, the possibility of an upset developed because of Lamar's status under the Fourteenth Amendment and the unexpected appearance of two independent candidates in the race. By emphasizing the question of Lamar's eligibility and the possibility that Congress might refuse to seat him, the independents and Flournoy might split the Democratic vote and bring about Lamar's defeat.[19]

Lamar's campaign also suffered when in mid-October he fell

17. Lamar to A. Y. Donaldson, August 12, 1872 (in possession of Miss Mary Donaldson, Box 84, Oakland, Mississippi). Lamar's contention that Republican leaders would permit him to be seated in Congress squares with a view held by John R. Lynch, Negro congressman elected in November, 1872, that the Republicans anticipated Lamar's election in advance. See John R. Lynch, *The Facts of Reconstruction* (New York, 1915), 67–68.

18. Hernando (Miss.) *Press and Times*, August 29, 1872; Jackson (Miss.) *Weekly Clarion*, August 29, 1872; Jackson *Weekly Mississippi Pilot*, August 24, 1872; Memphis *Daily Appeal*, August 19, 1872. No complete account of the convention has been located.

19. Jackson (Miss.) *Weekly Clarion*, September 12, 26, 1872.

sick while delivering a speech at Corinth. He suffered "symptoms of paralysis" and his doctor "prescribed absolute rest & quiet & said that I could not speak again without peril to my life—at best for several weeks." Against these grave warnings and the likelihood of another stroke Lamar continued his immediate engagements. But he felt "nearly used up" and compelled to cancel his last scheduled appearances.[20]

Prospects brightened, however, late in October when both independents withdrew from the race and threw their support to the Democrats. Then Lamar's problems virtually ended when Flournoy obligingly pledged not to take the seat if Lamar should be forced to resign after winning the election. Lamar now felt sufficiently recuperated and confident enough to leave the state to campaign for Horace Greeley in St. Louis.[21]

The Republican victory in Mississippi on November 5, 1872, surprised no one. Grant won a majority of 34,887 votes of 129,-163 cast. Republicans also won easy victories in five of six congressional districts. But the first district elected Lamar by a two to one majority. He lost in his home county of Lafayette, but that only demonstrated the nature of the contest throughout the district. Flournoy's lead in Lafayette was based on an important white Republican minority and a large black population. Lafayette's 42 percent black population was much larger than that of any other county in the district and made even more conspicuous the crucial importance of the heavily white electorate in the counties north and east of Oxford.[22]

The election won, Lamar traveled to Washington to seek the

20. Lamar to E. D. Clark, October 19, 1872, in Lamar Papers, University of Mississippi Library.

21. Jackson (Miss.) *Weekly Clarion*, September 12, 26, October 17, 1872; Hernando (Miss.) *Press and Times*, September 12, 1872; Memphis *Daily Appeal*, September 24, October 29, 1872; R. W. Flournoy to Lamar, n.d., quoted in Mayes, *Lamar*, 173–74.

22. Figures provided by Political Research Consortium. It is interesting to note that the first district as constituted before 1872 would have returned a vote of 11,953 to 7,443 in favor of Lamar's opponent. This comparison is based on the presidential vote of 1872. On the racial composition of the district see *Ninth Census*, I, 42–43. On the importance of Negro and white Republicans in Lafayette County, see Warren A. Ellem, "Who Were the Mississippi Scalawags?," *Journal of Southern History*, XXXVIII (May, 1972), 225, 229.

removal of his political disability. Recommendations from the
governor and other prominent Mississippi Republicans accom-
panied his petition and there seemed little reason to doubt its
success. Only one Mississippi congressman, carpetbagger Le-
grand W. Perce of Natchez, could not abide the move and tried
to prevent it. The House passed the necessary legislation on
December 9, 1872, with only thirteen negative votes cast. Two
days later the Senate concurred, and the Confederate record of
L. Q. C. Lamar was officially closed.[23]

Lamar now permanently reentered public life and never again
attempted to earn his livelihood or reputation outside the government. His experiences as lawyer, planter, and teacher would
not be repeated. And as if to mark this milestone in his career,
Lamar's health gave way under the strain. He immediately fell
sick of a violent attack of vertigo and very nearly died. Again his
recovery left him temporarily crippled. After a few days of treatment at the home of his old friend, A. T. Bledsoe, in Baltimore,
Lamar returned to Mississippi on crutches.[24] Ill and worn-out,
he told his friend E. C. Walthall of his despondency: "I do not
honestly expect to live twelve months. I believe I shall go off . . .
before anybody suspects that much is the matter." [25]

Fortunately, Lamar had time to recover fully. Mississippi's
irregular political calendar caused him to wait a year before fill-
ing his congressional post. By the summer of 1873 he felt able
to make one of his periodic trips to Georgia where he visited his
ailing mother and renewed old friendships.[26]

23. New York *Times*, December 7, 9, 10, 19, 1872; *House Journal*, 42nd Cong.,
3rd Sess., 39, 53–54; *Congressional Globe*, 42nd Cong., 3rd Sess., 91, 129, 260; *Journal
of the Senate of the United States* (hereinafter cited as *Senate Journal*), 42nd Cong.,
3rd Sess., 48, 50–51, 53. President Grant signed the bill into law December 17,
1872.
24. Mayes, *Lamar*, 175–76.
25. Lamar to E. C. Walthall, n.d., 1873, quoted in Mayes, *Lamar*, 561. A
photograph given by Lamar to Mrs. Clay on March 4, 1873, in C. C. Clay Papers,
showed him apparently underweight and in obviously poor health. Mrs. Clay's
comment on the reverse side gave her judgment: "I sadly fear I never shall look
upon his loved face again!"
26. Lamar to Beck [?], March 4, 1874, in Lamar Letters, University of North
Carolina Library; Lamar to A. H. Stephens, August 19, 1873, in A. H. Stephens
Papers, Manuscript Division, Library of Congress.

The Mississippi political situation did not, however, allow Lamar to concentrate exclusively on personal matters or on his approaching removal to Washington. The course of reconstruction reached a major turning point during 1873 in the open break between moderate Republicans (mostly native whites of Union-Whig background) and the radical Republicans (predominantly the carpetbag and Negro population). The division crystallized in the 1873 gubernatorial race when moderate Republican and former governor James Lusk Alcorn took leave from the Senate to run against carpetbagger Adelbert Ames.[27]

Since most Democrats believed they had no chance of defeating the Republicans, they were forced to choose between these two men. The Democratic party organization therefore nominally supported Alcorn and placed no candidate in the race against him. Though many saw little reason to prefer Alcorn to Ames, Lamar considered the election profoundly important. In a long letter justifying his support of Alcorn, whom he had opposed in 1869, Lamar made his motives clear. Alcorn had, he wrote, "assumed the leadership of the conservatives in this State. Whatever may be his personal motives, the public ones are laudable & patriotic, and these with the bold & gallant style in which he has thrown himself at the head of his old opponents entitle him to . . . cordial & unstinted support." [28]

The effort proved futile. Ames commanded an unbeatable combination of carpetbaggers, Negroes, and Democrats who saw Alcorn's defeat as the primary issue. The result gave Ames a comfortable majority of 20,467 votes. Lamar's support had helped Alcorn carry Lafayette County, however, and perhaps that was some consolation.[29]

27. David Donald, "The Scalawag in Mississippi Reconstruction," *Journal of Southern History*, X (November, 1944), 447–60, *passim*; Pereyra, *James Lusk Alcorn*, 121–63, *passim*; Ellem, "Who Were the Mississippi Scalawags?," 217–40, *passim*.

28. Lamar to E. D. Clark, October 14, 1873, in Lamar Papers, University of Mississippi Library. Lamar amplified his views on the election in a second letter to Clark, October 16, 1873, *ibid.*

29. Donald, "The Scalawag in Mississippi Reconstruction," 452–53. Figures from Political Research Consortium show that Alcorn's majority in 1869 was 38,089—considerably larger than Ames's in 1873.

As a consequence of the 1873 election, Lamar represented a state controlled by a much more radical government than when it had elected him one year earlier. The anomaly of a secessionist and Confederate in Congress from a Republican state thus became even more ironical. Little wonder that Lamar would become the spokesman of the dormant Democracy.

Lamar quietly took his seat when the Forty-third Congress convened in December, 1873. Unobtrusiveness seemed proper for a congressman formerly associated with secession and representing a state which in his opinion was still governed by foreign elements. Thus he chose inconspicuous but important work such as promoting a Democratic candidate in a dispute arising over a contested West Virginia House seat. Efforts of this kind brought him some satisfaction and notice, but Lamar himself confessed that his achievements were unimposing.[30]

Lamar's status among Mississippi Democrats did not long depend solely upon the singularity of his election or upon transient efforts, as in the West Virginia case. He had worn his new humility well and therefore became a likely choice, or volunteer—the method of selection is not clear—to eulogize upon the death of Charles Sumner, the leading Senate Radical. After that short speech—in effect a plea for sectional amity—Lamar was no longer simply an aberration from Republican Mississippi, nor did he limit his constituency to that state. Though his listeners could not have known it, he then assumed a place as spokesman for a conservative political philosophy which soon would command a large following throughout the nation.[31]

30. *Congressional Record*, 43rd Cong., 1st Sess., 45–46, 842–46, 876–77, 889–90, 963; *Biographical Directory of the American Congress,* 785; Lamar to Mrs. Lamar, n.d., quoted in Mayes, *Lamar,* 179; Lamar to T. J. Wharton, December 25, 1873, quoted, *ibid.,* 179–80.

31. Mayes, *Lamar,* 183; and Cate, *Lamar,* 156, maintain that the Massachusetts congressional delegation invited Lamar to present a eulogy. John R. Allen, "Bishop Paine in Texas," *Texas Methodist Historical Quarterly,* I (October, 1909), 172 ff., extract in Lamar Letters, University of North Carolina Library, states that Lamar told him personally that a meeting of southern statesmen decided who should give the eulogy with its plea for the South.

The sentiments expressed by Lamar in eulogizing Sumner and pleading for an end to war-born emotions were by no means spontaneous. From the events of 1865 and the following years he had learned a great truth; and having learned it well, he made it a master-credo which governed his entire postwar career. Defeat in war and the subsequent political humiliations left Lamar no choice but to look upon reconciliation as the only corrective for the South's plight. To serve the South, a statesman should above all else profess devotion to the Union. Patriotism, therefore, became the basis of a pragmatic political policy, and Lamar made the achievement of that policy his life's work.[32]

Despite apparent humility, Lamar was no less bitter than other conservative Southern Democrats in his reaction to the federal government's policies. His distinction lay only in the fact that he usually allowed pragmatic considerations to overcome the bitterness. Lamar expressed the necessity of a reconciliationist view to a friend as early as July 15, 1872, several months before his election to Congress: "Our people are under the supreme necessity of getting into harmonious relations with the Federal Government," because "grim despotism flares upon us at every point. Spies and secret detectives swarm through the country." Therefore, the question "is not how to restore the constitutional faith of our fathers, but how to get rid of these creatures, defiled by blood, gorged with spoil, cruel, cowardly, faithless, who are now ruling the South for no purposes except those of oppression and plunder." [33]

Such harsh words reflected Lamar's absolute refusal to think of Republican activities as legitimate. He ignored the fact that the Republican party represented the honest aspirations of many southerners—white as well as black—and that many did not con-

32. Lamar's notions of sectional accommodation may have been fed by personal contact with like-minded individuals during this period. James Longstreet visited him at least once and may have made this suggestion. See Oxford (Miss.) *Falcon*, August 30, 1866; and Thomas R. Hay and Donald B. Sanger, *James Longstreet: Soldier and Politician* (Baton Rouge, 1952), 334. Edward Mayes, Lamar's son-in-law, also believed in the necessity for reconciliation and may have been influential. See Wade, *Longstreet*, 357.

33. Lamar to Charles Reemelin, July 15, 1872, quoted in Mayes, *Lamar*, 170–72.

sider it a pernicious intruder from the outside. Instead, he wrote as if the South were a conservative Democratic monolith and insisted that there remained no necessity for continued intervention by the Republicans since the South would willingly accede to the results of the war. The defeated states had accepted the northern interpretation of the Constitution and the freedmen's political and civil equality with whites. Despite the Grant administration's refusal to accept the South's good intentions, Lamar wishfully informed his correspondent "that there is a large majority of the Northern people . . . disposed to treat the South . . . with gentleness and justice, and even with magnanimity." [34]

In this revealing and at times perceptive letter Lamar described the almost impossible difficulties facing a Southerner who attempted to promote sectional understanding. The man who could effect the reconciliation "indeed would be a patriot and benefactor." [35]

After his election Lamar began to think of himself as the patriotic benefactor of a contrite and anxious South. And it is important to note that he now, for perhaps the first time in his life, seized the initiative and acted as a leader rather than a follower of other men and their political theories. War and reconstruction pressed maturity upon the survivors. Longstreet and Davis could no longer point the direction for the South.

On November 4, 1872, he already saw himself as a vehicle of the great mission: "If I say or do anything, it will be to give to the North the assurance it wants that the South comprehends its own great necessities, and wishes to be no longer the agitating

34. *Ibid.* Lamar made essentially the same observations on the goodwill of northerners in a letter written shortly after the address. See Lamar to C. C. Clay, September 5, 1874, in C. C. Clay Papers, and published in Mattie Russell (ed.), "Why Lamar Eulogized Sumner," *Journal of Southern History,* XXI (August, 1955), 374–78.

35. Lamar to Charles Reemelin, July 15, 1872, quoted in Mayes, *Lamar,* 182. Paul H. Buck, *The Road to Reunion, 1865–1900* (Boston, 1937), 128, observed: "To play this role of patriot benefactor became so strong a desire in Lamar's ambition as almost to be an obsession."

and agitated pendulum of American politics." [36] With this objective in mind, Lamar asked advice from a number of northern men. The results of his inquiry supported his own concept of moderation and sectional goodwill.[37]

The evolution of Lamar's appeal was virtually complete when he went to Congress in December, 1873, but he felt he must bide his time. Careful timing was especially important since Lamar knew that southern conservative spokesmen were suspected by northern Republicans and therefore almost never attained a hearing either in Congress or in the northern press.[38] At first he prepared a speech on the civil rights bill then before Congress, but decided not to give it because of the antagonism the subject would create. He noted that placation of the North had been attempted ineffectually by Alexander H. Stephens and others whose efforts had been clouded by controversy. As he explained to his good friend, Clement Clay of Alabama: "What was wanted, was an *occasion* on which they would *listen* & listen with something of a feeling of *sympathy*. I thought the death of Sumner was such an occasion." [39]

Lamar's choice of an "occasion" showed considerable political instinct.[40] Sumner was an admirable subject since the North, and especially those most antagonistic toward the South, would read

36. Lamar to Associate Justice E. G. Peyton, Mississippi Supreme Court, *ca.* November 4, 1872, quoted in Mayes, *Lamar*, 175.

37. Michael C. Kerr to Lamar, March 15, 1873, in Lamar-Mayes Papers, and published in Willie D. Halsell (ed.), "Advice from Michael C. Kerr to a Reconstructed Rebel Congressman," *Indiana Magazine of History*, XXXVII (September, 1941), 257–61. Mayes, *Lamar*, 176, suggests there were others in addition to Kerr.

38. Lamar to C. C. Clay, September 5, 1874, in C. C. Clay Papers; Lamar to T. J. Wharton, December 25, 1873, quoted in Mayes, *Lamar*, 179–80.

39. Lamar to C. C. Clay, September 5, 1874, in C. C. Clay Papers. See also Lamar to Mrs. Lamar, April 28, 1874, quoted in Mayes, *Lamar*, 188–89.

40. James G. Blaine, *Twenty Years in Congress* (Norwich, Conn., 1884), II, 546, wrote: "It was a mark of positive genius in a Southern representative to pronounce a fervid and discriminating eulogy upon Mr. Sumner." Adelbert Ames later held that Lamar had two speeches ready to deliver: his choice depending upon circumstance. One was a bitter attack on the North, the other a plea for reconciliation. See Adelbert Ames to James G. Blaine, February 15, 1876, cited in Willie D. Halsell, "Note on a Phase of L. Q. C. Lamar's Career," *Journal of Mississippi History*, IX (January, 1947), 21.

every word said about the abolitionist champion. And Sumner
had another special quality in that he had shown a measure of
generosity toward the South in his advocacy of a general amnesty
for former Confederates. Thus he might serve as an example for
the North, and at the same time a southern representative might
with some justification eulogize the dead man.

Lamar honestly appreciated Sumner's call for amnesty, but
more importantly it could be used to advance a larger cause. He
assured a confidant that his eulogy "was dictated by no *pseudo*
'magnanimity,' but by a concern for the Southern people, a love
for them with their helpless families." [41] He thus simultaneously
served two causes and two loyalties. For a time the nationalistic
aim of reconciliation coincided with pragmatic southern sectionalism. This was his mission: by glorifying the union, he better
served the cause of the South. The day after the eulogy, he put
it plainly to his wife: "I never in all my life opened my lips with
a purpose more single to the interests of our Southern people
than when I made this speech." [42]

The eulogy itself was a very short speech and probably was
more effective for its pointedness. Lamar's remarks about Sumner served as a setting for his main theme. After alluding to
Sumner's moral stature and intellect, Lamar spoke of the senator's relationship to the South. On the antebellum slavery question he carefully praised Sumner as a man utterly dedicated to
individual liberty, but at the same time avoided any indication
that the South had been wrong on the question. Then he staged
his real thrust by noting Sumner's sympathy toward the southern people after the war. At this key moment Lamar skillfully
expanded Sumner's position to make it the vehicle of his own
message:

> Charles Sumner in life believed that all occasion for strife and dis-
> trust between the North and South had passed away, and there no

41. Lamar to C. C. Clay, September 5, 1874, in C. C. Clay Papers. Lamar gave
essentially the same reasoning in a conversation with J. R. Allen. See extract from
Allen, "Bishop Paine in Texas," 172 ff., in Lamar Letters, University of North
Carolina Library.
42. Lamar to Mrs. Lamar, April 28, 1874, quoted in Mayes, *Lamar*, 188–89.

longer remained any cause for continued estrangement between these two sections of our common country. Are there not many of us who believe the same thing? Is not that the common sentiment, or if it is not ought it not to be. . . . Shall we not, over the honored remains of this great champion of human liberty, this feeling sympathizer with human sorrow, this earnest pleader for the exercise of human tenderness and charity, lay aside the concealments which serve only to perpetuate misunderstandings and distrust, and frankly confess that on both sides we most earnestly desire to be one . . . in feeling and in heart?

Years of Methodist sermons had not been lost on Lamar. The imagery was ingenious: if the heroic Sumner had died believing a cause to be noble, then how could the North reject that cause. In his peroration Lamar nimbly transferred Sumner's cross to the shoulders of the suffering South:

The South—prostrate, exhausted, drained of her life-blood, as well as of her material resources, yet still honorable and true— accepts the bitter award of the bloody arbitrament without reservation, resolutely determined to abide the result with chivalrous fidelity; yet, as if struck dumb by the magnitude of her reverses, she suffers on in silence.

The North, exultant in her triumph and elated by success, still cherishes, as we are assured, a heart full of magnanimous emotions toward her disarmed and discomfited antagonist; and yet, as if mastered by some mysterious spell, silencing her better impulses, her words and acts are the words and acts of suspicion and distrust.

Would that the spirit of the illustrious dead whom we lament today could speak from the grave to both parties to this deplorable discord in tones which should reach each and every heart throughout this broad territory: "My countrymen! *know* one another and you will *love* one another." [43]

When Lamar finished, a "spontaneous burst of applause went up from Republicans and Democrats alike." The northern press responded with the same enthusiasm which swept over Congress.[44]

43. *Congressional Record*, 43rd Cong., 1st Sess., 3410–11.
44. New York *Tribune*, April 28, 1874. For other examples of favorable press response see: New York *Times*, April 28, 1874; Brandon (Miss.) *Republican*, May 14, 28, 1874; Jackson (Miss.) *Weekly Clarion*, May 7, 14, 1874. The *Clarion* articles

Lamar had achieved a spectacular personal triumph.[45] The popularity of his speech, however, was rooted in the nation's state of mind, both North and South. The experiment with reconstruction had already worn thin by 1874, and public opinion was fast becoming more sympathetic with the white, conservative South. The change which ultimately negated Republican political power in the South had already begun, and a great upsurge of sentiment for national unity was underway.[46]

Both circumstance and ability placed Lamar at the forefront of these momentous changes. In this national mood of accommodation, Lamar's past, by its very contrast to the Sumner eulogy, did a great deal to establish his new role. His career as antebellum planter, secessionist, Confederate, and then silent and contrite sufferer during reconstruction cast Lamar ideally as a conciliator. His image as a representative of the "natural" ruling class of the South qualified him to speak authoritatively for a new order. As the New York *Tribune* put it: "No one could be better qualified to speak for the class which ruled the South before the war, and which still embraces nearly all the education and social refinement of that unfortunate region." [47]

This altered climate of opinion meant that Lamar's bold dec-

---

provide excerpts from eight northern papers; and Mayes, *Lamar*, 189–97, provides excerpts from these and six others. See also Francis Pendleton Gaines, *Southern Oratory: A Study in Idealism* (Tuscaloosa, 1946), 53–56; and Buck, *Road to Reunion*, 129, on the press reception of the eulogy. Mayes, *Lamar*, 188, states that Speaker of the House James G. Blaine literally wept on hearing Lamar's words. Buck, *Road to Reunion*, 129; and Gaines, *Southern Oratory*, 55, repeat the story, but no earlier source has been found.

45. Lamar's delicate treatment of this subject is suggestive of W. J. Cash's interpretation of the South's position at the end of reconstruction: "For twenty years to come the South must balance precariously between what is necessary to establish full sway for the Democratic Party and to divorce the Negro from the ballot, and what would inevitably bring the bayonets back again. For twenty years those perpetually impending Yankee threats will have to be circumvented with elaborate caution." See W. J. Cash, *The Mind of the South* (New York, 1941), 148–49.

46. Kenneth M. Stampp, *The Era of Reconstruction, 1865–1877* (New York, 1966), 187–89, 191–94, 206–209; Buck, *Road to Reunion*, 96–98.

47. New York *Tribune*, June 10, 1874. See also Stampp, *Era of Reconstruction*, 156–58.

laration did not jeopardize his career, as would have been the case only a few years before. Actually numerous signs foretold that Mississippi would tolerate his position. Old-line Whigs, of course, had aimed at reconciliation from the first. And leading Democrats, including former governor and congressman John J. McRae and antebellum secessionist senator Albert Gallatin Brown, counseled reconciliation as early as 1867. Jacob Thompson, another Democrat whose stature certainly eclipsed Lamar's, publicly favored the "New Departure" more than two years before the Sumner eulogy. Furthermore, newspaper evidence suggests that the white population generally was willing even in 1867 to accept a policy of reconstruction which would permit Negro voting.[48]

On the subject of Sumner's death, the Democratic state legislators in Mississippi had joined Republicans in a tribute one month before Lamar's speech. And a major Democratic newspaper, the Jackson *Clarion*, also anticipated Lamar's "occasion" by praising Sumner's attitude toward the South.[49]

All this is not to say that Lamar earned unqualified support for his effort. There were critics certainly, and Lamar himself declared "that the time had come for me to stake my political life." [50] Even among his friends the first news of his speech caused hesitation and distress.[51] And some journalists who could brook no compromise with the Republicans categorically inter-

48. Oxford (Miss.) *Falcon*, August 18, 1871; Memphis *Daily Appeal*, August 15, 1871; Harris, *Presidential Reconstruction In Mississippi*, 241–42.

49. McNeily, "War and Reconstruction," 287; Jackson (Miss.) *Weekly Clarion*, March 19, April 30, 1874.

50. Lamar to C. C. Clay, September 5, 1874, in C. C. Clay Papers.

51. Lamar's letter to Clay, September 5, 1874, *ibid.*, answered his friend's gentle criticism. Mrs. Clay, who found his explanation adequate and even "eloquent," asked permission to publish the letter. Lamar declined saying "my Sumner Speech must be 'justified by faith' rather than by any reasons formally set forth." See Lamar to Mrs. Clay, December 20, 1874, *ibid.* James Z. George wrote Lamar twice in two days on this subject, first expressing "some apprehension" and then "wonder at the complete success attained by you." And still George did "not agree with you entirely in all you said of him." See J. Z. George to Lamar, May 3, 1874, in Lamar-Mayes Papers.

preted any moderate remarks on abolition or abolitionists as treasonous.[52]

In total impact, however, the reaction to the eulogy confirmed Lamar's belief in a tempered approach to postbellum statesmanship.[53] He had advocated the South's claim to honor and forthrightness in war and reconstruction, but had couched his contentions in tones of conciliation, and the North had generally accepted it. Little more than a month would pass before he would rise again before the House to employ the same tactics.

52. Brandon (Miss.) *Republican*, May 28, 1874, thought the Columbus (Miss.) *Democrat* the only paper which denounced Lamar. Mayes, *Lamar*, 191, lists the Canton (Miss.) *Mail* and the Meridian (Miss.) *Mercury* as critics. Out of state papers such as the Richmond *Dispatch* and the Savannah *Morning News* also reproached him. See *The Morning News*, June 17, 1874, in Scrapbook: 1872–1875, p. 107, John Emory Bryant Papers, Duke University Library.

53. Lamar to Mrs. Lamar, *ca.* April 29, 1874, quoted in Mayes, *Lamar*, 188; Lamar to Mrs. Lamar, May 5, 1874, quoted, *ibid.*, 191–92. In the letter of May 5, he said: "The whole world is my audience."

The House of Representatives: Elaboration of a Creed

Lamar served in the House of Representatives from December, 1873, until he succeeded James Lusk Alcorn as senator in March, 1877. When considered in conjunction with his efforts in Mississippi during this same period, there is reason to consider these the most decisive years of his career. He was closely attentive to Mississippi and southern affairs and to party needs throughout this period, and his health and vitality were sufficient to allow his talents full sway. After moving to the Senate he found fewer opportunities, and his declining physical condition prevented strenuous exertion. His reputation and his oratorical ability sustained him as an important force in politics, but historic occasions and heroic responses were not part of the story.

The difference in the House and Senate years was only partially personal. Probably more important was the fact that during his first years in the House the great political struggle over reconstruction reached its culmination. Lamar was deeply engaged in that struggle and played a significant role in reversing Republican achievements. When he entered the House in 1873, some parts of the South were still restive under the anomalous influence of troop-supported Republican governments. The attempt to alter this situation challenged him to the peak of his achievement. When this struggle entered into a less critical phase after the election of 1876, the possibility of real achievement was greatly diminished.

While appealing to men to rise above sectional prejudices in his Sumner eulogy, Lamar himself turned to the great matter of achieving Democratic power in both national and southern affairs. He husbanded the party's fortunes not only as a sectionalist seeking home rule for the South, but also as a committed and lifelong Democrat. As an antebellum congressman he had been notably regular in his support of the Democratic position, and after the war he continued to identify sectional and national interests with party politics. As a Democratic partisan Lamar took a special interest in state contests and devoted a good deal of energy to the numerous elections disputed before the House. As a member of the Committee on Elections in the Forty-third Congress (but not in the Forty-fourth Congress) he also had an official capacity in which he could give assistance to Democratic claimants.[1]

Three congressional elections of 1872—West Virginia, Louisiana, and Arkansas—commanded particular attention. The debates concerning these disputed seats were all quite technical insofar as both sides attempted to employ statistics and legal obfuscation; and they were conducted in a highly partisan fashion. As a member of the elections committee, Lamar served his party through long and caustic wrangling. With apparent competence and good fortune too, he saw all three of these elections ultimately decided in favor of the Democrats.[2]

Lamar's service to the Democratic party during his House years included almost constant electioneering in Mississippi and outside the state. The national elections of 1874 were unimportant in Mississippi, since congressional seats were not vacated until 1875; but Lamar took advantage of the fall recess to speak to his constituents and advise them of his own course in Con-

1. *House Journal*, 43rd Cong., 1st Sess., 62.
2. On the West Virginia election see *Congressional Record*, 43rd Cong., 1st Sess., 45–46, 842–46, 876–77, 889–90, 963; and *Biographical Directory of American Congress*, 785. On the Louisiana election see *Congressional Record*, 43rd Cong., 1st Sess., 4701, 5316; and *Biographical Directory of American Congress*, 202. On the Arkansas election see *Congressional Record*, 43rd Cong., 1st Sess., 1192, 1339, 1563–67, 1574–77; and *Biographical Directory of American Congress*, 1828.

gress.[3] During the following spring he campaigned outside the South. He and his good friend John B. Gordon of Georgia traveled into New Hampshire and Massachusetts to work for the party ticket in a canvass widely covered in the national press.[4] Almost as soon as he returned to Mississippi, Lamar participated in the "redemption" of his state from the Republicans, an effort which extended throughout the summer and fall of 1875. Owing to the odd election year in 1875, Mississippi underwent another general election in 1876; and Lamar campaigned vigorously and successfully throughout the state for the presidential electors of Samuel J. Tilden.[5]

Perhaps because of his eulogy and his partisan services or maybe in recognition of growing Democratic strength in the South, Lamar became chairman of the Democratic caucus when his party organized the Forty-fourth Congress in December, 1875. It was a great honor for one so recently returned from political oblivion, and it marked the pinnacle of his position within the Democratic party. In the Senate he never attained such an elevated status in party councils. After the election of 1876 and the accompanying partisan bitterness, the veneer of party regularity was somewhat worn. In 1875, however, his service as caucus chairman brought prestige and contributed to his image as a nationalist rather than a narrow sectionalist.

Lamar made a lengthy speech on the occasion of his election as caucus chairman. The sentiments expressed were primarily a political indictment of the Republican party. In addition, they indicated that Lamar sympathized sufficiently with the dominant views within the Democratic party so that he could speak for himself and the national organization at once. The principles he proposed included civil service reform, public economy, reduction in the tariff, and reform of the currency system. These were stated in general terms, of course, and could not have of-

3. Mayes, *Lamar*, 203–204. A draft of a speech to Marshall County voters, apparently given at this time, is in the Lamar-Mayes Papers. No newspaper coverage is available.

4. New York *Times*, March 7, 1875; New York *Tribune*, March 9, 1875.

5. The elections of 1875 and 1876 are detailed in subsequent chapters.

fended any large portion of the Democratic party. Besides these national goals, Lamar dedicated the Democrats to the cause of sectional amity, declaring that the party should strive to restore the Constitution to its "pristine strength" and to make it the protector of all sections and all individuals without regard to race or geographical location.[6]

Party victories and personal recognition were important to Lamar, but these were less significant than the advancement of his broader political and economic objectives. In both major areas Lamar's own blend of sectionalism and nationalism transcended other considerations. He pleaded for Union and reconciliation, and earnestly advocated a nationalistic program of economic development financed by the central government. On the other hand, he remained a staunch disciple of the traditional states' rights doctrine on all political questions. This paradoxical combination presumed compatability between economic nationalism and political decentralization. Lamar either did not notice or did not care about the inconsistency of his positions. Consistency was not that important to his pragmatic approach to statesmanship.

During the Republican Forty-third Congress (1873–1875) political issues seemed more important to Lamar than economic questions. Persistence of the Republican threat to home rule determined this basic priority. The platitudinous Sumner eulogy provided no immediate solution for the fundamental problems which divided the sections. At best its reception was only an indication of changing attitudes and motives. Congress was preoccupied with southern state governments and with the Negro's political fortunes after the eulogy the same as before. Immediately after the Forty-third Congress convened, civil rights legislation was introduced, and the struggle for its passage intensified as its fate became less and less certain.

Lamar helped obstruct various early Republican efforts at

6. For examples of press coverage see New York *Times*, December 5, 1875; Chicago *Daily Tribune*, December 7, 8, 1875; Memphis *Daily Appeal*, December 15, 1875; and the Jackson (Miss.) *Weekly Clarion*, December 8, 1875.

passing civil rights legislation[7] and then took advantage of a contested Louisiana congressional election to make his first major speech following the Sumner eulogy. He hoped to seat the conservative, George A. Sheridan, rather than the Negro radical, P. B. S. Pinchback, but the issue had larger implications. Democrats claimed that the Republican administration in Louisiana retained its power only by federal support. Success in seating Sheridan would publicize an alleged election discrepancy which southerners could claim as proof of radical treachery.[8]

Lamar's support of Sheridan provided a platform in Congress from which he attacked Republican reconstruction imposed upon the South and offered reconciliation in its place. This combination of partisanship with statesmanship made for an interesting speech; but some wary radicals must have thought reconciliation little better than enmity when Lamar threatened: "No party . . . can long bear the responsibility of . . . these grotesque caricatures of government." [9]

Lamar reminded the House of his remarks on Sumner and insisted again that the South had accepted the constitutional amendments in good faith. The sentiments of the Sumner eulogy had "not met one dissent throughout the whole extent of the Southern land." He must have strained even the credulity of well-wishers when he vowed: "Every black man of twenty-one years possesses a vote. . . . There is not a trace of privilege throughout the land. . . . Negro liberty is universal, thorough, and complete; and their equality before the law is without an exception." [10] Of course, Lamar did not say whether the Negro's alleged equality would survive the removal of federal troops.

In his argument for federal withdrawal Lamar sought to divert attention from the Negro and the basic problem of assimilation to the "real" issue of "constitutional government and

7. *House Journal*, 43rd Cong., 1st Sess., 83–84, 1030, 1080, 1131.
8. Sheridan was finally seated, but not until March 3, 1875. See *Biographical Directory of American Congress*, 202.
9. *Congressional Record*, 43rd Cong., 1st Sess., App., 426–31.
10. *Ibid.*

representative liberty." The great question was not that of racial antagonism, he said, since that conflict would resolve itself in time. Antagonism would disappear as the natural increase in white population and foreign immigration reduced the Negro's importance. Under these circumstances "it does not call for a scientist to calculate how long it will take for the weaker or smaller race to disappear before the more populous and stronger." [11]

An influential segment of the northern and border state press appreciated Lamar's speech and agreed with him. By 1874 rationalization had become statesmanship. According to the New York *Tribune*, Lamar "spoke with honest indignation of the outrageous abuse of the federal power" and his claims were "strictly true and most proper." The Louisville *Courier-Journal* thought that "even Northern Republicans could take no exceptions." The New York *Times* and *World*, the Boston *Advertiser*, and the St. Louis *Times* agreed that Lamar had hit upon a truth too long ignored.[12] Such praise echoed Lamar's own insight: "I believe, sir, that this spirit [of radical reconstruction] is passing away even from the minds of my friends on the other side. It is condemned by the spirit of the age." [13]

Lamar's exegesis on the spirit of the age did not go unchallenged. During the fall and winter of 1874 a highly volatile crisis in Vicksburg, Mississippi, threatened military intervention and irreparable damage to the still tender bonds of reconciliation. Racial and political tensions arising from alleged government malfeasance had heightened until an armed clash resulted in the death of two whites and twenty-nine Negroes.[14]

11. *Ibid.* Cf. Guion Griffis Johnson, "The Ideology of White Supremacy," in Dewey W. Grantham, Jr. (ed.), *The South and the Sectional Image* (New York, 1967), 66, which describes a theory of Negro retrogression and extinction as a result of competition with whites.

12. New York *Tribune*, June 9, 10, 1874; Louisville (Ky.) *Courier-Journal*, June 9, 1874; St. Louis *Times*, June 8, 1874, reprinted in New Orleans *Daily Picayune*, June 12, 1874; and New York *Times*, June 9, 1874. See also complimentary excerpts collected in Mayes, *Lamar*, 198–99.

13. *Congressional Record*, 43rd Cong., 1st Sess., App. 426–31.

14. Garner, *Reconstruction in Mississippi*, 328–37, *passim*. Wharton, *The Negro in Mississippi*, 190, sets the total at "about thirty-five."

Congress received news of the Vicksburg outbreak with more than usual interest. The fall elections had placed the first Democratic majority in the lower house since the war, and the Forty-fourth Congress scheduled to meet in December, 1875, promised to be less than amenable to Republican policies. Lamar believed that Grant wished to provoke an incident in the South so that Congress would provide him additional authority before March 4. And even more crucial in the long run, the presidential election of 1876 was already on the horizon. Republicans of the radical variety fell back on their surest weapon—the "bloody shirt" style of oratory which recalled southern treachery against the Union.[15]

Republican representative George C. McKee of Mississippi called for an investigation of the Mississippi troubles. Lamar tactically countered by supporting the move and declaring that the facts would vindicate the white citizens of Vicksburg.[16] He had already contacted friends in Mississippi who advised him of the whites' position. They described the situation as grave, and one correspondent declared himself "astonished at the moderation of our people." [17]

Under these circumstances, and assuming that the Republican dominated investigation committee would look for the worst in Vicksburg, Lamar decided to remain in Washington for the Christmas holidays and to direct from there the defense of Vicksburg whites. As he wrote Mrs. Clay, he must stay because "the wolf (at the White House) is panting for the blood of our people." [18] And with this vision in mind Lamar kept in close contact with Mississippi acquaintances, especially his old friend and former law partner, E. D. Clark.

15. Lamar to E. D. Clark, December 23, 1874, in Lamar Papers, University of Mississippi Library.
16. *Congressional Record*, 43rd Cong., 2nd Sess., 77.
17. W. P. Harris to Lamar, December 16, 1874, quoted in Mayes, *Lamar*, 236–37. See also Lamar to E. D. Clark, December 21, 1874, in Lamar Papers, University of Mississippi Library, in which he refers to Clark's last letter and the news of Vicksburg. See also B. G. Humphreys to Lamar, January 3, 1875, in Lamar-Mayes Papers.
18. Lamar to Mrs. Clay, December 26, 1874, in C. C. Clay Papers.

Lamar's first contribution to Vicksburg's defense came with the appointment of a Democratic minority to the investigating committee. At Lamar's recommendation, Speaker James G. Blaine appointed R. Milton Speer of Pennsylvania and William J. O'Brien of Maryland. Lamar then put the Democratic members in touch with Clark in Vicksburg.[19] Through the last days of December and early January, he maintained almost daily contact with Clark, providing arguments for the investigating committee and obtaining information for a speech in the House of Representatives.

Clark was advised to make a hard and fast case to prove Republican corruption in Vicksburg, with supporting evidence that the area suffered from a ruinous level of taxation. Misgovernment should be blamed directly on Governor Ames since he supported the accused officials. The defense should also argue that violence might have been averted if armed Negroes had not approached Vicksburg intent on trouble. Although Republicans would attempt to prove otherwise, Clark should "concentrate much force at this point. Show that there was no wanton or very little needless slaughter of negroes." [20]

Lamar went on to recommend lawyers for the job, and to suggest that the Democratic press in Vicksburg follow a moderate line so that spirited utterances could not be turned against them.[21] Further, it would help "if Governor Humphreys . . . would stop the Iuka Gazette, & the Southern States & some other papers of the same kind from their loud opposition to me until after the Vicksburg affair is settled. . . . McKee has said, & he will say . . . that I am not the true *Representative of the Democratic* sentiment in Miss. & will quote their denunciations of me to prove it." [22]

As Lamar must have anticipated, the five-man investigating

19. Lamar to E. D. Clark, December 21, 1874 (two letters), in Lamar Papers, University of Mississippi Library.

20. *Ibid.*

21. *Ibid.*; Lamar to E. D. Clark, December 26, 1874, *ibid.*

22. Lamar to E. D. Clark, December 23, 1874, *ibid.* See also Lamar to Clark, December 24, 1874, *ibid.* For the entire series of letters see: Lamar to Clark, December 21 (two letters), 23, 24, 26 (two letters), 1874, January 11, February 1, 1875, *ibid.*; S. J. Randall to Lamar, December 25, 1874, *ibid.*

committee divided according to party and filed both a majority and a minority report. He had, however, done his best to preserve the image of a beleaguered South which he had worked to create. Lamar unquestionably believed in that image, but it is equally clear that violence against the Negro mattered less than political objectives: it was enough for him "that there was no wanton or very little needless slaughter of negroes." [23]

The publicity given the Vicksburg riot and investigation prompted the New York *Herald* to invite an open letter from reconciliation's spokesman. Lamar's studied reply of January 9, 1875, attempted to placate the northern public while only thinly disguising the Negro's true fate. He vowed that under home rule in Mississippi the freedman's personal security and property would be completely protected by both law and public opinion. Suffrage, office holding, and jury duty would likewise be safe, although Lamar admitted that "in the exercise of them there might be some slight occasional disturbances." [24]

These remarks clearly substituted northern wish for southern intent. Lamar came much nearer his own concept of the proper relationship between the races when he further explained that the Negro's political rights would inevitably be affected by his poverty and ignorance. New York *Herald* readers were told that whites would naturally dominate Mississippi politics, but that home rule would allow party division without regard to race. These remarks failed to explain the process by which the Negro could be divided between parties and did not anticipate the possibility of a two-party system with the Negro as a potential balance of power. In vagueness calculated to calm a crisis-weary public in the North, he said, "leave our population to the responsibility of local self-government . . . and all that is now deranged and disorderly will certainly and permanently arrange itself." [25]

23. Lamar to E. D. Clark, December 21, 1874, *ibid.*
24. Lamar to editor, New York *Herald*, January 10, 1875, quoted in Jackson (Miss.) *Weekly Clarion*, January 28, 1875.
25. *Ibid.* The Jackson (Miss.) *Weekly Clarion* approved the statement. See also Jackson (Miss.) *Weekly Clarion*, January 23, February 11, 1875.

The *Herald* letter was Lamar's last extended statement on civil rights and the Negro during the Forty-third Congress. He had been preparing a speech on the Vicksburg troubles but for some reason did not deliver it. Possibly he decided that the acridly partisan atmosphere could yield nothing of worth. Indeed, Lamar explained to the House that his comments would serve no purpose and that he therefore declined to speak.[26]

This resolve against speaking, however, failed to save him from the impassioned struggle over civil rights during February, 1875. Such a vital and emotional issue could not be disregarded. He became so heated when the Republicans moved to censure John Young Brown of Kentucky for intemperate language, that he imputed discourtesy and cowardliness to Brown's accusers. Such a display of temper prompted a press report that Lamar had reached for a pistol. In a personal explanation he assured the House that this was not true.[27]

Lamar also joined in dilatory tactics against the administration's efforts to settle the southern question before March, 1875, when the House majority would change hands.[28] In desperation the Republicans finally moved to suspend the writ of habeas corpus in Louisiana, Arkansas, and Alabama, and thus to extend presidential power to the degree held under earlier enforcement acts. After opposing this bill through many stormy votes, the Democrats lost; the session ended, however, without final action in the Senate.[29]

26. At this time and on one other occasion Lamar asked permission to have his views recorded in the *Congressional Record*, but he did not turn over a speech to be printed. See the *Congressional Record*, 43rd Cong., 2nd Sess., 952, 1922. In one instance during the Forty-fourth Congress, Lamar again accepted discretion as the better part of valor. When the Republicans put forward a bill to amend the United States Constitution to forbid payment of Civil War claims to disloyal persons, Lamar failed to vote even though he was present in the House. See the *House Journal*, 44th Cong., 2nd Sess., 101, 181. Northern Democrats voted against the South on this last question and thus the issue had peculiarly sectional overtones. See C. Vann Woodward, *Reunion and Reaction* (Boston, 1951), 143–44.

27. *Congressional Record*, 43rd Cong., 2nd Sess., 989–90; New York *Times*, February 5, 1875; New York *Tribune*, February 5, 1875.

28. *House Journal*, 43rd Cong., 2nd Sess., 536–37, 548–76, 586–601.

29. *Ibid.*, 43rd Cong., 2nd Sess., 586–601; W. A. Dunning, *Reconstruction, Political and Economic 1865–1877* (New York, 1907), 254–55; New York *Times*, February 26, 28, 1875.

Obstructionism also delayed a civil rights bill guaranteeing public accommodations and jury service; but in this case the filibuster failed. For more than seventy votes Lamar stood fast, but the bill passed the House on February 4, 1875, and went to the Senate where Charles Sumner had initiated in 1872 the main Republican civil rights effort. On March 1, 1875, just before the Republican Congress dispersed, the battered remains of Sumner's civil rights bill became law. The Civil Rights Act of 1875 marked the end of an era. Advocates of freedmen's protection would not achieve another victory in the nineteenth century, and ultimately even this last accomplishment would be declared unconstitutional by the United States Supreme Court.[30]

The much heralded Democratic Forty-fourth Congress which convened in December, 1875, proved anticlimactic in the field of southern affairs. Lamar supported desultory efforts aimed at relieving the few remaining Confederates who were disfranchised by the Fourteenth Amendment[31] and at condemning the use of federal troops in the South;[32] but otherwise the change in party majority quieted the agitation. He voted against a Republican proposal to investigate the quality of public school education for Negroes in the South, a proposal which had no chance of passing.[33]

Despite the calm atmosphere in Congress during 1876, Lamar found several situations which suited his method and message. The first occurred on January 25 during debate on an appropriation bill for the national centennial celebration. The patriotic impulse invoked by the proponents of the appropriation provided Lamar another golden opportunity for promoting national unity and goodwill. His speech in support of the legislation was motivated, he said, by the "law of my career" before which "cherished purpose . . . all others . . . sink into insignificance." What Lamar wanted was "the pacification of these sections—to

30. *House Journal*, 43rd Cong., 2nd Sess., 252–55, 271–403; Dunning, *Reconstruction*, 255.
31. *House Journal*, 44th Cong., 1st Sess., 185–86.
32. *Ibid.*, 44th Cong., 2nd Sess., 181, 299.
33. *Ibid.*, 44th Cong., 2nd Sess., 177.

see my people of the South restored to the proud position of dignity and equality in this Union. . . . to live . . . in peace and perpetuity in a restored and fraternal Union." [34] Press response indicated that Lamar had again found the proper "occasion" for acquainting the Congress and the public with his mission of reconciliation. The friendly Louisville *Courier-Journal* related that the speech "fairly shook the house." The Chicago *Times* declared that the impact left the "Republicans . . . in stupefaction." [35]

A highly publicized summer riot in Hamburg, South Carolina, which resulted in the deaths of six blacks and one white, forced Lamar to shift his concern from reconciliation to home rule and caustic partisanship once more. In opposing use of federal troops to quiet racial antagonism, he employed arguments developed during the somewhat similar Vicksburg crisis. [36] Violence occurred, he reminded Congress, only "because these so-called Republican governments have . . . encouraged it by giving it impunity through their imbecility and cowardice, and often by actually inciting it." [37] The disorder had nothing at all to do with voting rights and was purely local in nature. It was the reprehensible activity of a lawless element of men who should be punished for their heinous crimes—but that responsibility properly belonged to state authorities. [38]

As recess approached, with the presidential campaign to follow, Lamar made on August 2, 1876, what James A. Garfield

34. *Congressional Record*, 44th Cong., 1st Sess., 630–31.

35. Louisville (Ky.) *Courier-Journal*, January 26, 1876. Mayes, *Lamar*, 276, quotes the Chicago *Times*. On the highly flattering reaction of Mississippi's leading newspaper to the speech, see Jackson (Miss.) *Daily Clarion*, February 1, 1876, and Jackson (Miss.) *Weekly Clarion*, February 2, 1876. The *Daily Clarion* said: "On Col. Lamar, more than any man, or all others combined, the hopes of the people who have suffered from the proscriptive rule of a vindictive party, are centered."

36. Cf. Lamar to E. D. Clark, February 1, 1875, in Lamar Papers, University of Mississippi Library, where Lamar outlined a speech which he did not give.

37. *Congressional Record*, 44th Cong., 1st Sess., 4709–11.

38. *Ibid.* Lamar's condemnation of the men responsible for the Negroes' deaths was commended by the New York *Tribune*, July 19, 1876. The Chicago *Daily Tribune*, July 19, 20, 1876 was more critical. For an example of Mississippi comment see Jackson (Miss.) *Weekly Clarion*, July 26, 1876.

called "a dangerous attack upon the Republican party." [39] In his last important House speech dealing with the sectional question, Lamar defended his section's solid support of the Democrats as a logical response to political realities and denied that the South controlled the party. A Democratic presidential victory, he said, would in no way jeopardize enforcement of constitutional amendments or the newly won rights of freedmen.

Here Lamar clearly intended to allay the suspicions underlying northern thought. He had no desire to suspend Negro suffrage, he said, but believed that true freedom and equality could not exist under "party tyranny" as practiced by the Republicans in the South. The Democrats and home rule offered a permanent solution: "Take the question out of national politics, and it can be settled on a basis which would consolidate all the rights of the black man, make him free and equal with every citizen before the law, protected in the fruits of his labor, safe in his person, happy in his household, secure in the enjoyment of whatever he can in fair competition achieve . . . and thus secure to him a higher and better life than he now leads as the misguided and deluded constituency of dishonest officeholders." [40]

This "dangerous attack" combined the major goals and political values of Lamar's career during this period. He wished to win northern acceptance of the South's good intentions and he desired, more than anything else, to gain home rule founded upon renewed confidence in the South's integrity. To achieve these ends he combined statesmanship of a high order and bald deception of the northern people who badly wanted to believe what he said. Probably this paradox reflects honest ambivalence in Lamar's convictions. Nothing in his correspondence indicates willful hypocrisy, and no inconsistency appears between his public and private declarations.

On the other hand Lamar's adroit manipulation of northern

39. James A. Garfield to Mrs. Garfield, *ca.* August 3, 1876, quoted in T. C. Smith, *The Life and Letters of James Abram Garfield* (New Haven, 1925), I, 607.
40. *Congressional Record*, 44th Cong., 1st Sess., 5087–94. The Memphis *Daily Appeal*, August 3, 1876, calls this "the grandest effort of his life." There are notes for this speech in the Lamar-Mayes Papers.

opinion certainly betrayed callousness toward the plight of the Negro. It also reflected his instinctive opinion that the freedman was a victim and tool of the Republicans. Even as a political strategy, however, Lamar's treatment of the Negro showed distressing shortsightedness. He claimed that the Negro would eventually follow white leadership and would divide into competing political parties. Thus a balanced two party system would emerge. That the Negro might have an additional political role or that he might prefer block voting in the future seems never to have occurred to Lamar. As a working politician, immediately concerned with the grasp of power, the distant future played only a small part in his judgments. His half developed ideas on ultimate solutions to the problems of politics and race were politically useful but of no practical consequence in the postreconstruction South.

The House of Representatives:
An Economic Corollary

Lamar and his fellow legislators were not entirely preoccupied with sectional matters during the Forty-third and Forty-fourth Congresses of 1873–1877. Economic questions also received their attention. Although the Mississippi press did not give economic problems sensational treatment, Lamar's voting record indicates that he diligently applied himself to the issues that he thought significant. His effort to carry out a consistently conservative program was of importance since the mid-seventies were years of deep economic difficulty in the United States.

A severe depression had swept the land after the railroad boom collapsed in the fall of 1873, and a cry arose for remedial action. Lamar believed that the trouble resulted partly from a shortage of money in circulation, and he at first thought that an increase in the money supply might serve to some extent as a corrective.[1] On occasion he also supported inflationary legislation as a means of expressing solidarity with other southern Democrats. Thus, in April, 1874, he joined an attempt to convert a Republican banking bill into a greenback (fiat money not redeemable in gold) expansion measure.[2] As the debate on the monetary issue

1. *House Journal*, 43rd Cong., 1st Sess., 264–65, 645–48.
2. *Ibid.*, 43rd Cong., 1st Sess., 771. Irwin Unger, *The Greenback Era: A Social and Political History of American Finance, 1865–1879* (Princeton, 1964), App. B, 409, shows that thirty southern Democrats voted for this effort while only three voted against it. On the other hand eastern Democrats voted eleven against and four for. Southern Republicans opposed the move twenty-four to four.

continued, however, Lamar's position in the Forty-third Congress emerged as a fundamentally conservative one based on maintaining existing levels of legal tender and United States notes that were redeemable in gold. He resisted efforts by both those who favored significant inflation and those who would decrease the money in circulation.

Lamar demonstrated his true position on currency in the showdown vote on the so-called Inflation Bill which occurred on April 14, 1874. This crucial bill established a clear line between conservatives and expansionists. Actually the measure was not extreme and in no sense represented a capitulation to the inflationists. Staunch conservatives strongly opposed it, nonetheless, because they looked upon even a moderate concession as a breach in their defense of sound money. The measure provided for a $46 million increase in national bank notes and allowed expansion of legal tender in circulation to $400 million, or about $18 million over the legal ceiling at the time. Taken together, the increases in circulation would not have amounted to more than $64 million—a modest change. The halfway solution earned the almost unanimous opposition of eastern Democrats as well as that of most eastern Republicans. On the other hand, the majority of western Democrats voted for the bill, as did two-thirds of the southern Democratic delegation. The bill passed the House, though Lamar sided with the easterners and opposed it.[3]

The Inflation Bill ultimately passed both legislative branches, but faced tougher opposition in the White House. Urged on by prominent conservatives including Charles Francis Adams, Sr., Edward Atkinson, Whitelaw Reid, and Cyrus Field, President Grant vetoed the measure as dangerously inflationary.[4] Lamar's vote clearly placed him in agreement with these men on the currency problem. The bill Grant later signed made only very mild concessions to the soft money men and passed by a large biparti-

3. *House Journal*, 43rd Cong., 1st Sess., 801–802; Unger, *The Greenback Era*, 235–36, App. C, 410.

4. Unger, *The Greenback Era*, 240–42.

san majority. The greenback limit was set at $382 million, the amount then outstanding. Lamar voted his approval.[5]

During the second session of the Forty-third Congress the Resumption Act of 1875 succeeded the Inflation Bill as a focus for House debate. The measure provided for a return in 1879 to a currency entirely secured by gold reserves and should have pleased all hard money advocates. The bill originated, however, as a partisan effort to consolidate different views within the Republican party before the coming presidential election. Consequently, the vote against resumption by Lamar and many other conservative Democrats may have reflected defensive party maneuvering rather than personal conviction.[6]

The currency question subsided somewhat after the Republicans secured passage of the Resumption Act, but it continually cropped up as efforts were made to repeal that legislation. Since the Democrats controlled the House when the Forty-fourth Congress convened in December, 1875, Lamar clearly felt less constrained by party considerations. Thus, he moved toward a consistent hard money position and voted against efforts to repeal the Republican sponsored bill.

In opposing repeal Lamar regularly voted with Mississippi Republicans John R. Lynch and G. Wiley Wells, while other Democratic members of the state delegation dallied and then finally voted with the national party on August 5, 1876, to suspend the 1879 resumption date.[7] Lamar's own criticism of the Resumption Act, in contrast to that of his Democratic colleagues, attacked the 1879 date as an unwarranted delay, and he voted for a commission to study "what measures are necessary and practicable in order to bring about the resumption of specie payments at the earliest possible time." [8]

---

5. *House Journal*, 43rd Cong., 1st Sess., 1260–61. Lamar's five Republican colleagues on the Mississippi delegation all voted for the final version.

6. *Ibid.*, 43rd Cong., 2nd Sess., 138. Unger, *The Greenback Era*, 252–55, 259, shows that only two Democrats voted for the measure.

7. *House Journal*, 44th Cong., 1st Sess., 202–203, 899–900, 1280, 1392.

8. *Congressional Record*, 44th Cong., 1st Sess., 5230–31; *House Journal*, 44th Cong., 1st Sess., 1391.

Lamar did not, of course, consider his deflationary position antithetical to party or sectional interests. He simply placed another interpretation, which he did not then explain, upon the abstract monetary principles involved and upon the effects of monetary policy in the South. In his view credit and the general economic climate would benefit from a conservative fiscal program.

Before the Forty-fourth Congress adjourned, a movement for currency inflation through the coinage of silver dollars had begun to displace the greenback solution as a panacea for the continuing economic slump. The silver issue would not reach its ultimate importance until a later day, however, and Lamar's opinion evolved with the changing circumstances. At this time his dedication to a stable currency was bimetallic, and he favored restoration of the legal tender status of the silver dollar which had been dropped from the mint list of 1873.[9] Though this attitude would change, he then desired only to see the people relieved of the "evils of an irredeemable currency." [10]

Lamar's record on economic issues during his postwar tenure in the House of Representatives revealed a consistent bias in favor of federal projects requiring expenditures of national funds. The enthusiasm and tenacity with which he advocated federal subsidization of the American economy made this the most outstanding principle of his economic philosophy.[11]

This position seemed to contradict Lamar's public attitude favoring retrenchment in both state and national government. He had spoken on this issue in various election campaigns in Mississippi and as chairman of the Democratic caucus during

9. *House Journal*, 44th Cong., 2nd Sess., 72.

10. Lamar's address to the Democratic caucus. See New York *Times*, December 5, 1875; and Memphis *Daily Appeal*, December 15, 1875.

11. A low tariff position was Lamar's greatest economic concern during his previous service in the House. This predilection for free trade or at least a downward revision continued into the postbellum period. In the Republican Forty-third Congress he generally voted with the minority. See *House Journal*, 43rd Cong., 1st Sess., 1073–76; 2nd Sess., 229–30, 526–29. The tariff, however, played a small part in the voting record described in this section.

the Forty-fourth Congress.[12] A free spending economic philosophy was nonetheless reasonable and not unlike that of many of his fellow congressmen from the South and from the Mississippi valley. The area's great need for material rehabilitation after the Civil War simply could not be satisfied without help from federal coffers. A policy of retrenchment appealed to the northeastern wing of the party which had long fought expenditures for public and private developments; but such an attitude from Lamar would have been doctrinaire and unrealistic. Consequently, he often voted with the Republican majority on these questions during the Forty-third Congress and with the minority when the Democrats won control of the House of Representatives in the elections of 1874.

Such economic alignment was ironic. Former Confederates sought reunion and reconciliation through the auspices of the Democratic party; and yet many of these same leaders shared little in common with their Democratic brethren in the Northeast in terms of economic policy. Conversely, the party of reconstruction and military intervention more willingly supported the material needs of the South than did the niggardly northern Democrats. For these reasons some southern spokesmen conspicuously associated themselves with Republican economic policies and forthrightly pleaded for capital support from the northern business community as well as for governmental aid. While Lamar remained rhetorically loyal to the Democratic party and did little to popularize this capital-seeking facet of the "New South" creed, his political contribution clearly complemented such efforts to rehabilitate the region.[13]

12. New York *Times*, December 5, 1875.

13. For a suggestive roll call analysis of voting on economic issues see John Kent Folmar, "The Erosion of Republican Support for Congressional Reconstruction in the House of Representatives, 1871–1877" (Ph.D. dissertation, University of Alabama, 1968), 194, 231, 337. In economic "scalograms" showing vote distribution Folmar places Lamar in a pattern of party regularity during the 43rd Cong., 1st Sess. and then shows him moving far toward Republican economic positions during the 43rd Cong., 2nd Sess. and the 44th Cong., 1st Sess. During the 43rd Cong., 2nd Sess. Lamar scaled nearer the Republican position than any other southern Democrat except one and nearer than any non-southern Demo-

A resolution offered on December 15, 1875, by Democrat William S. Holman of Indiana perhaps best illustrated the Democratic party alignment on subsidy appropriations. The measure stipulated that henceforth "no subsidies in money, bonds, public lands, indorsements, or by pledge of the public credit, should be granted by Congress to associations or corporations engaged or proposing to engage in public or private enterprise." The measure passed by a vote of 223 to 33. Southerners, including Lamar, constituted all but seven of the opposition. Only two northern Democrats voted against it along with a few Republicans.[14]

Lamar perhaps most earnestly represented the South's need to avoid undesirable retrenchment in the field of internal improvements. Because of the geographical location of his constituency, he received a place on the Select Committee on Mississippi River Levees when the Forty-third Congress met in December, 1873.[15] In this capacity Lamar tried to establish a special commission on reclamation of the river delta[16] and consistently favored improvements along the Mississippi. During the Forty-third Congress these far reaching projects included construction of a toll free canal shortening the distance from New Orleans to the Gulf of Mexico, improvement of the Mississippi River for navigation, and construction of a canal connecting Lake Michigan to the Mississippi River. Interestingly, the entire Mississippi delegation agreed upon the desirability of these economically beneficial improvements. Lamar voted with his five Republican colleagues in

crats except four. During the 44th Cong., 1st Sess. Lamar scaled nearer the Republican position than any other Democrat. These scalograms showing voting distribution are composite pictures, it should be noted, and combine various economic issues such as currency, railroad legislation, tariff, etc.

14. *House Journal*, 44th Cong., 1st Sess., 65–66; Woodward, *Reunion and Reaction*, 62. The Mississippi delegation divided four to two in favor of the resolution. Three Democrats and one Republican voted for the measure. Lamar and one Republican voted against.

15. *House Journal*, 43rd Cong., 1st Sess., 94.

16. *Congressional Record*, 43rd Cong., 1st Sess., 2929. The favorable response of his constituency may be judged in Jackson (Miss.) *Weekly Clarion*, April 16, 23, 30, 1874.

each instance. For Mississippians, party lines were not relevant
to the question of internal improvement.[17]

River improvement projects did not fare as well during the
Democratic Forty-fourth Congress as they had during the Republican Forty-third. The changed attitude of the legislature resulted mainly from the dominant role played during the 1875–
1877 sessions by the economy-minded northeastern wing of the
Democratic party. The differences between northern and southern Democrats (especially from the Mississippi valley) became
graphically evident when the House voted by roll call on a comprehensive bill to rebuild Mississippi levees, reclaim alluvial
lands, and improve navigation. After having deliberately put
off the legislation until near the end of the second session, northern Democrats helped defeat the measure 72 to 113. Only 18 of
124 northern Democrats voted with the southerners, and 10 of
these came from the border states. By contrast, southern Democrats voted 27 to 10 (with 20 not voting) in favor of the bill.

The Republican party also divided along sectional lines.
Southern Republicans voted 13 to 1 in favor of river improvements while northerners supplied only an additional 14 yea votes
as opposed to 50 votes against the measure. Mississippi's two remaining Republican congressmen joined the Democrats to make
the state's delegation unanimous in its support of the measure.

In all, southerners supplied 40 of the 72 affirmative votes; only
11 voted against the legislation. Clearly southerners were wedded
in an unequal struggle against the more thrifty northern representatives. The South at this time could expect nothing from
the northern Democrats and not a great deal from the northern
Republicans.[18]

Lamar's unstinting advocacy of internal improvements
reached far beyond the major expenditures favored for the Mississippi River system. During the Forty-third Congress he also
supported such projects as the construction of the Louisville and

17. *House Journal*, 43rd Cong., 1st Sess., 1114–17; 2nd Sess., 246–47.
18. *Ibid.*, 44th Cong., 2nd Sess., 668–69.

Portland Canal and the improvement of the economically unimportant Oostonoula River in Georgia. In the Forty-fourth
Congress he even parted company with the other three Democratic members of the Mississippi delegation to support a general
bill for the construction, repair, and completion of public works
on canals and rivers and presumably would have accepted more
of the same type of legislation if the House majority had been
more amenable.[19]

Lamar's penchant for disbursing federal funds did not stop
with public improvement legislation. He also voted with fair
consistency for government subsidization of private concerns—
most notably the railroads. Though aid to railroads at first glance
seems quite like the other federal expenditures which Lamar
favored, there was a difference because the beneficiaries—at least
the direct recipients—were private individuals rather than the
public.

By the mid-seventies Congress had soured on aid for railroad
companies because of such revelations as the Credit Mobilier
scandal of 1872, which had implicated important public figures.
Reformers in both parties now generally opposed railroad legislation and unfailingly attacked what they considered "jobbery."
Thus, in favoring generous government grants Lamar worked
against "reform" as well as against the economic policy of the
northeastern wing of his own party, which was more interested
in retrenchment than in government backed expansion. Here
again he appeared to oppose a principle which he publicly espoused in 1875 as chairman of the Democratic caucus.[20]

In favoring government financing for railroads, and most especially for a continental railroad along a southern route, Lamar
pursued a regional policy. His home state and other areas of the
South could not accept the position of the reformers and the
northern Democrats. During the spring of 1874 the Mississippi
legislature passed a resolution asking the state's congressional

19. *Ibid.*, 43rd Cong., 1st Sess., 882–83, 949–50; 44th Cong, 1st Sess., 778–79.
20. New York *Times*, December 5, 1875.

delegation to support a subsidy for the Texas Pacific Company in its proposed construction of a road from the Mississippi River to the Pacific Ocean. By the end of 1875 the legislature of every former Confederate state except Virgina and Louisiana had passed such a recommendation. Chambers of Commerce speaking for the commercial community echoed this sentiment; and newspapers supported the venture to the extent that, in 1875, the Texas Pacific Company (controlled by Thomas Scott of the Pennsylvania system) could publish a pamphlet quoting more than forty editors writing in its behalf.[21] In light of this general commitment, Lamar's position was obviously a popular one.

It is also possible that Mississippi's most important railroad company stood to benefit from the increased traffic which a Pacific coast connection might bring. The chronically troubled Mississippi Central Railroad, for which Lamar had served as board member and attorney, had become hopelessly indebted to the Illinois Central Railroad in 1872. Only some drastic improvement in its economic situation could have saved the road from the disaster of a court ordered receivership in March, 1876, and foreclosure in 1877.

Despite considerable economic and political justification for support of the Texas Pacific, trouble developed; and Lamar became during 1876 and 1877 a central figure in the controversy which surrounded congressional consideration of railroad legislation. There are two apparent reasons for this association. First, Lamar served as chairman of the House Committee on the Pacific Railroad when the Democrats returned to power in that branch of Congress in December, 1875. As chairman he introduced and promoted legislation reported by his committee. And secondly, complications arose from the Tilden-Hayes election controversy of 1876, and the involvement of railroad interests in the matter implicated Lamar in the bargaining which resulted.[22]

21. Woodward, *Reunion and Reaction*, 78–81. For a similar analysis see the Memphis *Daily Appeal*, November 18, 1875. Support of the project may be followed in the river oriented Memphis *Daily Appeal*, October 28, 30, November 6, 14, 19, 20, 21, 1875. Memphis expected to be a terminal of the road.

22. The election will be treated in a subsequent chapter.

These factors and the timetable which raised the transcontinental bill as an important issue in the Forty-fourth Congress combined to give Lamar special prominence.

Lamar's first setback in his role as chairman of the Pacific Railroad Committee came when northern Democrats led by William S. Holman blocked his effort to extend construction time for the Northern Pacific Railroad. Though that bill did not claim Lamar's interest to nearly the extent that the southern transcontinental road would, the demonstration of strength by opponents of his prorailroad policy was portentous.[23]

Special difficulties clouded the South's hope for its own continental road. The claim of the Texas Pacific on the southern route was effectively challenged by Collis P. Huntington and his combined Central Pacific and Southern Pacific lobby. Despite the southern states' solid stand for the Texas Pacific, Thomas Scott could not hope for a congressional subsidy while Huntington offered to build the road without government funds; nor could Huntington expect to overcome Scott's laboriously organized southern support. To resolve the impasse, they agreed to coordinate their lobbying efforts and to divide the project and the proceeds of the federal subsidy which they hoped Congress would pass. After this compromise, the Texas Pacific bill went to a subcommittee, which included Lamar as a member, and emerged in its final form.[24]

On January 24, 1877, in the midst of the Hayes-Tilden election dispute, Lamar reported two bills from his railroad committee. First, he reintroduced a measure extending the allotted construction time for completion of the Northern Pacific before the road forfeited its government grant. Congressman Holman

23. *Congressional Record*, 44th Cong., 2nd Sess., 92–93.
24. Woodward, *Reunion and Reaction*, 114. The discussion of the Texas Pacific question which follows draws heavily upon Woodward's work. Lamar's part in the jockeying between Huntington and Scott is not fully explained by extant evidence. His sympathy with Scott is, however, made clear by a letter from Scott to Lamar, April 13, 1876, in Lamar-Mayes Papers, suggesting certain actions Lamar might take to frustrate Huntington's efforts to defeat the Texas Pacific Railroad.

objected to the move on grounds that an extension would amount to an appropriation, since without new legislation the original grant would be reclaimed by the federal government. Lamar denied Holman's contention, but the chair decided in favor of Holman. Despite Lamar's argument that default by the Northern Pacific would result in great and undeserved injury to honest and even penurious stockholders, Holman effectively prevented consideration of the legislation. Although Lamar made two last efforts to bring the bill to a vote by suspending the House rules, he failed, and the session ended without action.[25]

The second bill reported by Lamar on January 24 was the controversial Texas Pacific bill as compromised and ironed out by the Pacific Railroad Committee. He immediately requested that it be made a special order on the calendar. Passage would exempt the company from the forfeiture requirements of existing laws and would divide construction of the Texas Pacific system between the Scott and Huntington companies—both to share in the government grant. In addition to the subsidy, the government would guarantee the debts of the companies.[26]

Apparently feeling his bill would not pass on its own merits, Lamar presented the Texas Pacific as a means of reconciling North and South by making possible the physical reconstruction of a war-torn area and by establishing sectional goodwill upon a base of equality and mutual respect.[27] Since the North had built transcontinental roads largely at public expense during and after the Civil War, this argument was not unreasonable. But the magic of an appeal for reconciliation could not be stretched this far. Holman again objected, and the House refused to grant the unanimous consent necessary to make the bill a special order. Consequently there could be no hope of its passage before the end of the session.[28]

25. *Congressional Record*, 44th Cong., 2nd Sess., 922–23, 2004; *House Journal*, 44th Cong., 2nd Sess., 633–34.

26. *Congressional Record*, 44th Cong., 2nd Sess., 924; Woodward, *Reunion and Reaction*, 127–31.

27. *Congressional Record*, 44th Cong., 2nd Sess., 924.

28. *Ibid.*

Lamar suffered personally with his program's defeat. Though he had little hope for the Texas Pacific bill even when he introduced it,[29] the vituperative response must have been disconcerting for a man so accustomed to high regard. Northern Democratic papers jumped on him with both feet, and the usually sympathetic Liberal-Republican press did likewise. His antagonists included such influential papers as the New York *Times*, the Chicago *Tribune*, the New York *Sun*, the New York *Tribune*, the Washington *Union*, and the weekly *Nation*. Perhaps none was so unkind as the New York *Times* when it warned that Lamar's good name would not carry the bill and that his "effort is rendered especially odious by the character of the scheme with which it is associated." [30] Lamar could take some comfort from the Memphis *Appeal*'s attack upon hypocritical northern editors who criticized the "reasonable and honest Texas Pacific bill as if they had never countenanced the robbing scheme known as the Central Pacific." [31] But overall, his national image and his personal dignity suffered a stunning reversal.

The futile struggle for the Texas Pacific, and the election crisis of 1876 with which the railroad question became associated, marked the close of Lamar's service in the House of Representatives. Even though his constituents approved his action, the bitterness of the final debate was in stark contrast to the brighter days of the Sumner eulogy. The failure meant a great deal more to Lamar than the immediate need for a transcontinental railroad. An economic and political principle—federal subsidization of southern development—had faltered. But on the other hand, some solace might be taken from the tenacious survival of both the principle and the bill after the session's end. Linked to the political events of 1876–1877, the Texas Pacific resurfaced as a crucial issue after Hayes became president of the United States. At another time and in another place Lamar would again speak

29. Lamar to Mrs. C. C. Clay, January 24, 1877, in C. C. Clay Papers.
30. New York *Times*, February 18, 28. 1877; Woodward, *Reunion and Reaction*, 134–39.
31. Memphis *Daily Appeal*, February 2, 1877.

for the legislation he considered essential to the well-being of
Mississippi and the South.

Other economic issues which concerned Lamar in the House
during the Forty-third and Forty-fourth Congresses would also
recur; and from now on his attitude would be set. Like his commitment to political decentralization, the defense of federally
supported economic development, coupled with a predilection
for sound money, had in the course of four years hardened into
a fixed dogma for his entire career. New questions would arise,
but his general response would logically follow these ingrained
notions of economic right and sectional interest.

Revolution of 1875

In a very real sense political and economic principles at the national level were of secondary importance to Lamar during the early years of his return to public life. So long as Mississippi remained under the rule of the Republican party with freedmen providing the voting base, Lamar's pronouncements in Washington offered little of relevance to his Democratic friends and neighbors. To them and to Lamar the ultimate and irreducible question was that of home rule. This compelling need never left his mind for long throughout the Forty-third and Forty-fourth Congresses until Mississippi's redemption was completed. But home rule, he must have known, could not be achieved against the Republican majority through the ordinary election process. The overthrow of the Republican state organization became, therefore, the revolutionary object of Mississippi Democrats.

The peculiarities of the Mississippi election calendar rendered the Democrats powerless to act against their antagonists during Lamar's first term in the House. No statewide election had been held since he took his seat in 1873, and so the general election of 1875 assumed great importance not only to Lamar personally but to the Democratic party as the first promising opportunity to "redeem" the state.

When Lamar returned home from Washington to report to his constituents in January, 1875, public meetings and testimonials greeted his arrival.[1] Such activity suggested that he would

1. Jackson (Miss.) *Weekly Clarion*, January 7, 1875; and Jackson (Miss.) *Daily*

easily be reelected in the fall. The sometimes publicized threat to gerrymander him out of office did not seem to present a real danger, although it did point to the incongruity of his position in a Republican state.[2] His congressional seat remained in a sense gratuitous and subject to the administration's tolerance, and so long as Lamar alone represented the Mississippi Democratic party in Washington, he spoke for a limited constituency and possessed no real moral authority to speak for the state. Unless the Democrats could effect a revolution in the political climate of Mississippi, reelection would be an empty victory.

Lamar took hope from the situation in 1875. The Democrats could, he thought, reasonably expect success for the first time since they had defeated the proscriptive constitution of 1868. The federal government's amnesty policy following ratification of the Fourteenth Amendment had increased the white vote. At the same time many native white Republicans had found the racial policies of the Ames government repugnant and had joined the Democrats in increasing numbers after 1873. This defection from Republican ranks gave white Mississippi its first semblance of political unity since radical reconstruction had begun. Of importance too was the fact that many Negroes, including men of standing, had become disillusioned with Ames and with Mississippi Republicanism in general. They realized that Republicans were unwilling or unable to provide sufficient rewards for Negroes, and believed that continued alienation from the native whites would result in hardship for the landless and dependent.[3]

Along with these events in Mississippi, national political developments favored a Democratic revival. The election of a Democratic majority to the lower house in 1874 presumably indicated a change in popular attitude toward Republican reconstruction.

Clarion, January 18, 29, 1875, describe public meetings to honor Lamar in Tupelo and Oxford. See also Jackson *Daily Clarion*, January 30, February 12, 20, 1875.

2. Jackson (Miss.) *Daily Clarion*, January 30, 1875.

3. Donald, "The Scalawag in Mississippi Reconstruction," 454–55; Hiram R. Revels to Grant, November 6, 1875, quoted in Garner, *Reconstruction in Mississippi*, 399–400.

Also, Grant had decided to discontinue military support for the Republicans, and in states like Mississippi this policy reversal sealed the party's doom. Before Grant announced his historic decision not to send troops to police the Mississippi election of 1875, Lamar had written his wife: "I think the future of Mississippi is very dark. Ames has it dead." Lamar thought that Ames would provoke an attack upon his Negro troops and "then Grant will take possession for him. May God help us!" [4] Without troops, however, the future brightened immeasurably.

Under these changing circumstances, the determined Democratic party began its organization as early as January, 1875. On the seventh of that month a supposedly bipartisan taxpayers convention met in Jackson to propose fiscal reforms. The convention urged the organization of taxpayers leagues in each county to search out ways of reducing taxes and to expose peculation by government officials. Although the Democratic party did not officially sanction the meeting, the implications were certainly partisan. One need look no further than to the convention leadership to find the connection. Albert Gallatin Brown and Wiley P. Harris, antebellum senator and congressman, both addressed the gathering. James Z. George, who would spearhead the Democratic campaign in 1875, was also active in these proceedings. [5]

On March 3, 1875, the Democratic minority in the state legislature met in caucus to make plans for the party's reorganization. The group named John M. Stone as chairman of a forty-two man committee to direct the effort. Stone's committee issued a statewide call for a Democratic meeting on May 17, 1875. In the midst of these preparations, Lamar traveled to Jackson where he joined other Democratic leaders. Although he issued no statement, the press reported that he would return for the May conference. [6]

4. Lamar to Mrs. Lamar, February 15, 1875, quoted in Mayes, *Lamar*, 211.

5. Jackson (Miss.) *Weekly Clarion*, January 7, 1875. According to Rowland, *History of Mississippi*, II, 192, Lamar attended and helped to prepare the address of the convention. Hudson Strode, *Jefferson Davis: Tragic Hero—The Last Twenty-Five Years, 1864–1889* (New York, 1964), 399, also places Lamar at the convention. The Jackson (Miss.) *Clarion* lists the delegates, however, and does not include Lamar.

6. Garner, *Reconstruction in Mississippi*, 372–73; Jackson (Miss.) *Weekly Clarion*, April 21, May 5, 1875; Memphis *Daily Appeal*, May 8, 1875.

When the delegates to the organizational meeting gathered on May 17, 1875, they decided to hold a state convention on August 3 and to invite all conservatives and antiradicals without regard to party. This inclusion of traditional anti-Democrats, especially the old Whig element, provoked some petty quibbling. Finally the new organization accommodated those who could not bear to be labeled "Democratic" by calling itself the Democratic-Conservative party. Lamar remained inconspicuous at the gathering and declined to address the delegates. In his failure to speak and to join the provisional executive committee, Lamar displayed a predisposition which characterized his relationship with the Mississippi Democratic party: he generally left organizational matters to others. In the campaign to follow he would serve primarily as spokesman and totem for the party.[7]

Between May and August, Lamar took to the stump. Since his own nomination was virtually assured, he campaigned principally against the Republican state legislature. With this larger target in view, he spoke at numerous mass meetings throughout northern Mississippi.[8]

The Democratic-Conservatives in Lamar's upstate area concentrated their efforts on a meeting scheduled for July 15 at Falkner's Station in Tippah County. For this occasion special trains transported between two and three thousand people to the rally. These hardy partisans who braved ninety degree temperatures did not go away disappointed. Lamar harangued against Ames and the Republicans for three torrid hours, blaming them for creating the deplorable color line and for the perversion of white-Negro relations through discriminatory reconstruction laws. In addition to Lamar's speech, Democrats at Falkner's Station heard from state legislator Thomas Spight and W. C. Falkner, the author, speculator, railroad promoter, and politician, and at the same time enjoyed a giant barbecue and dance. In the midst of this gaiety the gathering chose its delegates to the

7. Jackson (Miss.) *Weekly Clarion*, May 19, 1875; Memphis *Daily Appeal*, May 20, 22, 1875.
8. Jackson (Miss.) *Weekly Clarion*, July 21, 28, 1875; New York *Tribune*, July 26, 1876.

state convention and also passed resolutions approving Lamar's actions in Congress.[9]

Other meetings throughout the district endorsed Lamar, so that the Democratic-Conservative congressional nominating convention which met on July 22 resembled a testimonial more than a nominating procedure. No opposition developed, and the convention obligingly passed the resolutions Lamar desired opposing the color line and inviting Negro support. The business of the day settled, Lamar treated the 5,000 people in attendance to a grand attack on the policies and maladministration of the Republican party.[10]

Lamar then traveled from his own district to Jackson, where he opened the state convention on August 3 with a speech which has been characterized as the "bugle call" for the revolution of 1875.[11] Though it perhaps merited such a description, the content of Lamar's message had been well tested on earlier occasions, and he simply said the same popular things over again in Jackson. The appeal was obvious, but irrefutable. One editor enthusiastically declared: "His arraignment of the Radical Southern government was terrible, and his dissection of Ames and his crew in Mississippi was pitiless." [12]

Lamar's "bugle call" stressed two main points. He denounced Republicans for their southern policy and at the same time pledged the goodwill and patriotism of Mississippi whites. He had found this combination irresistible in his congressional speeches and on the stump prior to the convention. Immediate enfranchisement of the Negro, he believed, had been a mistake. Federal interference in southern affairs was all wrong. By employing the Negro for political purposes, the Republican-con-

9. Memphis *Daily Appeal*, June 30, July 20, 1875; Jackson (Miss.) *Weekly Clarion*, July 21, 28, 1875; Mayes, *Lamar*, 250–51. W. C. Falkner was the great grandfather of novelist William Faulkner.

10. Memphis *Daily Appeal*, July 23, 1875; Jackson (Miss.) *Weekly Clarion*, July 28, 1875; New York *Times*, July 23, 1875; Brandon (Miss.) *Republican*, July 29, 1875.

11. Rowland, *History of Mississippi*, II, 195; Jackson (Miss.) *Weekly Clarion*, August 4, 11, 1875.

12. Memphis *Daily Appeal*, August 4, 1875.

trolled federal government had drawn the color line and had caused a war between the races. By using this approach Lamar ignored all differences in opinion within the white community and described a simple struggle between Negro and carpetbagger Republicans on one side and native whites on the other. As an alternative to reconstruction, Lamar preached reconciliation and goodwill based on Negro enfranchisement and home rule, an arrangement which would admit native whites to responsible leadership. Mississippi, he declared, fully accepted the United States Constitution and its amendments and opposed the color line which was unrepublican and immoral.

In all this, Lamar said little that was new or informative. On one point, however, he clearly revealed the underlying supposition of his political philosophy. The American people of both sections, he told his Jackson audience, wanted peace and reconciliation. Once convinced that the South would protect the Negro in his rights, the northern public would support local government.[13]

Lamar's reasoning dominated the platform adopted by the Democratic-Conservative convention. It recognized the civil and political equality of all men and espoused public education for all children. Other planks included governmental economy, tax reductions, and judicial reform. A provision asking federal aid for flood control indicated the distinction made between state economy and national spending. And finally, the convention invited men of both races to support these principles.[14]

Lamar's program did not go altogether unopposed. Resistance centered on the anti-color line proposition and on the inclusion of "Conservative" along with "Democratic" as a party designa-

13. Jackson (Miss.) *Daily Times*, August 4, 1875, clipping in SEN50B–A3, Record Group No. 46; Jackson *Weekly Mississippi Pilot*, August 7, 1875; Jackson (Miss.) *Weekly Clarion*, August 4, 1875; Memphis *Daily Appeal*, August 4, 1875. Lamar wrote A. J. Phillips, August 20, 1875, in A. J. Phillips Papers, Houghton Library, Harvard University: "There is no accurate report of my speech delivered at Jackson."

14. Jackson (Miss.) *Weekly Clarion*, August 4, 1875; Memphis *Daily Appeal*, August 4, 1875.

tion. Led by W. H. McCardle, editor of the Vicksburg *Commercial*, and A. J. Frantz, editor of the Brandon *Republican*, the opposition group generally represented the counties with large Negro populations where Republicans, white and black, were concentrated. McCardle and Frantz feared that extensive Negro voting would prevent their regaining control of their county governments. The vote of 162 to 33 on the platform, however, showed the one-sided nature of this conflict. Nevertheless, the difference of opinion was not forgotten, and it would rankle Democrats from time to time.[15]

The state convention's biracial plank in no way ensured implementation on the county level. Many whites had determined to carry the election even at the cost of intimidating Negroes and white Republicans, and they would not be dissuaded.[16] Under these circumstances Governor Adelbert Ames may have struck close to the truth when he described the convention to his wife: "The true sentiment of the assembly was 'color line' though the platform says nothing about it. The understanding evidently is that each locality can act as it chooses, but the state convention shall put forth a platform for Northern consumption." [17]

Governor Ames charged that the words of Lamar's speeches masked their true intent. He wrote his wife on September 7, 1875, describing as "incendiary" the efforts by Lamar and his friend, John B. Gordon, who had come from Georgia to assist him. "The language they use," he claimed, "is not of itself violent, but the conclusions they reach are that this election must be carried, even if violence be resorted to." [18] Ames undoubtedly spoke with some justification, but ironically many Negroes at-

15. Memphis *Daily Appeal*, August 4, 1875; New York *Tribune*, August 10, 1875; Willie D. Halsell, "The Bourbon Period in Mississippi Politics," *Journal of Southern History*, XI (November, 1945), 520–21.

16. Jackson *Weekly Mississippi Pilot*, September 4, 1875, a Republican paper, pounced on this inconsistency and printed the following from the Columbus (Miss.) *Democrat*: "WHITE MEN SHALL RULE MISSISSIPPI. Col. Lamar may fancy that he and his coajutors have crushed out the race issue. Vain, silly thought."

17. Adelbert Ames to Blanche Ames, August 4, 1875, in Blanche Butler Ames (comp.), *Chronicles from the Nineteenth Century* (n.p., 1957), II, 124.

18. Adelbert Ames to Blanche Ames, September 7, 1857, *ibid.*, II, 166.

tended those same speeches by Lamar and Gordon, and the speakers made a definite pitch for their votes.[19]

Lamar's true attitude toward Negro voting in 1875 embodied both the public image and the contradictory tactic of harassment. The election of 1875 was, in fact, part of a longer campaign begun in 1872 which had always included ambiguities and contradictions of this sort. In the Sumner eulogy and similar declarations Lamar pleaded for reconciliation and sectional unity. In doing so he spoke as a national patriot, but he also sought the termination of federal intervention in the South as an end in itself. In 1875 he supported the United States Constitution and its amendments and justice for the freedmen. Perhaps he spoke in 1875 as a patriot and as a political equalitarian as he claimed, but his immediate goal once again was to end federal power in Mississippi. Duality inevitably resulted from this contradition between an idealistic rhetorical adherence to the constitutional amendments and the practical necessity of defeating the Republican party. Lamar preferred to enlist Negroes in the Democratic party as a means of achieving his objective. But at the same time he could not and would not stop color line methods, and he lent his energy and reputation to obscuring the existence of political intimidation.[20]

Desire for Democratic government and Negro suffrage became further confused in Lamar's mind because his thwarted sense of moral responsibility impinged upon practical political matters. He acted with the conviction that the politically ignorant Negro

19. New York *Times*, September 8, 1875; Memphis *Daily Appeal*, September 7, 1875.
20. The Republican party charged Lamar personally with white line speeches; for example: "Even Col. Lamar, that sweetest singer in Bourbonic Israel, grows wild and desperate in his latest harangues." See Jackson *Daily Mississippi Pilot*, October 27, 1875. See also *ibid.*, July 27, October 26, 1875; and Jackson *Weekly Mississippi Pilot*, July 31, 1875. Lamar defended himself in Congress on July 25, 1876, against what he considered false charges in a Washington paper that he had favored the white line in speeches at Aberdeen and Scooba, Mississippi, during the campaign. See *Congressional Record*, 44th Cong., 1st Sess., 4878–79; and New York *Tribune*, July 26, 1876. But according to Wharton, *The Negro in Mississippi*, 186, a Democratic badge in Lamar's home county gave the Negro bearer protection from physical violence and the right to "boss" other Negroes.

must somehow be accommodated to the political system. Without an accommodation, racial conflict could not end and Republican rule based on a Negro voting majority would, perhaps, continue into the future.[21] Furthermore, the color line concept favored by men like McCardle offended a fundamental commitment to representative democracy. As Lamar told the August 3 convention: "It is not right. It is not Republican. One of the principles of Democratic government is that all parts of the body politic shall contribute to its support and control. Any race organization which seeks to assert the exclusive management of a country may have good government, but cannot have liberty. It is tyranny unmixed, and is fraught with disaster." [22]

Four days after making that speech Lamar wrote Charles Nordhoff of the New York *Herald* explaining the party's platform and asking his support. Regarding the color line movement, Lamar wrote: "Whatever you may have heard or believe, this principle (the sense of moral rectitude) is as strong in the soul of our people as in any on earth." [23]

Whatever may be said of the "moral rectitude" of white Mississippians, they did succeed in combining color line methods with high sounding principles. After the convention, three long months of campaigning lay ahead. Tactical direction of the canvass fell to James Z. George of Jackson and the state executive committee which he headed. This leadership proved so effective and the cause so popular that the entire state soon seethed with political activity.[24]

Lamar was not a member of the executive committee and apparently played only a peripheral role in organizing the cam-

21. Lamar to Charles Reemelin, August 25, 1875, quoted in Mayes, *Lamar*, 258–59.

22. Jackson *Weekly Mississippi Pilot*, August 7, 1875.

23. Lamar to Charles Nordhoff, August 8, 1875, in Charles Nordhoff Papers, Houghton Library, Harvard University. Charles Nordhoff, *The Cotton States in the Spring and Summer of 1875* (New York, 1876), 76, credited Lamar as a defender of Negro rights.

24. Garner, *Reconstruction in Mississippi*, 373.

paign. He contributed instead as an active orator[25] and as a rallying point for the rank and file members of the party. Lamar's unique status as Mississippi's Democratic representative in Congress may have induced many to agree with the suggestion of antebellum senator Albert Gallatin Brown who wrote on May 26, 1875: "I did not at first fully approve of Lamar's speech over the dead Sumner. But, having witnessed its good effects, I recant. It is now, I think, on every account our policy to make him our *recognized* leader. We thereby, amongst many other advantages, get the benefit of his conservative statements so often and so boldly expressed. By making him our leader we make these expressions our own, and thus disarm our Northern slanderers." [26] Brown provided Ethelbert Barksdale, editor of the Jackson *Clarion*, with an article praising Lamar. The *Clarion* printed the piece with a poem which must have been effusive even for that time and place. The verse aimed straight at the patriot's heart: "Press where you see his white plume shine, amid the ranks of war"; and, "Amidst the thickest of the fight will blaze, the helmet of Lamar." [27] Other newspapers echoed Lamar's role as Democratic figurehead—a symbol of national stature.[28]

By election time the combination of high toned rhetoric, intimidation, and violence had paid off. The contest was already over; the vote simply confirmed Democratic achievements over a period of months. Very little fraud occurred at the polls on November 3; and little was necessary. The revolution of 1875 ended quietly.[29]

25. Jackson (Miss.) *Weekly Clarion*, September 8, 29, October 6, 20, 27, 1875; Brandon (Miss.) *Republican*, September 2, 9, 1875. Judging from the James Z. George correspondence Lamar was the most sought after speaker of the campaign. See Garner, *Reconstruction in Mississippi*, 375n.

26. A. G. Brown to Ethelbert Barksdale, May 26, 1875, quoted in Mayes, *Lamar*, 248. As editor of the *Clarion*, Barksdale played an important role in the Democratic party.

27. Jackson (Miss.) *Weekly Clarion*, June 2, 1875; Mayes, *Lamar*, 248.

28. Memphis *Daily Appeal*, July 20, 27, 1875; Brandon (Miss.) *Republican*, August 19, 1875; Jackson (Miss.) *Weekly Clarion*, August 11, 1875. For instance, the press ballyhooed Lamar as a vicepresidential candidate on the abortive National Union party ticket with N. P. Banks.

29. Garner, *Reconstruction in Mississippi*, 392; Wharton, *The Negro in Mississippi*, 195–97.

The Democratic majority of almost 31,000[30] sufficed to elect a state treasurer (the only state office involved in the election), a majority of both houses of the state legislature, a majority of county officials, and four of six congressmen. Lamar himself ran without opposition, and his district returned all of its twelve counties for the Democratic party.[31] A Republican governor, lieutenant governor, and several lesser officials remained in office, but their power was spent and their humiliation imminent.

When the Democratic legislature met in December, Lamar had already left for Washington. In his absence state leaders demanded the immediate impeachment of Ames, Negro Lieutenant Governor A. K. Davis, and Negro Superintendent of Education T. W. Cardoza. Former governor Alcorn's term in the Senate would expire in 1877, and the new legislature would provide for his successor.

Lamar played no known part in the proceedings against Davis and Cardoza, though apparently he had no objections. Ames's impeachment, however, carried dangerous political overtones, and concerned him directly. Lamar presumed that the Republicans would seek to prove foul play in Mississippi and realized that if Ames were removed without absolutely irrefutable proof of cause, the Democratic victory would be vulnerable to federal counteraction.[32] In a letter remarkable chiefly for its uncharacteristic cynicism, he conveyed to E. D. Clark his determination to build a strong case. "It may subserve a useful purpose to employ [scalawag] Joshua Morris," he declared. "It is not necessary for me to state what my feelings towards that person are; but if he can be made useful by getting, through his peculiar capacity for finding carrion, information that is inaccessible to our people, such a man, should not be thrown away." [33]

30. Compared to a Republican majority of 20,467 in 1873.

31. Election figures furnished by Political Research Consortium. On the method and effect of voter intimidation see Wharton, *The Negro in Mississippi*, 185 ff.; and Sallis, "The Color Line in Mississippi Politics," 211–21.

32. Lamar to E. C. Walthall, February 23, 1876, quoted in Mayes, *Lamar*, 263.

33. Lamar to E. D. Clark, n.d., Lamar Papers, University of Mississippi Library. Republican Joshua Morris served as Mississippi's attorney general.

Ames's fate could also affect the choice of Alcorn's successor in the Senate—a matter of vital importance. Lamar's name had been mentioned in this connection as soon as the Democrats took over the legislature. County organizations passed resolutions, and newspapers endorsed senatorial candidates as early as December, 1875. Other prominent men including James George and Robert Lowry, both leaders in the revolution of 1875, received complimentary attention; but they withdrew their names from consideration, and the legislature elected Lamar without opposition.[34]

Ominously for Lamar and the revolution, Governor Ames refused to recognize the Mississippi legislative body, and Republican members declined to participate in the election of a senator on grounds that an irregular body could not so act. Meanwhile, Oliver P. Morton had introduced a resolution in the United States Senate calling for an investigation of the Mississippi election because of the widespread reports of fraud and violence.[35] More trouble developed when Ames refused to certify Lamar's election while the impeachment charges against Ames were pending.[36]

Ames's father-in-law, Ben Butler, assumed responsibility for managing his case in Washington. Ironically, the radical Butler and Lamar cooperated in a compromise which led to Ames's departure from Mississippi. Soon after Lamar learned that his

34. Both the Jackson (Miss.) *Clarion* and the Memphis *Daily Appeal* supported Lamar for the Senate. The latter showed a great deal more enthusiasm than the *Clarion*, printing resolutions from smaller papers and press excerpts from all over the country. See Jackson (Miss.) *Weekly Clarion*, December 1, 1875, January 12, 19, 1876; Jackson (Miss.) *Daily Clarion*, January 7, 1876; and Memphis *Daily Appeal*, December 11, 25, 1875, January 7, 19, 1876.

35. *Congressional Record*, 44th Cong., 1st Sess., 220. The Morton resolution resulted in the Boutwell Committee investigation. The Boutwell report did not touch Lamar with the exception of the Oxford courthouse affair in 1871. The resolution may have been put forth in Ames's behalf since Mrs. Ben F. Butler wrote to her daughter, Blanche Ames: "There is a chance that Morton's resolution in the Senate may stop further action against Gen. Ames, if Lamar has any fear about getting into the Senate." See Ames (comp.), *Chronicles from the Nineteenth Century*, II, 264.

36. Undated transcript of an interview between state senators Allen and Reynolds and Governor Ames, in Lamar-Mayes Papers; Reuben O. Reynolds to Lamar, February 16, 1876, quoted in Mayes, *Lamar*, 313–14.

election had not been certified, J. B. Beck and Jeremiah Black, northern Democrats in touch with Butler, informed Lamar that Ames would be willing to resign if the legislature dropped the impeachment issue. Otherwise, a strong defense would be made. They also suggested that Butler might kill the congressional investigation of election fraud in Mississippi. Beck and Black concluded that Lamar actually opposed Ames's impeachment and that he would undertake to stop the proceedings. Butler himself believed Lamar to be sincere.[37]

Lamar seems to have decided in favor of the compromise primarily to avoid further controversy and a damaging investigation by a Republican congressional committee. Ames's resignation, coupled with the removal of Lieutenant Governor Davis, would permit installation of the Democratic president pro tem of the Mississippi senate as acting governor. Lamar's election to the Senate, if he were really worried about it, could then be certified by the acting governor. Thus, nothing whatsoever could be gained by forcing the issue with Ames.[38]

After Ames's resignation on March 28, 1876, John M. Stone became Mississippi's acting governor and Lamar's election was certified. Lamar immediately wrote Stone outlining the most vital issues facing the new administration. First, he urged the appointment of a distinguished judiciary;[39] second, he counseled

37. Lamar to E. C. Walthall, February 23, 1876, quoted in Mayes, *Lamar*, 263–64; Ben Butler to Adelbert Ames, February 25, 1876, in Ames (comp.), *Chronicles from the Nineteenth Century*, II, 304–305.

38. Lamar to E. C. Walthall, February 23, 1876, quoted in Mayes, *Lamar*, 263–64. Ames's distrust of Lamar in this matter and his bitterness is indicated by his letter to Ben Butler just two weeks before he resigned: "I am free to confess I have no faith in Lamar's political integrity. . . . My opinion of the man is—I know him well—that he deceives," and that "he is one thing here and quite another in Washington." See Adelbert Ames to Ben Butler, March 14, 1876, quoted in Halsell, "Note on a Phase of L. Q. C. Lamar's Career," 21. Ames's wife wrote to her mother on March 14, 1876: "The warmest friends of Lamar here are the most violent for impeachment—and Mr. Lamar is a double dealer on whom no dependence can be placed, as it is well known that in all matters political he does not hesitate to be false"; and "if he really wishes to be of service, let him call off the dogs—which he can easily do." See Ames (comp.), *Chronicles from the Nineteenth Century*, II, 344.

39. Lamar had already written Stone urging the appointment of his close

sale of the executive mansion: "The people will hail it as a return to Republican economy & simplicity of living"; and third,
the governor "ought not to countenance any funding measures
that even squint toward Repudiation." Stone at once replied
in agreement with all these suggestions.[40] Such policies did not,
of course, constitute the revolution of 1875. The election itself
had already achieved the major objectives of the Democratic-
Conservatives. Home rule had been won and the Negro voting majority had been brought under white conservative domination. Fiscal reforms and other adjustments in governmental
policy would follow quietly and without effective Republican
opposition.

The tone and the early date of the Lamar-Stone letters suggested that Lamar might play an active role in the state's redemption government. Surprisingly, however, he did not continue the
supervision of Mississippi's return to austere Democratic government. National problems in the House of Representatives and
then in the Senate claimed his attention instead. Reinforced by
the end of Republican rule in Mississippi and most other southern states, Lamar resumed his place as spokesman and diplomat
for the South on the national scene.

---

friend Edward Walthall to a circuit judgeship. See Lamar to John M. Stone,
March 29, 1876, in John M. Stone Papers.

40. Lamar to Governor Stone, March 31, 1876, in Governor's Papers: John M.
Stone, Series E, MDAH; John M. Stone to Lamar, April 1, 1876, in Lamar-Mayes
Papers.

Revolution of 1876 and the New Departure

Lamar looked toward the national election of 1876 with understandable optimism. Weakened by the schism of 1872, and by economic depression beginning in 1873, Republicans had already lost control of the House of Representatives and had suffered the scandals of Grant's second administration. The Democrats benefited from these political developments and stood to gain even more from the emergence of the South as a potent force in the electoral college. Democrats also believed that their nominee offered a striking contrast to Grant. Samuel J. Tilden's reputation as reform governor of New York and his professed goodwill toward the South were viewed as a powerful combination, and Republican Rutherford B. Hayes did not appear strong enough to stop him. Lamar had long anticipated and worked toward such a change in the course of national politics.

Mississippi's recently enthroned Democrats took courage from these propitious circumstances and hoped to carry their state for the first time in a presidential election since the Civil War.[1] And if the state should go for Tilden, Mississippians would at the same time also complete their own revolution. Congressional elections were to be held again in 1876, and the chances of defeating the remaining two Republican congressmen appeared good.

1. James Z. George, Chairman, State Executive Committee, to Lamar, September 11, 1876, in Lamar-Mayes Papers.

Lamar's fragile health failed during the spring and summer, but by September he felt like campaigning in earnest. Judging from the returns, he might have rested more easily. The election sent a solidly Democratic delegation to the national House of Representatives and handed Tilden a majority of almost 50,000. No gubernatorial elecion would be held until 1877, but Democrats won all other executive positions; and the Democratic state legislature reflected the overwhelming rout of the Republicans.[2]

National election results on the other hand confounded both Democrats and Republicans. Each side claimed victory and great confusion replaced the usual postelection calm. Soon, however, it became clear that disputed returns in Louisiana, South Carolina, and Florida would decide the presidency, and both parties sent representatives scurrying south to protect their interests.[3] As Congress would not convene to count the electoral votes until December 4, the journey of the "visiting statesmen" took on great importance. During the intervening weeks both Democratic and Republican parties had their work to do.

Lamar traveled with other Democratic watchdogs to New Orleans. They immediately found cause for concern and advised Tilden that he should consult directly with Hayes. These observers believed that a conspiracy to deprive Tilden of Louisiana's votes existed already and that the best hope of thwarting that plan lay in appealing to Hayes's sense of honor. Tilden, however, disregarded the suggestion and the mission could offer no better solution.[4]

2. Abram S. Hewitt to Lamar, October 20, 1876, in Lamar-Mayes Papers; Memphis *Daily Appeal*, March 12, April 2, 1876; Jackson (Miss.) *Weekly Clarion*, August 23, 1876. For Lamar's speaking engagements see: James George to Lamar, October 19, 1876, in Lamar-Mayes Papers; Memphis *Daily Appeal*, September 9, 23, October 13, 27, 1876; and Jackson (Miss.) *Weekly Clarion*, November 1, 5, 1876. Election figures furnished by Political Research Consortium.

3. An electoral vote from Oregon, disputed on technical grounds, is not germane to this aspect of the story.

4. Samuel Randall, L. Q. C. Lamar, Henry Watterson, Oswald Ottendorfer to S. G. Tilden, November 14, 1876, in "Testimony before the Select Committee on Alleged Frauds in the Presidential Election of 1876, in relation to Cipher Telegraphic Dispatches," *House Miscellaneous Documents*, 45th Cong., 3rd Sess., No. 31, p. 336; telegram from Lamar to E. C. Walthall, n.d., quoted in McNeily, "War

En route back to Washington for the congressional session which would decide the presidency, Lamar revealed his misgivings to W. H. Roberts of the New Orleans *Times*, who was traveling on the same train. Roberts' immediate destination was Cincinnati; and from there he planned to go to Columbus, Ohio, for an interview with Governor Hayes. Undoubtedly he listened willingly to Lamar's impressions. Both Roberts and Lamar stopped off in Cincinnati to visit with another interested party, Murat Halstead of the Cincinnati *Commercial*. As they both knew, Halstead was on very friendly terms with Hayes and was actively promoting his succession to the presidency.[5]

Lamar declined an invitation to accompany the two newspaper men to Columbus,[6] but he talked freely enough so that they could relate his general position to Hayes. Lamar claimed, as they reported, that the South wanted no civil disruption and would "not oppose an Administration which will favor an honest administration and honest officers in the South." [7]

Lamar's indirect message does not seem to have constituted an offer to support Hayes's election. Despite immediate newspaper allegations and charges by a congressional investigating committee, neither Hayes nor Lamar understood that a bargain had been proposed and struck.[8] Hayes gave no hint in his correspondence or in his diary to support such a conclusion. And La-

---

and Reconstruction," 487. In an interview given the New Orleans *Times*, Lamar mentioned the possibility of having the vote counted by honorable men of both parties. He stressed, however, his belief that the Democrats carried Louisiana by 7,000 votes. See Memphis *Daily Appeal*, November 15, 16, 17, 1876, citing the *Times* on Lamar's interview; and his telegram to Walthall quoted in McNeily.

5. Testimony of W. H. Roberts, in "Report of the Investigation of the Presidential Election of 1876," *House Miscellaneous Documents*, 45th Cong., 3rd Sess., No. 31, p. 881.

6. *Ibid.*; Murat Halstead to Lamar, December 20, 1876, in Lamar-Mayes Papers.

7. T. Harry Williams (ed.), *Hayes, The Diary of a President, 1875–1881* (New York, 1964), 52.

8. The rumor of collusion cropped up almost immediately and was persistent. New York *Times*, December 3, 4, 1876, gave accounts of the episode but disputed the charges of political dealing. Memphis *Daily Appeal*, December 9, 1876, cited the New York *Herald* on this point, and raised the subject again on January 9, 1877. Jackson (Miss.) *Weekly Clarion*, January 10, 1877, carried the story.

mar even refused to take seriously the assurances from Hayes, conveyed through W. H. Roberts, promising a lenient policy toward Democrats in the South. A sympathetic policy, Lamar thought, would be altogether impolitic and therefore impossible for Hayes. Though their assessment of Hayes's remarks varied somewhat, both Roberts and Lamar seemed interested only in knowing Hayes's intentions and in assuring him that if he did become president, he would be acceptable to the South so long as he treated the section justly. Nothing more happened at the time.[9]

From Cincinnati Lamar traveled into the crisis atmosphere which hung over Washington in December, 1876. Party spirit bred tension and divided the capital into political war camps. Republicans adamantly maintained that the electoral vote in the South belonged to Hayes. Democrats were just as convinced that Tilden had been elected and that the Republicans would unjustly refuse to honor the popular mandate.

Democratic party solidarity broke down under the pressure and gave way to bitter division. The northern wing generally opposed compromise, and some of its members threatened armed resistance as a last alternative to defeat. The southern wing, chastened by defeat in war, counseled a more moderate course.[10] The real ability of Democratic extremists to arm their party against Republican efforts to install Hayes cannot be measured. But more to the point, many men, including Lamar, thought the danger of civil conflict to be real, and this conviction weighed heavily upon them during the days of decision.[11]

9. Testimony of W. H. Roberts, in "Report of the Investigation of the Presidential Election of 1876," *House Miscellaneous Documents*, 45th Cong., 3rd Sess., No. 31, pp. 881–82; Williams (ed.), *Hayes, Diary of a President*, 52–53; Murat Halstead to Rutherford B. Hayes, December 10, 1876, in Rutherford B. Hayes Papers, Hayes Memorial Library, Fremont, Ohio; E. A. Angier to Hayes, December 16, 1876, *ibid.*

10. Woodward, *Reunion and Reaction*, 32–33.

11. Lamar to Burton N. Harrison, March 8, 1877, in Mrs. Burton Harrison's Scrap Book, 1859–1909, Burton N. Harrison Papers; Lamar speech of n.d., 1879, quoted in Mayes, *Lamar*, 297–99. D. D. [?] to Captain Alfred E. Lee, December 25, 1876, in Rutherford B. Hayes Papers, credited Lamar with fear of trouble if Tilden was not inaugurated.

Believing Tilden elected, but fearful of violence or war, Lamar sought a safe solution to the controversy. On December 10, 1876, he claimed in an interview that the Constitution provided an answer. It required agreement of the two houses of Congress on the election of a president through the electoral college system. The vice president, who presided over the joint session, lacked authority to accept or reject disputed votes on his own volition. He must leave the choice to the two houses, and if they should fail to agree to the election of a candidate then the houses should "immediately proceed in their respective duties— one [House] to elect the President and the other [Senate] the Vice President. Let the constitution be maintained inviolate, and there need be no disorganizing collisions and no necessity for resorting to force." [12]

Lamar realized, of course, that his constitutional solution would not be acceptable to the Republicans. As chairman of the House Democratic caucus and then as chairman of a joint House-Senate committee formed on December 11, he remained in close touch with the developing controversy. From this vantage point he saw that the impasse would not be resolved through any such simplistic application of established law as he had suggested.[13]

Lamar's rather hollow proposal actually exposed the failure of the Democrats to develop a viable strategy. Unfortunately, the situation did not immediately improve. During the Christmas recess, which began on December 19, Lamar went with Senator Thomas F. Bayard to visit Tilden. The meeting did nothing to resolve the dilemma. Tilden presented no plan of action and gave no indication of his intentions. Lamar must have returned deeply shaken in his hope for a peaceful Democratic inauguration. Without leadership from the party's candidate a catastrophic debacle was likely. In light of Tilden's earlier rejection

12. Interview of December 10, 1876, quoted in McNeily, "War and Reconstruction," 492. The same quote is in Memphis *Daily Appeal*, January 6, 1877.
13. New York *Times*, December 8, 9, 1876; Allan Nevins, *Abram S. Hewitt, with Some Account of Peter Cooper* (New York, 1935), 351.

of the "visiting statesmen's" advice to meet with Hayes, this interview offered anything but reassurance.[14]

Since the holidays yielded no master plan from Tilden, and no intimation of compromise came from Hayes's people, the Democrats returned to Congress somewhat unsettled. The inclination toward violent resistance among northern Democrats grew during the first two weeks of January. This belligerence was abetted by rumblings from Roscoe Conkling's anti-Hayes clique, which threatened to desert the Republican candidate.[15] At the same time moderates, including Lamar, sought a middle way—a means of arbitration which would satisfy partisans and give a cloak of legality to a president whose claim to office could at best be tenuous.

As a member of the Democratic advisory committee and as a leading moderate, Lamar became deeply involved in the effort which finally led to a solution of the election impasse. Since the Republican Senate and Democratic House of Representatives could never be expected to agree, the proponents of compromise decided that a bipartisan electoral commission should be named with membership from both legislative bodies and from the Supreme Court as well. Presumably such a group would have some claim to objectivity, because Justice David Davis, a professed Independent, would round out the Supreme Court delegation.

The electoral commission bill came to a vote in the House on January 26, 1877. Lamar justified the legislation in a speech chiefly notable for its appeal to calm statesmanship. He defended the measure's constitutionality with reasoned argument and then proceeded to show its applicability to the crisis at hand. By establishing a commission, he said, a "thoroughly considered and

---

14. Edward Spencer, *Public Life and Services of Thomas F. Bayard* (New York, 1880), 261, describes the visit. This account is accepted by Nevins, *Abram S. Hewitt*, 335 and Charles C. Tansill, *The Congressional Career of Thomas Francis Bayard, 1869–1885* (Washington, 1946), 156–57. L. C. Weir to Rutherford B. Hayes, February 7, 1877, in Rutherford B. Hayes Papers, asserts that Tilden provided Lamar and Bayard with an actual plan of war to insure his inauguration. Weir gave Halstead as his source. Tansill, 150, discounts this version of the conference.

15. Woodward, *Reunion and Reaction*, 110.

impartial opinion" would be guaranteed and the country secured against the existing defective system of presidential election. Lamar then noted that resistance had been widely discussed as an alternative. By contrast, the bipartisan commission would allow a decision without "either fraud or force." And the defeated party would be spared humiliation.

Lamar assumed his familiar peacemaking posture in presenting the machinery for an orderly presidential succession. The proposed electoral commission bill would be, he explained, a "declaration" that future crises would be resolved without military force. Lamar also suggested that the new president should, to an extent, consider himself above party obligation. By implication, a nonsectional policy appeared to be the condition required for election.[16] The bill became law, and a few days later Lamar nominated five members (his part in their selection is not known) to represent the House of Representatives.[17] Once the commission's membership was chosen, little remained except to wait.

Though Lamar in his speech perhaps promised more than the commission bill explicitly provided, he stated his position completely, or almost completely. Later in a letter of explanation to his friend and former protege Burton N. Harrison, Lamar repeated the argument given in the debate of January 26 and added a clinching support to his reasoning: "When I got to Washington I found that Tilden was defeated—his inauguration an impossibility."[18] Conditions in New Orleans and Washington had convinced Lamar of the hopelessness of his party's cause.

This realistic appreciation of Tilden's situation encouraged Lamar's peace efforts and influenced his Democratic colleagues who voted 186 to 18 for the electoral commission. The South's even greater support for the bill indicated that its representa-

16. *Congressional Record*, 44th Cong., 2nd Sess., 997–99.
17. *House Journal*, 44th Cong., 2nd Sess., 309–31.
18. Lamar to Burton N. Harrison, March 8, 1877, in Mrs. Burton Harrison's Scrap Book, 1859–1909, Burton N. Harrison Papers. Apparently Harrison was convinced and wrote his sister that Lamar acted patriotically and wisely. See Harrison (ed.), *The Harrisons of Skimino*, 214.

tives indubitably wanted a peaceful inauguration. More confident of their man, the Republicans voted eighty-five to fifty-two
against passage. They believed with Hayes that the plan was unnecessary to their victory.[19]

Lamar's pronouncements did not go well with those who insisted that Tilden's inauguration be the price for peace. In Mississippi a large number of prominent Democrats fresh from the
fires of the 1875 revolution opposed him. Influential editors, including Ethelbert Barksdale of Jackson and W. H. McCardle
of Vicksburg, belonged to the dissidents. Barksdale, editor of the
Clarion, and usually a Lamar supporter, voiced the opinion of
this faction most strongly. The resulting bitterness made political enemies of the two men for years to come.[20] Outside the
South, Montgomery Blair's Washington *Union* went further
and clearly inferred that Lamar had been guilty of collusion.
For several days Blair had accused Hayes of soliciting southern
Democrats with promises of political advantage and sympathetic
consideration of their favorite legislation. Then he attributed to
Lamar a willingness to permit the Republican Senate, through
its presiding officer, the right to count the electoral votes. Blair
retracted and apologized for his inaccuracies, but the charge persisted as the election crisis developed.[21]

Lamar personally believed that attacks coming from the northern press had no direct connection with the presidential question. He had indeed aroused the enmity of influential journalists
and politicians by his continuous support of the subsidy bill for
the Texas Pacific Railroad, a project detestable to many non-

19. Woodward, *Reunion and Reaction*, 151–52; Harry Barnard, *Rutherford B. Hayes and His America* (Indianapolis, 1954), 362–63; *House Journal*, 44th Cong., 2nd Sess., 309.

20. Mayes, *Lamar*, 301–302; William H. McCardle to Jefferson Davis, February 27, 1877, in Rowland (ed.), *Jefferson Davis, Constitutionalist*, VII, 525.

21. Washington *Union*, January 3, 5, 6, 1877. Jackson (Miss.) *Weekly Clarion*, January 10, 1877, quoted the St. Louis *Republican* to the effect that Lamar first answered Blair's charge with a belligerent note amounting to a personal challenge, but that friends dissuaded him from sending it. The *Union* retracted its charge on January 6.

southern Democrats.[22] On January 24, during the debate on the
commission bill, Lamar led an effort opposed by northern Democrats to report legislation favorable to the railroad. As in the
case of the electoral commission bill, he pleaded for passage in
the name of sectional reconciliation—in this case through economic reconstruction; but the northern wing of his party helped
to defeat the effort. Since the Hayes Republicans befriended
Lamar's Texas Pacific bill, enemies of both the railroad subsidy
and the election compromise, quite frequently the same people,
quickly drew the logical conclusion. Suspicions were aggravated
when news reports and gossip linked Lamar to the so-called
"Scott Plan" for making Hayes's inauguration conditional upon
Republican support for the Texas Pacific.[23]

Stories of such a plan began as early as mid-January, when
Hayes's supporters had sought common cause with the Texas
Pacific Railroad lobby which was at the time stymied in the
House. According to the most generally accepted historical interpretation, the Hayes Republicans and the Texas Pacific lobby
together formulated a promising arrangement, the "Scott Plan,"
to lure southerners away from their party's northern wing. The
basic understanding provided that Thomas Scott's economic influence in the South would be used to insure Hayes's inauguration, and, in return, Hayes would look with a sympathetic attitude toward the Texas Pacific.

In addition to the "Scott Plan" there evolved a political understanding involving a number of southerners and Hayes Republicans which was potentially of far more importance. It provided
that southerners would see the electoral count through, would
aid Republicans in organizing the House of Representatives, and
would assist Hayes in reestablishing a Republican party based
on white conservative support in the South. In return, Hayes's
supporters promised to end reconstruction, to restore home rule
in South Carolina, Louisiana, and Florida, to appoint a south-

22. Jackson (Miss.) *Weekly Clarion*, January 10, 1877.
23. Woodward, *Reunion and Reaction*, 66–67, 119, 127–36.

erner to the cabinet, and to cooperate with southern conservatives in the distribution of federal patronage. This exchange of favors overlapped and complemented the "Scott Plan," and together they greatly improved Hayes's prospects in the House. Doubtless many southern leaders agreed to such an arrangement either in full or in part. Others who were not party to an actual understanding at least had wind of Hayes's lenient attitude toward the South.[24]

The package was an attractive one. Lamar had built his postwar career around "redemption" of the South, and the arrangement placed this objective within his grasp. He had also consistently favored internal improvements and federal subsidies for the South; and he had enthusiastically supported the Texas Pacific Railroad. The Hayes people felt with good reason that Lamar would be willing to cooperate.[25] No wonder that speculators hearing of this bargaining should assume that Lamar was a participant.

Early in February these two vital issues—the election and the Texas Pacific—came up for House consideration. As the electoral commission began to count the controversial votes, efforts at passing the Texas Pacific Railroad bill were redoubled. Then on February 10 the commission announced its decision on the disputed Florida returns. In a strict party division—eight to seven—the Hayes electoral votes were approved.[26] Tilden's defeat in the remaining states could hardly be doubted. Before the fears of Tilden's partisans could be fully realized, Lamar joined a Democratic party move later that same day to recess the House.[27] When the House reconvened on February 12, 1877, Lamar indignantly voted against acceptance of Florida's vote for Hayes despite the commission's decision. The Democrats carried

24. *Ibid.*, 174–75.

25. *E.g.*, Murat Halstead to Rutherford B. Hayes, December 21, 1876, in Rutherford B. Hayes Papers; James M. Comly to Hayes, January 8, 1877, *ibid.*

26. Justice Davis, who presumably was politically independent, had meantime been elected to the Senate and so declared himself ineligible for the commission. A Republican, Justice Joseph Bradley, replaced Davis.

27. *House Journal*, 44th Cong., 2nd Sess., 419.

their defiant gesture 168 to 103. On February 14 he again supported a resolution claiming that the Tilden-Hendricks electors represented the legally chosen ticket in Florida and must be
counted in opposition to the commission's ruling. Having helped
create the commission, Lamar seemed unwilling to accept a decision opposing his own party.[28]

Lamar's actions during the crucial days which followed were
not always consistent or decisive. On February 17, when the electoral commission announced its readiness to report on the Louisiana vote, Lamar moved to recess until the nineteenth. The
Democrats carried the motion and the count was delayed.[29] On
the evening of the seventeenth the Democrats met in caucus. One
group, whose members were almost exclusively from the North
and West, proposed a filibuster to prevent further congressional
action and Hayes's victory. Southerners, including Lamar, voted
to complete the count, and they carried the caucus. On the nineteenth, after the House reconvened and debated all day, the
Democratic caucus met again to consider strategy. The same
obstructionism was attempted, but once again Lamar and the
southerners prevailed.[30]

Lamar's attitude still had not become clear. After temporarily blocking House action and committing himself against a filibuster, he wrote Thomas Bayard of a revolt reported to be brew-
ing among Senate Republicans who opposed Hayes's policies.[31]
Perhaps the developing Republican opposition to the electoral
commission suggested a future opportunity to guarantee withdrawal of troops from the southern states.

Whatever his plans, they still did not include effective obstruction of the vote count. On February 20 he supported a House
resolution against counting the Hayes ballots from Louisiana.
But more importantly, he refused that same day to accommodate
a filibustering move to recess the House and to postpone com-

28. *Ibid.*, 423, 444.   29. *Ibid.*, 465–67.
30. Woodward, *Reunion and Reaction*, 177–80.
31. Lamar to Thomas F. Bayard, February 19, 1877, in Thomas F. Bayard
Papers, Manuscript Division, Library of Congress.

pletion of the Louisiana count.[32] The second vote was more decisive and indicated that Lamar stood by the caucus decision not
to filibuster. Thus, he seemed an aggressive opponent of the commission's Republican findings, but at the same time he refused
to help block the procedure which led inexorably to Hayes's
victory.

Lamar's somewhat ambiguous course on February 20 also
included a highly suggestive letter to his friend, John E. Ellis,
congressman from Louisiana. Lamar advised Ellis to meet with
Stanley Matthews, Hayes's brother-in-law, and to ask for Hayes's
assurance that, if inaugurated, he would not sustain the Republican government in Louisiana. The Ellis letter later appeared
in newsprint and was cited in a congressional investigation as
evidence of collusion involving Lamar, Ellis, and Hayes. The
note is of special interest in a broader context because it suggests
that Louisiana and other Republican southern states had not
received binding assurances regarding the federal government's
future policy. In light of this letter it would appear that either
Lamar was not already a party to a bargain with the Republicans, as was sometimes charged by the press, or that he lacked
confidence in the assurances which had been given. Lamar still
retained some of the early skepticism regarding Hayes's intentions which he had confided to W. H. Roberts of the New Orleans *Times*. In this, his position had changed little since his
arrival in Washington in December. He admitted the probabil-
ity of Hayes's inauguration but wished for definite assurances
regarding the South. Unless Lamar blatantly misrepresented the
situation to Ellis as a cover for clandestine activities, he was not
a party to any previous deal.

In his letter to Ellis, Lamar stated that Matthews had authorized a spokesman to say that Hayes would not support the Republican government in Louisiana. Lamar's information indicated that Hayes was seeking a way to drop the Republican state
regime. Lamar went on:

32. *House Journal*, 44th Cong., 2nd Sess., 488, 492.

Now, Ellis, this is the first thing I have ever heard as coming from
Hayes worth acting upon by any Southern man. We do not want
the offices, but we do want to get our states and our people free
from carpet bag government. Ought you not, if an available opportunity offers, to spring forward at once and see if you can't free
your state? I think you should at once see Mr. Stanley Matthews
and ask him if Hayes will give you some assurance that he will not
maintain Packard in his domination of our people.[33]

Ellis did not immediately follow Lamar's advice. Meanwhile,
an article in the Columbus (Ohio) *State Journal,* a paper close to
Hayes, attacked Louisiana whites for their intimidation of Negroes. A tremor passed through the ranks of southern Democrats
who mistakenly assumed that Hayes had approved the piece.
Fearful that Hayes had reversed himself and would now support
the Louisiana Republicans, Lamar and the southerners voted
with the northern wing of their party to force a recess on February 23. In the caucus which followed Lamar further pursued his
new course and stood by the filibusterers in favor of an additional
recess on February 24. On that day the filibuster failed temporarily despite the fact that Lamar and forty-one other southerners
moved to recess; but a dangerous shift of votes had started, and
Lamar was for the moment a participant. With the South in rebellion, the House recessed for the weekend to reconvene on
February 26.[34]

On the afternoon of the twenty-sixth Lamar went to the
House chamber with a changed attitude. His view now reflected
the results of several conferences earlier that day involving prominent Louisianians and Republican leaders. Apparently satisfied
with the assurances given, Lamar and fourteen other southerners broke with the filibusterers and voted against a recess which
would have again delayed the count. His shift actually preceded
further guarantees given the night of the twenty-sixth at the

33. Lamar to John E. Ellis, February 20, 1877, in "Report of the Investigation of the Presidential Election of 1876," *House Miscellaneous Documents,* 45th
Cong., 3rd Sess., No. 31, pp. 896–97, 973–74.
34. *House Journal,* 44th Cong., 2nd Sess., 521, 530, 539; Woodward, *Reunion
and Reaction,* 186–90.

Wormley House but followed an assurance by President Grant to the Louisiana group, presumably known to Lamar, that the Louisiana Republican state government would not be protected.[35]

The filibusterers, led by Louisianians, continued the delay until they could clarify certain points with the Republican congressional leaders and with Grant, including an agreement for the withdrawal of troops. In the two days following, while these conversations continued, Lamar consistently voted with a large majority to keep the House in session. Finally, on March 2, 1877, the Louisianians were satisfied, the roll calls were halted, and the count continued to its fateful conclusion.[36]

Most Americans were gratified by the passing of the great crisis. Chaos had been avoided. The traditional system of election by the electoral college had been preserved intact, even if somewhat battered. Lamar shared this general satisfaction, and as a spokesman for the southern section he had additional cause for pleasure. The region's most cherished objectives had been promised and a national government not unfriendly to the South had been installed.

Lamar generally thought that national and regional well-being were compatible. A peaceful succession to the presidency was central to this well-being. He perceived, however, that a favorable compromise from the southern Democrats' weak position depended upon negotiation and even on opportunism. He consequently responded as rapidly changing circumstances dictated, and at times he seemed to be confused and to behave with ambivalence. He curiously shifted from sponsorship of the electoral commission bill to the dilatory tactics of the obstructionists and back again. As a member of Democratic strategy committees he played an influential role, and he made a substantial effort on the House floor for the electoral commission bill. Despite this

35. Woodward, *Reunion and Reaction*, 194–98; *House Journal*, 44th Cong., 2nd Sess., 547.
36. Woodward, *Reunion and Reaction*, 198–202; *House Journal*, 44th Cong., 2nd Sess., 574, 589, 592–95, 613.

support for the commission, he engaged in obstruction and privately considered a negative vote on the final decision.[37] By advising Ellis to see Stanley Matthews, and by helping hold up House action, he played at least a peripheral role in the final understanding of February 26 at Wormley House, and yet he withdrew from Ellis' filibuster effort after the twenty-sixth. And finally, his support of Thomas Scott's Texas Pacific Railroad scheme during the crucial period added another dimension to his behavior.

If, on the other hand, consideration of Lamar's position is extended to include the entire election history rather than just late January and February, a less ambivalent picture appears. From this perspective, Lamar can be seen to have made his commitment almost two years earlier. In March, 1875, he told Henry W. Grady in Atlanta that the Republicans could be defeated only by a coalition of Democrats, Liberal-Republicans, and other anti-administration men. He believed that either Liberal-Republican Charles Francis Adams or Justice David Davis, an Independent, could win under the Democratic banner. Of the regular Democrats, Thurman, Hendricks, or Bayard might be able to draw sufficient support from outside the party if the platform made concessions to the Liberal-Republicans.[38]

Lamar favored making the coalitions and compromises necessary to secure a victory over Grant's policies. As in the past, he would willingly sacrifice rigid party regularity for higher political values. His logic had been the same when he favored Grant's brother-in-law, Louis Dent, for governor of Mississippi in 1869 and when he subscribed to Republican Alcorn's campaign against Ames in 1873. The paramount need was the state's redemption, and other considerations bowed before that objective. Likewise, in national politics Lamar had supported the

37. Mayes, *Lamar*, 699–701, reprints an address written in February, but never delivered, which supported a vote against final acceptance of the electoral commission's decisions. Lamar made clear, however, his intention of submitting to Hayes's succession.

38. Atlanta *Herald*, quoted in Mayes, *Lamar*, 224–28, and summarized in New York *Times*, April 8, 1875.

Liberal-Republicans in 1872 as the most promising means of defeating Grant. In each case a desire for conservative home rule guided him. "Our nominations and our platforms," he wrote in 1873, "were all made with a view to these Federal & external relations & exigencies." [39]

The prospect of civil violence in November, 1876, eroded Lamar's party regularity further. Despite his hopes for a Democratic victory, he believed that incumbent Republicans held the upper hand in an election impasse. In addition to the state returning boards, Republicans controlled the army and other governmental machinery. It seemed unlikely that Hayes could be convinced to relinquish the presidency.[40] By disquieting contrast, Tilden offered little in the way of leadership or plan of action. It would therefore be better to compromise with Hayes than to go down with Tilden.

Lamar's efforts developed along two lines. He advised Tilden from New Orleans to meet with Hayes to discuss an honorable resolution, and when that failed he promoted compromise legislation which would allow an acceptable and legal vote count. At the same time Lamar accurately anticipated the ultimate victory of Hayes and set about making the best of it. Soon after the election he sent word to Hayes through Roberts and Halstead that the South would "not oppose an Administration which will favor an honest administration and honest officers in the South." [41] Lamar also sought assurances that Hayes, if inaugurated, would follow a friendly policy toward white Democrats in the South. He received the assurances indirectly and piecemeal and then helped carry out the electoral commission's findings. There is no evidence that Lamar's cooperation depended upon any specific guarantees in relation to the Texas Pacific Railroad. It is true, however, that he staunchly promoted the road throughout the crisis, as did most of his southern colleagues, and it is obvious

39. Lamar to E. D. Clark, October 14, 1873, in Lamar Papers, University of Mississippi Library.

40. A speech by Lamar in Mississippi, n.d., 1879, quoted in Mayes, *Lamar*, 297–98.

41. Williams (ed.), *Hayes, Diary of a President, 1875–1881*, 52.

that Republican offers of help could not have displeased him.

Lamar favored a compromise course in respect to the election controversy well before the formulation of the so-called "Scott Plan." And, as a matter of fact, the press attacked Lamar for collusion prior to that time. Early in December the New York *Herald* and *Times* presented the accusations, and the loyal Memphis *Daily Appeal* and the Jackson *Clarion* replied in his behalf.[42] The *Clarion* carried Lamar's countercharge that the press attacks were vindictive and that they originated in his support of the Texas Pacific Railroad bill. Lamar himself made the connection between the election and the railroad question; his press critics had not mentioned a deal involving the Texas Pacific. The "Scott Plan" may have been talked about in some circles during the first week of January, but it was not finally agreed upon until later.[43] Lamar's advice to Tilden to confer with Hayes and his conversations with W. H. Roberts and Murat Halstead indicate his willingness to compromise from the beginning of the crisis in November.

Even after the Scott-Hayes lobby made its determined effort in February, Lamar filibustered temporarily and wrote a speech against the electoral commission's findings. Unless these be discounted entirely as diversionary tactics, he suffered at that late date personal misgivings about the dependability of Hayes's southern commitment.

Hayes's correspondence during the crisis also fails to document a definite understanding with Lamar beyond an expression of mutual goodwill. These letters in fact contain a large amount of criticism of Lamar. Pennsylvania congressman W. D. Kelly advised Hayes against taking such men as Lamar into his confi-

42. New York *Times*, December 3, 4, 1876; Memphis *Daily Appeal*, December 9, 1876, January 9, 1877; Jackson (Miss.) *Weekly Clarion*, January 10, 1877.

43. Extant Lamar correspondence provides no help in this matter. The only Thomas Scott letter to Lamar bears the date April 13, 1876; the only Collis Huntington letter to Lamar is dated November 16, 1876. The Murat Halstead-Lamar correspondence does not mention the Texas Pacific or its managers. The Hayes Papers contain circumstantial evidence to connect Lamar with the group interested in Hayes's election and the Texas Pacific, but the information is inconclusive.

dence.[44] Wilson J. Vance, the Cincinnati *Commercial's* Washington correspondent, warned that southerners friendly toward Hayes "don't go much on Lamar's sincerity . . . and the Lamar crowd will, I think myself, bear a little watching." [45] Even the central figures in the engineering of the Scott-Hayes plan distrusted Lamar. Within a week of Hayes's inauguration, Andrew Kellar of the Memphis *Avalanche*, head of the southern portion of the "Scott Plan," wrote Joseph Medill of the Chicago *Tribune* that "Lamar will not do in an emergency." [46] And Thomas Donaldson, confidant of Hayes, felt that Lamar "is one grand Humbug." [47] These men clearly did not think of Lamar as a partner in their project to make Hayes president.

Lamar found no relief from criticism even after the Hayes-Tilden controversy ended. Two days after the inauguration, on March 4, 1877, he heard from a constituent that "our people are very much depressed here, cursing everybody, you with the balance." [48] And Lamar was not insensitive to the news from home either. Almost pathetically he wrote that "men who have loved me are beginning to grow cold in their affections; I know that men who have trusted me have begun to falter in their confidence." [49]

The threat to Lamar's carefully cultivated political image spread far beyond Mississippi. In Washington, more trouble awaited him when he chaired the Democratic caucus assembled to plan strategy under another Republican president. The vola-

44. W. D. Kelly to Rutherford B. Hayes, December 17, 1876, in Rutherford B. Hayes Papers.

45. Wilson J. Vance to Murat Halstead, January 5, 1877, *ibid.* According to Vance, these friendly southerners thought Lamar "only anxious to get his seat in the senate—after that he will show different colors."

46. Andrew Keller to Joseph Medill, March 20, 1877, in William Henry Smith Papers, on microfilm, Hayes Memorial Library.

47. Thomas Donaldson to Rutherford B. Hayes, February 18, 1877, in Rutherford B. Hayes Papers.

48. Mr. Goar to Lamar, March 6, 1877, quoted in Mayes, *Lamar*, 304.

49. Lamar to Rutherford B. Hayes, March 22, 1877, quoted in Mayes, *Lamar*, 307–309. A copy in the Hayes Papers does not include the quoted passage. Lamar apparently thought better of it before posting the letter.

tile B. B. Douglas of Virginia charged Lamar with sacrificing the presidency to secure a seat in the Senate. The New York *Tribune* reported the abuse so severe that "but for the intervention of friends Mr. Lamar would undoubtedly have shot him." [50]

When the Senate met to swear in its new members, uncompromising Stalwart-Republicans led by Oliver P. Morton challenged Lamar's admission on grounds that the Mississippi legislature of 1875 was illegally constituted. Stalwart tactics failed, however, because of support that Lamar received from other Republicans—notably James G. Blaine and Blanche K. Bruce. As Mississippi's senior senator and the only Negro in the upper House, Bruce greatly eased Lamar's embarrassment and his help inspired a lasting cordiality between the two men. For his part, Blaine took the floor and argued vigorously in opposition to Morton. In the end confirmation was easily gained. The security of six years in the Senate must have been welcome to Lamar, especially at a time when reelection to the House might have been uncertain.[51]

The Senate, having sworn in its new members, turned to the business of President Hayes's cabinet appointments. Important policy considerations—especially concilation of the South and government reform—affected Hayes in his choice of an official family. And these same policies excited opposition to the appointments from the Stalwart wing of the Republican party which stood for sectionalism in politics and the spoils system in government.

Some favored Lamar for southern representation in the cabi-

50. New York *Tribune*, March 5, 1877; New York *Times*, March 4, 1877. Both papers declared Douglas to be drunk at the time.

51. *Congressional Record*, 45th Cong., 1st Sess., 2, 5–15; Samuel D. Smith, "The Negro in the United States Senate," in Fletcher M. Green (ed.), *Essays in Southern History Presented to Joseph Gregoire de Roulhac Hamilton* (Chapel Hill, 1949), 61; Melvin I. Urofsky, "Blanche K. Bruce: United States Senator, 1875–1881," *Journal of Mississippi History*, XXIX (May, 1967), 134; Lynch, *The Facts of Reconstruction*, 186–90; New York *Tribune*, March 7, 1877. Besides other problems, Lamar's letter to Ellis suggesting a meeting with Stanley Matthews was published in the New York *Tribune*, March 30, 1877. The Memphis *Daily Appeal* carried the Ellis letter March 30, 1877.

net, but there is no evidence that Hayes took this advice seriously. Instead, the nomination of David M. Key, a Democrat from Tennessee, as postmaster general came before the Senate. To implement his pledge against corruption Hayes selected reformers William Evarts and Carl Schurz for the State and Interior departments. The Stalwarts rallied to stop confirmation of all these men. The split within Republican ranks might well have been decisive if sympathetic southern senators had not moved to the president's support. Hayes himself thought that Lamar and the southerners had saved him from defeat. The cooperative spirit which had proven so important in February thus sustained Hayes in his first presidential difficulty.[52]

Lamar certainly had no call to join the "bloody shirt" obstructionists in the cabinet struggle. To the contrary, he had good reason to think kindly of Evarts, Schurz, and Key. He must have remembered Evarts as a reformer and as defender of Andrew Johnson against Senate radicals during the impeachment proceedings of 1868. Schurz had proven himself a friend of the South in 1872 in the founding of the Liberal-Republican movement, and Lamar had always considered him to be a man above sectional prejudice. Although Lamar did not care for Key personally, he would hardly have opposed a conservative Southerner under such circumstances. In short, Lamar had every reason to support Hayes in his appointments and none for opposing him.[53]

After the irritating cabinet nominations Senator Lamar took up a matter which concerned him a great deal more. Despite assurances from Grant and Hayes, federal troops still remained in Louisiana and South Carolina where they protected Republican state governments. Provoked by the delay, Lamar wrote Hayes

52. Whitelaw Reid to Rutherford B. Hayes, February 21, 1877, in Rutherford B. Hayes Papers; E. D. Morgan to Hayes, February 22, 1877, *ibid.*; Irving W. Lyon to Hayes, February 24, 1877, *ibid*; Williams (ed.), *Hayes, The Diary of a President*, 80–81.

53. Lamar to E. D. Clark, March 30, 1877, in Lamar Papers, University of Mississippi Library. The friendly relationship with Schurz continued through Lamar's tenure in the Interior Department. Lamar called Key "mere *locum tenens*."

on March 22: "The position . . . taken by Southern Senators, *in solido*, rests upon the foundation of your inaugural Address: viz—that you would not consent to sustain by unconstitutional interposition of the Federal forces State Governments which had no support. . . . They felt that this resolution, promptly and firmly carried into effect, gave to the South that for which she had most earnestly contended." [54] Lamar had Hayes in a spot here, and both men knew it. He cleverly combined pressure for fulfillment of pledges to the South with an implied threat to Hayes's self-conceived role as leader of all the people and all the sections. Hayes "is full of the idea of being a great Pacificater" Lamar wrote E. D. Clark. [55] And he told Hayes: "I regarded you Mr. President as the one who was to open to us a new era—an era illustrious as one of peace, prosperity, nationality." [56]

Although Hayes left no record of his reaction to Lamar's forceful solicitation, on the day following receipt of the letter he invited South Carolina's Wade Hampton and Daniel Chamberlain to Washington. That conference presaged the carpetbagger Chamberlain's downfall. A few days later a commission traveled to Louisiana to review the situation. After further delay the troops were finally withdrawn on April 24, 1877. [57]

Hayes's unwillingness to immediately satisfy the Southern re-

54. Lamar to Rutherford B. Hayes, March 22, 1877, in Rutherford B. Hayes Papers. This fascinating letter marked *"Strictly private & confidential"* had several suggestive but inconclusive phrases. On the question of withdrawal Lamar said, "we thought you had made up your mind and indeed you so declared to me." One cannot help wishing Lamar had said *when* Hayes so declared. From the tone of this letter and one written to E. D. Clark, March 30, 1877, in Lamar Papers, University of Mississippi Library, it appears that Lamar saw Hayes after the inauguration and not before. As noted above W. H. Roberts testified under oath that Lamar never saw Hayes. Cate, *Lamar*, 288, holds that Lamar saw Hayes in February.

55. Lamar to E. D. Clark, March 30, 1877, in Lamar Papers, University of Mississippi Library.

56. Lamar to Rutherford B. Hayes, March 22, 1877, in Rutherford B. Hayes Papers.

57. Woodward, *Reunion and Reaction*, 219, 221. Actually there were only 3,280 troops stationed in the South (omitting Texas) at the end of fiscal 1876. Hayes's orders left these men in the states where they were assigned, but returned them to their regular barracks. See Kenneth E. Davison, *The Presidency of Rutherford B. Hayes* (Westport, Conn., 1972), 137–38.

deemers on the troop question pointed up a basic difficulty in his "new departure" program. He wished to rebuild the Republican party in the reconstructed states by appealing to the best element of whites. But he could not bring himself to entirely desert the regular Republicans, Negro and white, or to fully relinquish political control to native Mississippians.

Many southern leaders observed this dilemma and knew what Hayes was doing. Lamar, for one, understood, and he meant to make the most of it. He was willing to cooperate with a friendly Republican administration, but this goodwill included no sympathy for Hayes's efforts to absorb part of the Democratic party; and certainly Lamar had no plans to help him. Late in March he wrote to E. D. Clark that public opinion and the admitted failure of reconstruction had placed the Republicans in a new frame of mind. "Knowing this," he said, "it has been my aim to get these ideas in the Republican Party developed into active political forces." But he had no confidence in the permanence of those "forces." And consequently, "as a mere party question" the South must continue to be Democratic: "A Southern Statesman can never be a power in the Republican Party." [58]

Lamar's judgment would certainly have been disquieting to the usually optimistic Hayes. And it would have been puzzling too, for Lamar admitted the existence of the common ground which Hayes claimed for Republicans and southern conservatives. Lamar himself seemed a bit confused when he declared that "the Democratic Party of the nation is the natural ally of our people. . . . But the intellect, courage, literature, moral ideas . . . and aggregations of wealth . . . at the North are all arrayed against the Democrats." [59]

To a man of Lamar's mentality, forged as it was in sectional controversy, the proposition that the Democratic party should remain the "natural ally" required no debate. And furthermore, how could the South hear such debate while the Republican

58. Lamar to E. D. Clark, March 30, 1877, in Lamar Papers, University of Mississippi Library.
59. Ibid.

party's image included Negro equality and "bloody shirt" political tactics. The South's overriding political needs simply could not be gained by alliance with Republicans. Hayes and members of his cabinet did not understand the South, Lamar reported to a friend: "They are not *enrapport* with us in a single sentiment. They feel more natural & easier with Morton than they do with me. They love Chamberlain, they can understand his dialect & appreciate his aims & enter into his plans—whilst they regard Hampton as an embarrassment. They want to conciliate the whites of the South, but the real object of interest to them is the Negro & they look with misgivings to the result of any policy which terminates federal survellance [*sic*] over the former & federal protection over the latter. Even those who have no sentimental interest in the negro, have not lost their estimate of his value to them as a voter." [60]

Lamar hardly did justice to Hayes in this analysis, but the rejection stood as his final word. In this judgment he established a rule of conduct for the remainder of his public career; and in fact, he spoke for a future far beyond his own life. The South would cooperate with the Republicans in things conservative, but she would defend her home rule and white supremacy from within the Democratic party. Despite charges by Stalwart Roscoe Conkling that Lamar was a chief advisor to Hayes, there is no evidence that their relationship ever became intimate on either a political or a personal basis. There existed no chance that Lamar would become a Hayes man or a Republican. [61]

Hayes's hopes and expectations for winning over the South apparently never included Mississippi to the same extent that they did other Confederate states. [62] The patronage policy of

60. *Ibid.*
61. Hayes mentions Lamar only twice in his diary and apparently never corresponded with him. Lamar letters to Hayes are few and sustain this generalization. On Conkling's charge see Stanley P. Hirshon, *Farewell to the Bloody Shirt: Northern Republicans and the Southern Negro, 1877–1893* (Bloomington, 1962), 43.
62. There is only indirect evidence on this point. *E.g.*, a letter from Hayes to W. D. Bickham, May 3, 1877, cited in Vincent P. DeSantis, *Republicans Face the*

conciliating white Democrats was therefore probably never fully employed in Mississippi, and Lamar's connection to the administration, in this respect, was not as close as that of men such as Stephens and Gordon in Georgia.[63]

Hayes had ample justification for neglecting the "new departure" Republican movement in Mississippi. The regular party organization had already fatally divided between white leadership and the Negro rank and file. Refusal to satisfy Negro demands for office and influence had thoroughly discredited white leaders and drove many of the disillusioned into the Democratic party. This split, combined with the general demoralization suffered after the defeats of 1875 and 1876, proved decisive. The party formally disbanded in 1877 and failed to offer a ticket in the election of that year.

Negroes revived the Republican organization without the whites, and a new political reality emerged in Mississippi. White Democrats and Negro Republicans "fused" in a relationship which promised the blacks some material rewards but assured their utter subordination. In this arrangement the Democrats, including Lamar, helped Negroes retain control of the Republican organization and the patronage of the national Republican

---

Southern Question: The New Departure Years, 1877–1897 (Baltimore, 1959), 66, shows that Hayes hoped for results in North Carolina, Maryland, Virginia, Tennessee, Arkansas, Louisiana, South Carolina, and Florida, while expressing no opinion at all on Mississippi. Davison, *The Presidency of Rutherford B. Hayes*, 138, also omits Mississippi from Hayes's list of hopeful states. Hayes in his goodwill tours in the South failed to visit Mississippi and included no prominent man of that state in the president's party. See Hirshon, *Farewell to the Bloody Shirt*, 38–39.

63. The evidence is again indirect. Extant Lamar letters relating to patronage are very few (only three letters in addition to three petitions which he signed) and suggest this conclusion by their small number. DeSantis, *Republicans Face the Southern Question*, 91–93; Woodward, *Reunion and Reaction*, 225–26; and Hirshon, *Farewell to the Bloody Shirt*, 36, all discuss Hayes's appointment policy in the South without including Mississippi in their generalization that Hayes gave about one third of the offices in the South to Democrats. There is also some contrary evidence: James Lusk Alcorn to Kenneth Rayner, February 6, 1878, cited in Pereyra, *James Lusk Alcorn*, 186, complained that Republicans got no support from Hayes. DeSantis, *Republicans Face the Southern Question*, 92, cites a similar complaint from an unnamed Mississippi Republican.

party. In return, Negroes supported conservative Democrats at election time. In a political milieu so harshly realistic and cynical as this, Hayes could expect little from his "new departure" patronage policy.[64]

The role of Mississippi's senior senator, Blanche K. Bruce, a Negro and a Republican, added an additional dimension to the evolving Mississippi party structure. It is perhaps part of the irony of Lamar's relationship to the Negro that he respected and even admired Bruce while participating in the political subordination of his race. Shortly after entering the Senate, Lamar invited Bruce to his residence in Washington for a discussion of their mutual interests and especially that of federal patronage. In a "Private and Confidential" letter concerning their conference, Lamar wrote that Bruce "is a sensible, self-poised man who has purposes of his own & is not timid about following them & adhering to them. He strikes me too as a man of truth, & the fact is I believed him to be a noble negro." [65]

In that cordial conversation the two Mississippi senators reached a tentative understanding. They agreed, Lamar said, upon the desirability of removing "Carpetbaggers & corrupt mischievous white men." While concluding that Bruce could not be exploited for Democratic party purposes, Lamar did believe "he will go with me into any reasonable plan of so distributing the Federal offices as will give recognition to both races." As a start, Lamar suggested to Bruce that the carpetbagger postmaster in Vicksburg might be replaced by a Negro Republican, "whose bond should be *secured* by our people, & who should put a man chosen by his securities in charge of the money orders & other

64. Lamar's participation in the fusion movement was not as conspicuous as it might have been. His home county and congressional district were predominantly white, and Negro votes there were not essential. Elsewhere he moved with care and discretion. For a recent description of fusion politics see William C. Harris, introduction to John R. Lynch, *The Facts of Reconstruction* (Indianapolis, 1970), xlvi–xlviii.

65. Lamar to E. D. Clark, March 15, 1877, in Lamar Papers, University of Mississippi Library.

important business of the office—a Southern democrat acceptable to our people." [66]

There is reason to believe that this relationship remained effective throughout Hayes's administration. In the only two known pieces of Lamar-Bruce correspondence Lamar asked favors in patronage matters but indicated respect for Bruce's political needs. In a letter addressed to "My respected Colleague," Lamar asked for help on the appointment of a white "mild" Democrat rather than a nonresident to the Meridian post office. But the request was tentative and subject to Bruce's approval since, as Lamar said, "I do not wish you to do anything that would bring you into a damaging conflict with your party friends." [67]

This political détente, if known to Hayes, must have destroyed any dream of a successful white Republican party in Mississippi. The fusion principle, inadvertently supported by Hayes's appointment policy, strengthened Democrats while the machinery of the Republican party went to relatively acquiescent Negroes. The Negro majority was neutralized, while little incentive remained for white Democrats to succumb to Hayes's appeal to join the opposition party. Mississippi had her "home rule" and white domination.

Bitter-enders found Lamar's tactics compromising and despicable, but there can be little doubt that he accurately and effectively represented the majority of his white constituents in achieving these goals. As spokesman for his people and executioner of their wishes, Lamar's career found its ultimate fulfillment during the time between the Sumner eulogy and the complete Democratization of Mississippi. This period of politi-

66. *Ibid.*
67. Lamar to B. K. Bruce, October 18, 1879, in Blanche K. Bruce Papers, Howard University Library. Lamar signed the letter "With great respect & the kindest wishes for your prosperity & happiness." See also Lamar to Bruce, October 27, 1879, *ibid.*, asking consideration for an appointee. On Bruce, see Urofsky, "Blanche K. Bruce," 118–41.

cal effectiveness was also one of personal development. He possessed a maturity, self control, and realism which had not characterized his antebellum and war years. In his early manhood he had attached himself to local luminaries and generally contented himself with leadership by others. As a young man, he especially accepted with little question the doctrines provided by his father-in-law, Augustus Longstreet. Then during the sectional crisis and Civil War he publicly associated himself with Jefferson Davis, often to the extent that his own views merged almost completely with those of his mentor. The death of Longstreet, the more or less open break with Davis, and the harshly maturing experiences of the war and reconstruction ended this tendency to follow stronger men. During the 1870s Lamar emerged in his own right. Vacillation and indecision generally gave way to an overall consistency, and Lamar claimed a decisive position of leadership both in his own state and in the South, and to some extent in national affairs. Fifty-two years old in 1877, and with events etched upon a face that had known much trouble, he stood at the threshold of a Senate career.

The Senate, 1877–1880: Falling Back upon the Ways of the Fire-eater

Lamar returned to Mississippi after the special session of Congress adjourned in March, 1877. During the spring and early summer he made no public speeches, but his silence did not reflect tranquillity. Critics continued to question his course in the election controversy, and division imperiled the state Democratic party on the issue. Party rebellion also threatened over nomination of a gubernatorial candidate and as a result of persistent agitation for inflation of the monetary system. Lamar had an immediate interest in all these matters, and consequently he decided to personally represent Lafayette County at the Democratic state convention—a duty usually fulfilled by a lesser politician.[1]

Biting newspaper criticism did not deter Lamar from accepting a place on the crucial platform committee. In this capacity he successfully blocked mention of the currency question, allowing the issue to remain open, so members of the congressional delegation suffered no restraint or embarrassment. The issue would crop up again when Congress considered currency legislation at its next session, but the showdown was at least postponed.[2]

Lamar's presence counted for less when the convention undertook to nominate a gubernatorial candidate. Although he took

1. Memphis *Daily Appeal*, August 1, 1877.
2. Natchez (Miss.) *Democrat*, quoted in New York *Times*, August 13, 1877, also charged that Lamar blocked a plank on Hayes's southern policy, but there is no other evidence on this point. According to the Memphis *Daily Appeal*, August 3, 1877, he did announce confidence in Hayes.

no public position, Lamar favored his friend, E. C. Walthall, for
the office, and Walthall tentatively authorized use of his name if
circumstances seemed promising. But even after the convention
deadlocked for nine ballots the chief contenders did not with-
draw, and the Walthall forces apparently decided to hold back.
On the tenth vote Acting Governor John M. Stone won the
nomination.

At least one unfriendly paper declared the outcome a personal
defeat for Lamar. And certainly Walthall's failure belied the
charge by some journalists that Lamar controlled the convention with a dictatorial hand. Anxious to allay such bitterness
and to restore party harmony, Lamar warned the convention
against division as long as radical Republicans menaced home
rule.[3]

Conciliatory statements did not impress the dissident factions,
and a segment of the state Democratic press continued to condemn Lamar's role in the convention. The area's most influential newspapers—the Jackson *Clarion* and the Memphis *Daily
Appeal*—defended him,[4] but smaller papers reflected an ominous
dissastisfaction throughout the countryside.[5]

Such factiousness must have dismayed Lamar after his easy
election to the Senate only a few months earlier. It also suggested
that the party's machinery was not so malleable as he might have
expected. His committee victory in excluding a silver plank from
the platform seemed weak beside the failure to nominate Walthall and the personal criticism to which he was subjected. Lamar
never worked closely with the state organization, and when he

3. Natchez (Miss.) *Telephone*, quoted in Memphis *Daily Appeal*, September
11, 1877; Memphis *Daily Appeal*, August 1, 2, 3, 1877. See also Forester (Miss.)
Register, and Canton (Miss.) *Mail*, quoted in Albert D. Kirwan, *Revolt of the
Rednecks: Mississippi Politics, 1876–1925* (New York, 1965), 33.

4. *E.g.*, Memphis *Daily Appeal*, September 8, 1877; and Jackson (Miss.) *Weekly Clarion*, August 15, 1877. The Oxford (Miss.) *Falcon*, Lamar's hometown paper,
also supported him. See citation in Memphis *Daily Appeal*, September 8, 1877.

5. *E.g.*, Forester (Miss.) *Register*, and Canton (Miss.) *Mail*, quoted in Kirwan,
Revolt of the Rednecks, 33; Natchez (Miss.) *Democrat*, quoted in New York *Times*,
August 13, 1877; and Natchez (Miss.) *Telephone*, quoted in Memphis *Daily Appeal*,
September 11, 1877.

stepped from his place as titular head and spokesman his lack of control became painfully apparent. The venerable statesman's image had begun to crack even before he commenced work in the United States Senate.

After Stone's uncontested victory in the November election, Lamar headed back to Washington for the opening of the Forty-fifth Congress. The brief special session dealt primarily with disputed elections, especially those in South Carolina and Louisiana. Lamar always voted for the Democratic contenders and on one occasion he forcefully defended the seating of Marion C. Butler of South Carolina.[6] After a short break Congress convened for its regular session in December, 1877, and Lamar received the committee appointments which helped determine his senatorial role in the coming days. His two standing committee appointments included the Committee on Railroads, for which he was fitted by his experience in the lower house, and the Committee on Education and Labor, which suited him because of his earlier legislative experience and his career as a teacher.[7]

The Senate did not at first, however, turn to matters of railroads or of education and labor. The currency problem Lamar had faced in the lower house in 1873 and at the recent Mississippi convention obtruded to crowd other issues from consideration. The economic crisis which had begun in 1873 still hung over the land with depressing insistence, and many people felt that a substantial alteration of the nation's monetary system promised the best hope for relief. Debtors in particular, since they suffered most from the existing state of affairs, favored inflation as a means of revitalizing the market place through increased availability of money and corresponding price increases. On the other hand, conservative financial thinkers, including

6. *Congressional Record*, 45th Cong., Special Sess., App., 62–65. Voting may be followed in *Senate Journal*, 45th Cong., Special Sess., 79–109.

7. *Senate Journal*, 45th Cong., 2nd Sess., 26. He also was appointed to the Select Committee on Transportation-Routes to the Seaboard.

Lamar, questioned the connection of money to economic depression and decried efforts to debase the currency.

The money question in the Senate now focused upon silver: proponents of inflation believed that free coinage and the restoration of silver's legal tender value, suspended in 1873, would supply the necessary catalyst for economic recovery. On December 6 an effort giving a silver bill special order succeeded despite Lamar's opposition. And then Stanley Matthews of Ohio offered a resolution allowing payment of all United States bonds in silver dollars and restoring the legal tender nature of the silver dollars. Lamar voted against Matthews' resolution but he also opposed countermeasures requiring payment of all bonds in gold.[8]

Amid great public excitement Lamar gave his first major speech in the Senate on January 24, 1878, and declared his opposition to both silver and gold requirements for paying bonds, since either would unnecessarily commit the government to an inflexible policy. From that premise, he addressed his argument entirely to the Matthews resolution and the silver bill.

In Lamar's opinion silver should be remonetized only by cooperative action of interested nations and based upon fair and honest ratios with gold. Unilateral action by the United States, he said, would establish silver as "the exclusive ruling element of American currency" and would bring European silver to the United States. In effect, this would establish silver and eliminate gold from the currency; the cheap would drive out the dear. Lamar recognized the humanitarian instincts of many who contended that remonetization would relieve the depression, but he dismissed their reasoning as spurious.

He insisted that harmful gold hoarding would automatically cease as the hitherto undervalued greenback reached par value. This would be achieved under the government's existing policy of stockpiling gold reserves for the ultimate replacement of greenbacks. The implementation of the Resumption Act of 1875,

8. *Senate Journal*, 45th Cong., 2nd Sess., 31, 125–29. Unger, *The Greenback Era*, 357–64, describes the debate in the Senate on this resolution and the Bland bill which followed.

due in 1879, woud begin the substitution of hard money for paper and would end the currency crisis. Passage of the silver bill would reverse this desirable effect.

Remonetization of silver would, Lamar contended, hurt the laborers, debtors, and farmers whom its proponents claimed to favor. Wages would lag behind the inevitable inflation. Farmers would be hurt because their income would be determined abroad on a gold market, while their expenses increased as a result of remonetization and free coinage. And as a clincher, Lamar pleaded the ultimate argument of the sound money conservative: payment in silver of bonds purchased with gold would constitute an act of bad faith; paying back good money with bad would be injurious to credit both at home and abroad.

Lamar emphatically disputed silverite arguments that the money question pitted the capitalists against the laboring class. A class interpretation, he claimed, held no validity in a country where economic mobility allowed laborers to become capitalists and vice versa. In this Lamar seemed to purposely phrase his denial of class conflict in terms of industrial working men in the North. On the other hand he avoided entirely the economically pathetic and politically explosive situation in his own Southland, where radical agrarianism demanded inflation as a solution to chronic farm depression.

In this way Lamar associated himself with the conservative northeastern wing of the Democratic party and Hayes's following in the Republican party, which opposed the silver bill and favored implementation of the Resumption Act in January, 1879. He was at the same time true to the antebellum planter's tradition of soundness on fiscal matters and to the hard economic lesson learned during the rampantly unstable reconstruction era. But the farmers in Mississippi and throughout the South cared little for all that.[9]

Lamar's position thoroughly antagonized public opinion at home and again threatened a split in the Mississippi Democratic

9. *Congressional Record*, 45th Cong., 2nd Sess., 519–26.

party. As already recounted, he had as early as August, 1877, found himself at variance with a substantial number of Democrats in the state convention. Then in January, 1878, before Lamar's Senate speech, the farmer-dominated Mississippi House of Representatives passed a resolution instructing the state's congressmen to support the Bland-Allison silver bill to inflate the currency through coinage of silver. When Lamar ignored these instructions and voted against the Matthews resolution which also favored revaluation of silver, the Mississippi House struck back by thanking Negro Senator Blanche Bruce for his vote in support of remonetization. The Senate of Mississippi, however, declined to join in the rebuke until after Lamar spoke on January 24. Then on February 4 a resolution supporting the silver bill cleared both Houses.[10] The powerful and usually friendly Memphis *Appeal* and Jackson *Clarion* joined the silverites to complete Lamar's isolation.[11]

Since the Bland-Allison silver bill did not come up for final vote in the Senate until February 15, 1878, Lamar had sufficient time to reconsider and recant. Apparently he gave no thought to reversing his position. He wrote a member of the Mississippi legislature on February 8 expressing his regret that he must vote against the expressed wishes of his friends at home. Conscience and studied opinion, he said, dictated his course. In declaring his intention, Lamar indulged his penchant for turning a righteous phrase: "I would rather deserve than have their approval," he said.[12] And to his wife he wrote: "I cannot do it; I had rather quit politics forever." [13]

---

10. The House was controlled throughout the "Bourbon Period" by farmer interests favoring inflation. Lamar also received criticism from the *Patron of Husbandry*, organ of the state Grange. See Halsell, "The Bourbon Period in Mississippi Politics," 530–33; and Jackson (Miss.) *Weekly Clarion*, February 6, 1878.

11. Memphis *Daily Appeal*, January 25, February 2, 1878; Jackson (Miss.) *Weekly Clarion*, February 6, 1878. The *Weekly Clarion* of February 6 also thanked Lamar for his defense of the state against the charge of repudiation, thus pointedly avoiding a break with him.

12. Lamar to James Gordon, member of the Mississippi legislature from Pontotoc County, February 8, 1878, quoted in Mayes, *Lamar*, 332.

13. Lamar to Mrs. Lamar, February 14, 1878, quoted in *ibid.*, 333.

On February 15 Lamar voted for several dilutions of the Bland-Allison Act[14] and then rose to state his opposition to the bill's passage and to place on record the instructions of the Mississippi legislature. His short, high-toned justification was classic: "Mr. President," he said, "between these resolutions and my convictions there is a great gulf. I cannot pass it. Of my love to the State of Mississippi I will not speak; my life alone can tell it." In rhythmic rhetoric he talked of the generations of young men whose educations he had guided and said: "Upon them I have always endeavored to impress the belief that truth was better than falsehood, honesty better than policy, courage better than cowardice. To-day my lessons confront me. To-day I must be true or false, honest or cunning, faithful or unfaithful to my people." [15]

Lamar's vote against the Bland-Allison Act went almost unaccompanied among southerners. Democrats and Republicans alike, except Butler of South Carolina, Hill of Georgia, and Lamar, all agreed as to the desirability of silver.[16] Not surprisingly, Lamar reaped the wrath of the depression-minded populace. Indeed, the flood of emotion and resentment seemed to jeopardize his right to speak for his constituency.

The Jackson *Clarion* openly denounced his actions, and since editor Barksdale headed the Democratic State Executive Committee, and his paper served as an important party organ, this amounted to open warfare. The far ranging consequences of the split became clear when thirteen members of the Mississippi Senate scorned the judgment of Barksdale and the legislature and jointly assured Lamar of their confidence in his earnestness. By summertime, however, Lamar's own congressional district convention had passed a platform favoring silver remonetization and reissuing greenbacks. The convention also demanded an in-

14. *Senate Journal*, 45th Cong., 2nd Sess., 201–204.
15. *Congressional Record*, 45th Cong., 2nd Sess., 1061.
16. *Senate Journal*, 45th Cong., 2nd Sess., 209; *Congressional Record*, 45th Cong., 2nd Sess., 1112. Lamar later voted against overriding Hayes's veto, but the bill passed anyway. See *Senate Journal*, 45th Cong., 2nd Sess., 252.

vestigation of the frauds related to Hayes's election in 1876. The resolutions did not mention Lamar by name, but the rebellion had obviously followed him home.[17]

Lamar's dogged refusal to give in to critics of his monetary policy elicited grudging admiration from some. Besides the friendly Senate minority, the lieutenant governor of Mississippi wrote a personal letter congratulating Lamar on his stand; E. C. Walthall, though disagreeing on the silver vote, praised him for his courage and promised ultimate vindication; and the Vicksburg *Herald*, also disagreeing on silver, came to his defense.[18] Other moral support came from hard-money southerner, Ben Hill of Georgia, and from F. A. P. Barnard, Lamar's old colleague at the University of Mississippi and subsequently president of Columbia University in New York. He received encouraging letters from leading Republicans including former New York congressman William Phelps, Henry Clay Warmoth, who had been a reconstruction governor of Louisiana, and his old friend Charles Reemelin of Ohio.[19]

Lamar's situation had undoubtedly become uncomfortable. Many in Mississippi defended his integrity and right to vote his conscience, but a stand at variance with popular conviction was tenuous at best, and Lamar suffered misgivings about his future. Although he probably did not mean it, the moody Lamar even talked for a time of quitting politics. Letters to his wife expressed dissatisfaction and regret that he could not financially afford to

17. Jackson (Miss.) *Weekly Clarion*, February 20, July 31, 1878.
18. William H. Simms to Lamar, February 18, 1878, quoted in Mayes, *Lamar*, 336; E. C. Walthall to Lamar, February 16, 1878, *ibid.*; Vicksburg (Miss.) *Herald*, *ibid.*, 337. Mrs. Lamar wrote E. D. Clark, May 1, 1878, in Lamar Papers, University of Mississippi Library, thanking him for his article in the Vicksburg (Miss.) *Herald*.
19. Ben Hill to Lamar, March 7, 1878, in Lamar-Mayes Papers; F. A. P. Barnard to Lamar, January 29, 1878, *ibid.*; Barnard to Lamar, February 12, 1878, quoted in Mayes, *Lamar*, 332–33; William W. Phelps to Lamar, February 18, 1878, *ibid.*, 335; H. C. Warmoth to Lamar, February 16, 1878, *ibid.*, 335; Charles Reemelin to Lamar, February 16, 1878, *ibid.*, 336. Lamar's action also excited criticism outside Mississippi. See Robert Toombs to Alexander Stephens, January 25, 1878, in Phillips (ed.), *Correspondence of Toombs, Stephens, and Cobb*, 732–34. See also Memphis *Daily Appeal*, February 22, 1878; New York *Tribune*, February 16, 1878; and New York *Times*, February 16, 1878.

leave public life. Such sentiments tell more about Lamar's state of mind and of his dependence upon public office for a livelihood than they do about his intentions; but at any rate, he was unhappy.[20]

Actually Lamar's political future could hardly have been fragile enough to justify his despondency. His Senate term would run until 1882—four years away—a long time in politics. And his disregard of the legislature's wishes was not so drastic as it seemed. The antebellum doctrine of instruction had fallen into disuse after the Civil War, and there could be little argument that a senator should resign his seat if unwilling to accept the legislature's demands.[21]

Lamar temporized but little in his Senate voting on monetary questions throughout the remainder of the Forty-fifth Congress. He did vote during the second session to reconsider the retirement of legal tender notes, but then he favored making the notes receivable by the government although not otherwise acceptable as legal tender. He voted against repeal of the Resumption Act of 1875 and against a resolution making United States notes receivable on certain bonds. During the final session Lamar voted only once on a currency issue, and then he opposed the payment of pension arrears in legal tender notes withdrawn from circulation under a law of 1875.[22] His record for conservative money policy remained intact; and it also went virtually unnoticed by a Mississippi press which usually paid little attention to such questions except when writ large.

Lamar next concentrated his efforts in behalf of the Texas Pacific Railroad bill—substantially the same legislation which

20. Lamar to Mrs. Lamar, several letters, dated and undated, quoted in Mayes, *Lamar*, 341–42. An interesting but exaggerated assessment of Lamar's dilemma is in John F. Kennedy, *Profiles In Courage* (New York, 1964), 144–55.

21. W. E. Dodd, "The Principle of Instructing U.S. Senators," *South Atlantic Quarterly*, I (October, 1902), 326–32; George H. Haynes, *The Senate of the United States: Its History and Practice* (Boston, 1938), II, 1029–30; Clement Eaton, "Southern Senators and the Right of Instruction, 1789–1860," *Journal of Southern History*, XVIII (August, 1952), 319.

22. *Senate Journal*, 45th Cong., 2nd Sess., 479, 581, 688–89; 3rd Sess., 411.

he had promoted as chairman of the Railroad Committee in the House of Representatives. As a practiced expert on the question and now as a member of the Senate Committee on Railroads, Lamar spoke at considerable length in favor of the measure. He rehearsed the old arguments employed in the House, pleading that the Texas Pacific needed additional time under its original grant because of the depression of 1873, and that the federal government should guarantee the interest on bonds to be issued by the railroad to finance its construction. The South, he said, deserved the road since the previous transcontinental systems, located outside the South, had been subsidized by the national government. And he reminded the Senate that nearly every southern legislature supported the Texas Pacific proposal, and that the connection with the west coast would encourage needed industrial expansion.

In this infrequent, direct reference by Lamar to southern industrialization, he suggested that a cheap transportation system would provide the deficiency which had arrested the section's development. Echoing the gospel of Henry Grady, Lamar declared: "The South has every condition of soil, climate, and raw material for the development of a great industrial community." The region already possessed infant industries, "but, to develop these industries she must have free access to the markets of the world, and be able to attract to herself the skill and capital and the . . . machinery of the North." [23]

Lamar's speech also placed emphasis upon the nationalistic aspect of such a road. He undoubtedly intended to serve sectional interests by nationalistic arguments, as he had on many economic and political occasions, but the rhetoric was nonetheless noteworthy. The road, he said, would serve the government in its civil and military needs, and it would bring merchants and manufacturers into contact with the west coast, South America, China, and the Pacific islands. As he put it, in starkly Whiggish terms: "My purpose is to show that . . . its results will be to in-

23. *Congressional Record*, 45th Cong., 2nd Sess., 3653-59.

crease the national power, to develop the national interests, and to augment the wealth and prosperity of the people of the whole country." [24]

Lamar could not hope for success without assistance from either the Hayes Republicans who had promised Scott their support or from the northeastern wing of the Democratic party. This support never came. In June, just before Congress recessed, he pleaded his cause once more amidst personal attacks from the press for jobbery. Again he failed to get his way.[25]

Lamar's Texas Pacific speech forecast the attitude he would take on economic issues throughout the entire Forty-fifth Congress. As in the House of Representatives, he consistently advocated a program of government spending and subsidized economic development. Few opportunities to conspicuously support private efforts in the South occurred, however, and Lamar did not often publicize southern industrialization. He generally left spokesmanship for the "New South" doctrine to others, while he gave practical assistance in Congress whenever possible.[26]

Although Lamar achieved little for railroads and other private endeavors, he found many opportunities to promote improvement of the roads and public waterways. In this he joined other southern congressmen who deluged Congress with their legislation—forty such bills being introduced in the Senate alone between October and December, 1877.[27] Lamar remained inconspicuous since he did not serve on a committee formulating this legislation, but he and Republican senator Bruce consistently

24. *Ibid.*

25. *Ibid.*, 4129; New York *Times*, May 29, 1878. The Mississippi legislature and the Jackson (Miss.) *Weekly Clarion*, January 9, 1878, supported the Texas Pacific.

26. This reticence did not indicate indifference to southern industrial development. For example, Lamar favored sending an emissary to Europe in search of capital. See New York *Times*, December 21, 1877, which comments on and quotes from Lamar's letter to John B. Gordon on the subject. He also supported minor legislation favorable to the timber and turpentine industry and to railroads. He opposed enforcement of the 8-hour day. See *Congressional Record*, 45th Cong., 2nd Sess., 1398–1401; 3rd Sess., 518; and *Senate Journal*, 45th Cong., 2nd Sess., 677.

27. DeSantis, *Republicans Face the Southern Question*, 88.

voted for bills introduced by others. Of special significance, he supported enlargement of important rivers and harbors appropriations which came before the Senate.[28] And closer to home, Lamar offered an amendment to increase the allocation for improvement of the Pascagoula River; he had less luck with this, however, and the chair ruled him out of order. He also fought to establish a Mississippi River improvement commission, but this agency would have to await the next Congress.[29]

The Forty-fifth Congress also considered an issue new to Lamar's experience. As Lamar visited Mississippi between sessions, yellow fever struck New Orleans in late July, 1878, and spread rapidly along the Mississippi River northward. Through late summer and fall the sickness raged. By early December the little north Mississippi town of Grenada alone had reported over 1,000 cases of "yellow jack" and the death toll had reached 350. The town was virtually deserted as its citizens fled for safety—taking the dread disease with them—until finally the trains passed through with closed windows and without stopping. Just fifty miles south of Grenada, Oxford did not succumb to the epidemic, but Lamar and his family left town for the country, where the air might be purer. He remained there even though he had to forego the election canvass of 1878.[30]

Lamar arrived in Washington for the opening of Congress in December, and he moved immediately to establish a yellow fever commission. He was appointed a member of the new commission and later traveled in this capacity to Memphis and New Orleans. In December, 1878, Lamar introduced a bill for the establishment of a federal department of public health. Later in February, 1879, he supported legislation to combat infectious diseases

28. *Senate Journal,* 45th Cong., 2nd Sess., 632–33, 647, 655–56, 666–67; 3rd Sess., 433–47.

29. *Congressional Record,* 45th Cong., 2nd Sess., 4437; *Senate Journal,* 45th Cong., 3rd Sess., 468.

30. Marshall Scott Legan, "Mississippi and the Yellow Fever Epidemics of 1878–1879," *Journal of Mississippi History,* XXXIII (August, 1971), 205–206; Memphis *Daily Appeal,* July 14, August 2, October 29, 1878; Mayes, *Lamar,* 352–53. Gordon wrote for help in the Georgia campaign but apparently did not get it. See John B. Gordon to Lamar, October 7, 1878, in Lamar-Mayes Papers.

and to establish a federal bureau of public health.[31] In proposing federal attention to health as to economic questions, Lamar again reflected a major tenant of his political philosophy: a willingness to fall back upon the national government.

Lamar did not, however, entrust the federal government and national conscience with responsibility for all issues, Spring, 1878, also saw mild sectional debates involving home rule and civil rights, and here his position as a spokesman for conservative southerners logically required that limitations be placed upon federal authority. Therefore he helped restrict use of the army for Republican and civil rights' purposes in the South, and he also voted to continue limiting Negro enlistments in the army. But for a time he studiously avoided arguments which might damage sectional goodwill and even enhanced this ideal by supporting the pensioning of Ulysses S. Grant as General of the Army.[32]

The anti-Hayes faction of the Republican party, however, had determined before the fall election of 1878 to again base its campaign on the "bloody shirt." That deliberate affront to the South, plus widespread Democratic victories and obvious voting irregularities, caused virtual collapse of hope that reconciliation had been achieved. The remarkable Democratic coup of 1878 signaled the emergence of the "solid South," a clear hazard to Republican national hegemony. Understandably the Republicans responded to the challenge with bitterness.[33]

Lamar did not campaign vigorously in 1878 because of the yellow fever epidemic. Still, he became involved in subsequent partisan antics even before reaching Washington for the December opening of Congress. En route to the capital Lamar told the Cincinnati *Enquirer* of his confidence in Hayes's continued

31. *Congressional Record*, 45th Cong., 3rd Sess., 2, 35, 66; Memphis *Daily Appeal*, December 27, 31, 1878; Jackson (Miss.) *Weekly Clarion*, December 25, 1878, January 8, 1879; *Senate Journal*, 45th Cong., 3rd Sess., 362–64.

32. *Senate Journal*, 45th Cong., 2nd Sess., 406, 535, 541–42, 645.

33. Buck, *Road to Reunion*, 110–11; DeSantis, *Republicans Face the Southern Question*, 99–101.

goodwill toward the South. He maintained nonetheless that home rule remained the chief issue in southern elections and that the region would necessarily be "solid" on that account. He categorically denied that the Democratic victory had depended on Negro disfranchisement: "In my state they [elections] were as peaceable as any election in the world could possibly be. Not a human being was molested or made afraid." [34]

The interview made national news and immediately provoked charges of hypocrisy. The New York *Tribune* put it most plainly: "The South is solid, as the history of Mr. Lamar's own State proves only too conclusively, because Democratic assassins have driven Republican leaders out of politics or into their graves." [35] In the Senate, James G. Blaine, not always averse to baiting Southerners, picked up the cry. On the very first day of the session he introduced highly inflammatory resolutions calling for an investigation to determine whether any citizens had been deprived of their constitutional rights. Blaine's comments threatened punitive reduction of southern congressional representation as provided by the Fourteenth Amendment in case freedmen were denied the vote.[36]

Senator Allen Thurman of Ohio replied to Blaine, and then Lamar rose to conclude the Democratic rebuttal. In an unusual performance Lamar clearly acted on the defensive and resorted to disingenuous argument. He countercharged that lightly populated states in Blaine's New England area benefitted most from the American system of congressional representation to the disadvantage of larger population centers. He also flatly denied that Negroes were proscribed in the South. In his words, there was not "a single right of freedom or of citizenship belonging to the black race of the South that was not as secure and as well enjoyed as that of the proudest and freest white in the land." [37]

34. Cincinnati *Enquirer*, quoted in Memphis *Daily Appeal*, November 22, 1878; Jackson (Miss.) *Weekly Clarion*, November 28, 1878.

35. New York *Tribune*, November 29, 1878. See also *ibid.*, November 30, 1878; and New York *Times*, November 21, 1878.

36. *Congressional Record*, 45th Cong., 3rd Sess., 84–86.

37. *Ibid.*, 87–89.

Reiterating a tired rationalization once more, he explained that the natural leadership of whites resulted from their "intelligence and virtue and sagacity" as contrasted to the Negro's ignorance.

More striking even than this ill-considered and untruthful argument, sharp repartee, a mode of debate unbecoming the conciliator, became Lamar's outlet for frustration. Smarting from the sarcastic ridicule which Blaine heaped upon his reasoning, Lamar spleenfully replied: "That will do pretty well for wit and pretty well for the Senator's peculiar species of perversion, but it will not do for the truth." [38] The next day an unrepentant Lamar somehow found cause for comfort and wrote his old friend Henry Watterson to boast: *"My point told"*; and, *"I will give them more of it."* [39]

Lamar and Blaine continued their colloquy in the March, 1879, issue of the *North American Review* as participants in a symposium on Negro suffrage. The format was, of course, more formal and polite than their encounter in the Senate. In replying to Blaine's essay Lamar quietly granted that enfranchisement of the Negro had been necessary and desirable, but after that he disputed his antagonist point by point. Lamar contended that the Negro had learned through his political experience to look upon the white southerner as his natural ally and preceptor. But still "years must pass before the ballot will have educated him fully into self-restraint, temperate citizenship" and "at this state of its progress the negro vote cannot intelligently direct itself." Lamar believed however that in the not too distant future political issues would divide white men in the South and that the Negro vote would also divide—with the blessing of the whites.

38. *Ibid.* In an interview with the Washington *Post* a few days later, Lamar said of the "southern outrages" that "the recent election in Mississippi was as peaceable and orderly as any ever held in the Union. Every man, black or white, voted as he pleased, and every vote was honestly counted." The interview is quoted in Memphis *Daily Appeal*, December 26, 1878.

39. Lamar to Henry Watterson, December 12, 1878, in Henry Watterson Papers, Manuscript Division, Library of Congress. Lamar later wrote President-elect Garfield a long and complimentary letter recommending Blaine for secretary of state. See Lamar to James A. Garfield, January 3, 1880 [*sic*], in James A. Garfield Papers, Manuscript Division, Library of Congress.

Until then the Negro's freedom and equality before the law would be complete and his franchise a protection against exploitation. Lamar closed his essay with the judgment that when problems arise, "proper remedies for whatever of evil or error may attend the working out of this grave and critical experiment" should be left to home rule.[40]

Back in Congress, Lamar voted in support of this practical conclusion. There he opposed all measures fostering federal protection of Negro rights. He voted to kill a resolution to enforce the war amendments and for state rather than federal punishment under the Fifteenth Amendment.[41] Late in February, 1879, when an army appropriations bill came from the House, Lamar and the Democratic Senators voted to retain provisions which prohibited use of federal troops for policing congressional elections. Republicans succeeded in deleting the offending sections, but the Democratic House refused the Senate version. Congress adjourned without passing an army appropriations bill, thus forcing Hayes to call a special session to consider the matter.[42]

Another dispute arose between southern Democrats and Republican partisans just before Congress adjourned its regular term in the spring of 1879. This time the confrontation followed an effort to exclude former Confederates from a Mexican War pension bill.[43] After the attempt failed, Republican senator George Hoar from Massachusetts offered an amendment exempting Jefferson Davis alone from pension benefits. Davis' champion as always, Lamar immediately charged Hoar with wanton insult. The chair called him to order for his language—

40. Lamar, L. Q. C., et al., a Symposium: "Ought the Negro to be Disfranchised," North American Review, CXXVIII (March, 1879), 225–83. Other participants included: Wade Hampton, James Garfield, Alexander Stephens, Wendell Phillips, Montgomery Blair, and Thomas A. Hendricks. See Rayford W. Logan, The Betrayal of the Negro from Rutherford B. Hayes to Woodrow Wilson (New York, 1965), especially his chapter "The Negro as Portrayed in the Leading Literary Magazines," which discusses this symposium in perspective.

41. Senate Journal, 45th Cong., 3rd Sess., 163–64, 182, 218–22.

42. Barnard, Rutherford B. Hayes, 482; Senate Journal, 45th Cong., 3rd Sess., 359, 434–35.

43. Senate Journal, 45th Cong., 3rd Sess., 448.

only to be overruled by a Senate vote. Lamar then excoriated Hoar for the injustice to Davis, contending that all Confederates stood exactly the same in the matter of disloyalty.

The heat of the debate carried Lamar to extraordinary lengths in his impromptu assault against Hoar. "Sir," he said, "it required no courage to do that; it required no magnanimity to do it: it required no courtesy. It only required hate, bitter, malig‚ nant, sectional feeling, and a sense of personal impunity. The gentleman, I believe, takes rank among Christian statesmen. He might have learned a better lesson even from the pages of mythology. When Prometheus was bound to the rock it was not an eagle, it was a vulture, that buried his beak in the tortured vitals of the victim." [44]

Those slashing remarks which the Republican Chicago *Tribune* described as "unrivaled bitterness and malignity" [45] revealed a seldom exposed facet of Lamar's postwar political personality. Conciliation was now his trademark, but when goaded there appeared an instinctive grasp of the art of personal denunciation. Against Hoar he vented it fully.

The sectional debate continued unrelieved after Hayes called

44. *Congressional Record*, 45th Cong., 3rd Sess., 2227–29. In a letter of March 15, 1879, quoted in Mayes, *Lamar*, 371, Davis thanked Lamar for his defense. Their personal relationship during this period was, however, somewhat unsteady. Davis had written a letter critical of Lamar's refusal to abide by the Mississippi legislature's instructions on the Bland-Allison Act, and this was published in the Jackson (Miss.) *Clarion*, January 15, 1879. And even before that, Davis was apparently irritated by what he considered to be a slight from Lamar. In a letter to John B. Gordon, November 11, 1877, Lamar had urged Gordon to go to Europe as a representative of southern industry. Lamar had disqualified himself from the mission because antebellum Mississippi had repudiated certain debts and had thereby incurred an unenviable reputation for fiscal irresponsibility. For a time Davis took personal offense at this reference to repudiation. The difficulty was finally ironed out to the satisfaction of all after an involved round of letters. See Lamar to John B. Gordon, November 11, 1877, quoted in Memphis *Daily Appeal*, December 11, 1877; Lamar to W. T. Walthall, June 29, 1878, quoted in Rowland (ed.), *Jefferson Davis, Constitutionalist*, VIII, 22–23; Gordon to Walthall, August 21, 1878, *ibid.*, 258–59; and Jefferson Davis to Gordon, August 28, 1878, *ibid.*, 267–68. For a history of the repudiation issue see Vagn K. Hansen, "Jefferson Davis and the Repudiation of Mississippi Bonds: The Development of a Political Myth," *Journal of Mississippi History*, XXXIII (May, 1971), 105–32.

45. Chicago *Tribune*, March 3, 1879.

the newly elected Forty-sixth Congress into special session in April, 1879, to pass the stalled army appropriations bill. The Democrats, having taken control of the Senate, proceeded to pass the House bill with prohibitions against the use of the army and federal marshals in policing elections. Hayes vetoed the act. New measures followed without the objectional provisions about civilian authorities but still forbidding military interference at polling places. Hayes again used the veto and the wrangling continued. Finally, after the special session had dragged on until June 20, a compromise measure which amounted to a victory for the president became law.[46]

Lamar did not at first participate in the acrimonious debate over the policing of elections. While the Democratic Congress and Hayes were at loggerheads, he busied himself pushing through a measure to establish a Mississippi River commission. On June 18, two days prior to the army appropriations compromise, he received unanimous consent to bring the Mississippi River bill to a vote, and it easily passed. The Democratic majority then sought that same day (June 18) to force, over strenuous Republican objections, a vote on the army appropriations bill.[47] A stalemate dragged on until sometime around midnight when Roscoe Conkling of New York charged that the Democrats had betrayed an understanding that Lamar's bill could be brought up in return for a delay on the army vote. The accusation proved too much for Lamar, whose temper seemed ungovernable. His reply to the irascible Conkling went further even than the fiery exchanges with Blaine and Hoar. Fairly exuding anger, and according to the New York *Times* "in a voice almost choked with passion," [48] Lamar tersely explained his own understanding of the matter and then turned to Conkling: "With reference to the charge of bad faith . . . I have only to say that if I am not superior to such attacks from such a source I have

46. *Senate Journal*, 46th Cong., 1st Sess., 98–99, 106–107, 131, 136, 245; Barnard, *Rutherford B. Hayes*, 482–83.

47. *Senate Journal*, 46th Cong., 1st Sess., 226–35.

48. New York *Times*, June 20, 1879.

lived in vain. It is not my habit to indulge in personalities; but I desire to say here to the Senator that in intimating anything inconsistent . . . with perfect good faith, I pronounce his statement a falsehood, which I repel with all the unmitigated contempt that I feel for the author of it." [49]

Conkling retorted that if Lamar "did impute or intended to impute to me a falsehood, nothing except the fact that this is the Senate would prevent my denouncing him as a blackguard, and a coward." [50] According to the New York *Times*, "when Mr. Lamar rose to reply he was livid with passion and trembling with suppressed rage. He replied, however, with a calmness which was forced and a dignity which was assumed." [51] He said: "Mr. President, I have only to say that the Senator from New York understood me correctly. I did mean to say just precisely those words, and all that they imported. I beg pardon of the Senate for the unparliamentary language. It was very harsh; it was very severe; it was such as no good man would deserve, and no brave man would wear." [52]

Both the New York *Times* and the New York *Tribune* speculated about the possibilities of a duel between the two men; but apparently the principals made no plans for one. Lamar himself did not believe that Conkling would present a challenge but felt that "the matter is not yet over." "A great deal will depend on what the *Times, Tribune, Herald*, and *Sun* of to-day will say. If they say fight, he will do so; but if the sentiment at the North says he has done enough, he will resort to some other method to get me down." [53]

An interesting question arises as to Lamar's motivation in allowing himself to be involved in such an unseemly fray. His practice for years had been to uphold the highest standard of decorum and to remain aloof from participation in vituperative partisan struggles—especially those involving sectional questions.

49. *Congressional Record*, 46th Cong., 1st Sess., 2143–44.
50. *Ibid.*   51. New York *Times*, June 20, 1879.
52. *Congressional Record*, 46th Cong., 1st Sess., 2143–44.
53. Lamar to E. C. Walthall, June 20, 1879, quoted in Mayes, *Lamar*, 386–87.

At this time either he felt secure enough to fall back upon the ways of the fire-eater, or he had become weak enough to be dragged into an outburst totally inconsistent with his hitherto primary mission of reconciliation. Even granting, as Lamar maintained, that Conkling "had determined to make me take part in the silly and unwise discussions that our party has been carrying on," [54] the about face was a mysterious one.

A friend of Lamar's, S. A. Jonas, editor of the Aberdeen (Mississippi) *Examiner*, may have unwittingly touched upon the underlying explanation when he described the reaction to the speech in Mississippi. "You will remember that I assured you . . . that its effect would be to crystalize public sentiment . . . and rally your people in solid phalanx to you; but I had no conception of the strength of the sentiment until I reached home, and no idea that the enthusiasm . . . would be shared alike by friends and foes in politics; but so I found it. . . . The timely rebuke . . . was regarded as a vindication of Mississippi . . . and, as such, entitling you to the thanks of Mississippians 'without regard to race, color,' or political affiliation." [55]

Lamar may have had such a political motive, but there is no direct evidence to support the supposition.[56] There can be little doubt, however, that at this time he very much needed a boost among his constituents. He was under constant fire by 1879 for his position on the compromise of 1876–1877, his disobedience to instructions on the silver question, and his espousal of moderation in the face of provocation from northern "bloody shirt" politicians. It is also true that while campaigning on the hustings later in 1879 Lamar indulged in the same kind of reverse "bloody shirt" tactics—perhaps to convince the people of his soundness on vital sectional issues.

Fortunately, the record Lamar carried home did not depend entirely on name calling with radical Republicans. The special

54. *Ibid.*

55. S. A. Jonas to Lamar, July 1, 1879, quoted in Mayes, *Lamar*, 390–91.

56. To Walthall he wrote: "But for once in my life I feel that I am *right*, even in the most extreme alternative." See Lamar to E. C. Walthall, June 20, 1879, quoted in Mayes, *Lamar*, 386–87.

session of the new Congress yielded several important results. Since the Democrats controlled the Forty-sixth Congress, which first convened in March, 1879, Lamar improved upon his committee assignments. He succeeded senior Mississippi senator Blanche K. Bruce as chairman of the Mississippi River Committee and became a member of the Judiciary and the Railroad committees; and later in the session a vacancy permitted his return to the Education and Labor Committee. In addition to these standing committees he again served on the Select Committee on Epidemic Diseases. These appointments carried over through the second and third sessions and would guarantee him considerable influence.[57]

Lamar's proudest accomplishment in economic legislation was the establishment of the Mississippi River Improvement Commission, a body charged with planning the improvement of the river's channel and its banks.[58] As chairman of the Mississippi River Committee he initiated appropriate legislation in the Senate, and then he took up the House version and guided it through passage on June 18 amid the disrupting effects of the debate on army appropriations.[59] As a lesser achievement perhaps, but still important to river folk in the aftermath of the terrible yellow fever epidemic of 1878, Lamar triumphantly joined the Democratic majority in passing a bill to combat the spread of infectious diseases.[60] His earlier efforts in these areas now were rewarded. With this positive record behind him and the taste of the Conkling affair fresh in his mouth, Lamar headed home to see to his political fences.

When Lamar reached Mississippi in late June, 1879, he intended to vindicate his position in Congress and to shore up developing crevices in the state's Democratic organization. He realized that personal friction between himself and others within

57. *Congressional Record*, 46th Cong., 1st Sess., 15, 435; 2nd Sess., 19; 3rd Sess., 14–15.
58. Lamar to E. D. Clark, June 18, 1879, in Lamar Papers, University of Mississippi Library.
59. *Senate Journal*, 46th Cong., 1st Sess., 187, 226; *Congressional Record*, 46th Cong., 1st Sess., 34, 2099, 2103. Blanche K. Bruce also supported the bill.
60. *Senate Journal*, 46th Cong., 1st Sess., 162–63.

the party signaled a dangerous division on fundamental questions and that a third party movement might seize on these differences. In such a situation the Negro vote could possibly control the balance of power again. The results might return the radicals to office.[61]

Lamar made only one speech before a recurrence of yellow fever interrupted his campaign. The family traveled to Virginia where they were safe from the epidemic, while Lamar went on to Washington where he stayed until Mississippi affairs compelled his return in mid-September.[62] Though he concealed it from the press, Lamar was not well at this time; and in fact, illness may have prompted his journey as much as the yellow fever did. He underwent operations for a painful growth in his nose, but the growth returned causing his head and eyes to ache. The doctor believed it to be benign, and fortunately medical attention arrested the trouble.[63]

Lamar returned to Mississippi in September while the battle raged for control of the state legislature. He spoke extensively throughout the northern part of the state on behalf of the party's candidates.[64] He attacked the inflation minded Greenbackers and decried unseemly and self-destructive Democratic bickering. On these occasions he also defended himself against recurring criticism of his support of the electoral commission bill, claiming that he had been vindicated by the withdrawal of troops from the South. And more than anything else, he justified his recent course in ignoring legislative instructions and opposing the Bland-Allison Act in the Senate.

The crux of Lamar's defense was the denial that he had ever opposed the principle of silver remonetization. He insisted, to

---

61. Interview in Cincinnati *Enquirer*, quoted in Jackson (Miss.) *Weekly Clarion*, November 27, 1878. For the speech at Oxford see Jackson (Miss.) *Weekly Clarion*, October 8, 1879.

62. Jackson (Miss.) *Weekly Clarion*, July 2, 1879; Mayes, *Lamar*, 397.

63. Lamar to E. D. Clark, August 31, 1879, in Lamar Papers, University of Mississippi Library.

64. Jackson (Miss.) *Weekly Clarion*, October 8, 15, 22, 1879; Mayes, *Lamar*, 408; Lamar to Blanche K. Bruce, October 18, 1879, in Blanche K. Bruce Papers.

the contrary, that in the House of Representatives he had supported silver coinage and failed to do so in the Senate only because of changing financial conditions the world over. Because silver had been devalued internationally, he favored its restoration only if the dollar weight could be increased, or if by international agreement the value could be reset. To remonetize a devalued silver dollar would betray the national credit and honor. He reminded his constituents of the commitment he had made to sound money while serving as chairman of the national Democratic caucus in 1875; and he emphasized that he had been elected to the Senate after that commitment. And finally he pointed out the sectional implications of the Bland-Allison Act. The South's failure to support payment of the national debt with sound money would confirm the charges of those who claimed that former Confederates would never help retire union obligations incurred during the Civil War. He also feared economic damage to the South if the silver issue discouraged movement of capital into the area. As for the legislature's instructions, Lamar firmly held that instructions were not mandatory and could not take priority over conscience.[65]

Lamar also mended his political fences by means other than public speeches. In the spring and summer of 1879 he worked at placing supporters in postmasterships in Vicksburg and Meridian. For the Meridian job he asked help from Senator Bruce. The language of his request suggested a working relationship between the two men. Lamar said: "It will be a great help to me in this community if through your agency Mr. Smith can procure the apointment." [66] A few days later he again wrote Bruce asking him to keep a lady employee in office.[67] The extent of federal patronage available for use in Mississippi is not known,

65. Two accounts of speeches are available in detail. See Jackson (Miss.) *Weekly Clarion*, October 8, 1879, for the Oxford speech; and Mayes, *Lamar*, 342–48, for a speech without date or place of delivery.
66. Lamar to Blanche K. Bruce, October 18, 1879, in Blanche K. Bruce Papers. On the Vicksburg appointment, see Lamar to E. D. Clark, April 4, 1879, in Lamar Papers, University of Mississippi Library.
67. Lamar to Blanche K. Bruce, October 27, 1879, in Blanche K. Bruce Papers.

but the Republican administration may have given Lamar extra consideration even as late as 1879 in an effort to win support from the Mississippi Democrats. Or Bruce and other "fusionists" may have channeled jobs for Lamar's use without the knowledge of the national Republican party. Unfortunately, fusionists left little evidence of such activities.

Lamar again interrupted his efforts at personal vindication on October 31, 1879, when his mother died in Georgia, necessitating a trip there.[68] He arrived back in Mississippi after the state Democratic victory to face an entirely different but related political situation: the election by the legislature of a United States senator to succeed Blanche K. Bruce. A bitter factional and personal battle arose over the prize.[69]

Long before the Mississippi election Lamar had decided on his candidate for Bruce's place in the Senate. As early as February, almost a year before the election, he wrote E. D. Clark of the Vicksburg *Commercial*, commending E. C. Walthall of Coffeeville as the man for the job.[70]

In supporting Walthall, Lamar showed a surprising lack of perspicacity, especially for a politician already hurt by unpopular positions taken in 1876–1878. Walthall resided in the same area of the state as Lamar—only a few miles from Oxford—and therefore could not offer geographical balance to the Senate delegation. Furthermore, he was not nearly so prominent as several others who had made important contributions to the revolution of 1875 and to subsequent Democratic administrations. By contrast, both James Z. George and Ethelbert Barksdale resided in Jackson and could claim to represent southern and central Mississippi. Both men had been deeply involved in state politics and

68. Mayes, *Lamar*, 411.
69. The election chose only state legislators. The Democrats won control of the two houses with a combined 135 seats to 7 Republican seats and 16 National (Greenback) seats. Figures furnished by Political Research Consortium.
70. Unaddressed memorandum, February 18, 1879, signed by Lamar, in Lamar Papers, University of Mississippi Library; Lamar to E. D. Clark, February 20, 1879, *ibid.*

had strong claims upon the Democratic party because of its victory in 1875. George had directed the campaign as chairman of the state executive committee during the revolution of 1875–1876 and afterwards had served as chief justice of the state supreme court. Long influential in the Democratic party, Barksdale had edited the Jackson *Clarion* and had served as state printer and then as chairman of the state executive committee after George's retirement. Congressman O. R. Singleton appeared as a third obvious and willing candidate, whose political service dated back to the antebellum congressional delegation. In the face of these considerations Lamar had determined to support Walthall.[71]

Lamar apparently urged Walthall's candidacy for purely personal reasons. Their acquaintance dated back to the reconstruction period when the two men practiced law together in Coffeeville, and Lamar would have taken pleasure in honoring a close friend. Practically speaking, he would have benefitted from Walthall's personal loyalty, and the election of such a person could only be construed as a complete endorsement of his course in Congress. In a four and one-half page private memorandum on the subject Lamar did not really go beyond this explanation except to proclaim generally the man's great ability and integrity. If Lamar's professions on the matter can be taken at face value, he realized in advance that there would be strong opposition and that the opposition might be directed at him as Walthall's sponsor; he even claimed to understand that Walthall's election might endanger his own seat in the election of 1882.[72]

Lamar became so intent on pushing Walthall that he decided to stay home from Congress in December, 1879. Enlisting E. D.

---

71. Willie D. Halsell, "Democratic Dissensions in Mississippi, 1878–1882," *Journal of Mississippi History*, II (July, 1940), 126–27. Lamar also mentioned James R. Chalmers as a candidate, but he seems not to have been a strong contender. See Lamar to E. D. Clark, February 20. 1879, in Lamar Papers, University of Mississippi Library.

72. Unaddressed memorandum, February 18, 1879, in Lamar Papers, University of Mississippi Library; Lamar to a "friend" in Vicksburg, February 17, 1879, quoted in Mayes, *Lamar*, 411–12.

Clark of the Vicksburg *Commercial*, he promoted publication of a questionnaire to be put to all aspirants for the office. The questions were intended to pin down the candidates on leading issues of the day and to show Walthall in a favorable light. Lamar asked for specific answers on monetary policy in terms of greenbacks, silver coinage, payment of national debt, and specie resumption; and he wished to force the candidates into a position on the legislature's authority to instruct senators. Finally, he wanted the candidates queried on their attitude toward his own course in the Senate, and whether they would consider election a vindication or condemnation of his position.[73]

The questionnaire duly appeared in the *Commercial* on December 29, 1879, but the rather clumsy trap did not work. Walthall's answers in agreement with Lamar's position in Congress were printed in the *Commercial* and in the *Clarion*, but the other candidates declined to reply.[74] Probably Lamar had succeeded only in cementing the harmful identification between himself and Walthall. At the same time he burdened Walthall with the unpopular silver position which the inflationists found so offensive. The depressed farmer element had deferred to Lamar's leadership, but to ask that they support another of the same political breed, but without his redeeming features, proved too much.

Lamar threw off misgivings that his presence might hurt the cause and traveled to Jackson when the Democratic legislators caucused to nominate a senator.[75] Since his participation in the statewide convention of 1877 had caused criticism, he could surmise that attendance at a legislative caucus would provoke an even more bitter outbreak, especially because his electioneering for Walthall kept him from Congress, which was then in session. Even ordinarily sympathetic persons must have looked askance

73. Lamar to E. D. Clark, December 26, 1879, in Lamar Papers, University of Mississippi Library.

74. Vicksburg (Miss.) *Daily Commercial*, December 29, 1879, January 5, 14, 1880, cited in Halsell, "Democratic Dissensions in Mississippi," 126.

75. Lamar to E. D. Clark, December 31, 1879, in Lamar Papers, University of Mississippi Library.

at Lamar's continued truancy from the Senate in mid-January.

The trip to Jackson turned out to be an altogether unfortunate one. During six ballots on the first day Ethelbert Barksdale almost won the contest, failing by only two votes. The Walthall forces withheld his name from consideration to await a more favorable moment. That same night Lamar suffered an attack of paralysis apparently brought on by nervous tension and excitement. For a moment he seemed dangerously ill. A doctor applied leeches to his head, a respected treatment during the nineteenth century, but his condition remained serious. Lamar had paid a terrible price for his efforts without assuring his friend's victory.[76]

When word of these events reached Walthall, he joined Mrs. Lamar, and both made the trip to Jackson. He immediately placed his candidacy before the caucus, but lagged behind Barksdale as the voting dragged on for a week without a decision. Finally Walthall withdrew in defeat and his followers shifted their allegiance to James Z. George whose name was then brought forward. After Barksdale and George deadlocked through the ninth day of the caucus, Barksdale also retired in favor of George, and the struggle ended in a saving compromise.[77]

In a sense the struggle for the senatorship resulted in a standoff between Lamar and Barksdale. Neither had won, and George had been a compromise upon whom both sides could agree. Probably George's political complexion was even more acceptable to Lamar than it was to Barksdale, at least on the major issue of attitude toward the federal government and acceptance of reconciliation.[78] But still Lamar suffered a profound sense of loss. Back in Oxford and still on crutches, he told Clark on January 28 just how keenly he felt Walthall's defeat: "Barksdale

76. Memphis *Daily Appeal*, January 13, 1880; Jackson (Miss.) *Weekly Clarion*, January 21, 1880. The *Clarion* did not discuss Lamar's involvement but simply reprinted an article from the New Orleans *Picayune*.

77. Memphis *Daily Appeal*, January 13, 16, 17, 20, 22, 1880. Cf. Kirwan, *Revolt of the Rednecks*, 52.

78. Halsell, "Democratic Dissensions in Mississippi," 128; Kirwan, *Revolt of the Rednecks*, 52.

speaks with unwitting truth when he says I have met a 'signal punishment.' It is one which grows sharper & more bitter every day. It is my one great disappointment in my life, & the only one of a political nature that I could not have borne with composure." [79]

Lamar would never entirely cherish George's presence in the Senate and sometimes spoke unkindly of him to intimates.[80] The matter did not end with private regrets either. A critical press spearheaded by Barksdale's *Clarion* relentlessly attacked Lamar for his behavior while a number of smaller papers chimed in.[81] Broken in health and sorely put upon, he recuperated for a time in Oxford, and then in February, 1880, started for Washington for the remainder of the congressional session.

79. Lamar to E. D. Clark, January 28, 1880, in Lamar Papers, University of Mississippi Library. Lamar characteristically felt self-pity: "I want to tell the press & legislature that they need not trouble themselves about me, for I do not expect to want their support or votes. I have done about all in my power for the South & am ready to close my stewardship."

80. Lamar to E. D. Clark, May [or August] 12, 1882, *ibid.*; Mary F. Summers, "Edgar Wilson: The Mississippi Eagle, Journalist of the New South" (Ph.D. dissertation, Mississippi State University, 1962), 92.

81. Jackson (Miss.) *Daily Clarion*, January 28, 1880. Jackson (Miss.) *Weekly Clarion*, February 4, 11, 1880, quotes press coverage on both sides including: Yazoo City (Miss.) *Sentinel*, Yazoo City (Miss.) *Herald*, and Grenada (Miss.) *New South*. Halsell, "Democratic Dissensions in Mississippi," 128, cites: Raymond (Miss.) *Hines County Gazette*, Meridian (Miss.) *Lauderdale Review*, Vicksburg (Miss.) *Daily Commercial*, and Water Valley (Miss.) *Courier*.

The Senate, 1880–1884:
Absenteeism, Troubles at Home,
and National Prominence Regained

Lamar did not participate actively in the congressional session which commenced while the intra-party struggle raged in Mississippi. Obviously his prospects diminished somewhat in his failure to appear during the first two and a half months. And apparently he did not intend even then to take a conspicuous part in the proceedings. The voting record indicates that even after his initial Washington appearance in February, 1880, Lamar still did not attend Senate sessions for protracted periods. He did not vote at all for almost a month (late April to late May) and returned for only the last meetings and the more important votes. Lamar did not explain this irregularity; presumably illness was the cause, irritated by the numbing disappointment of his late defeat. Perhaps, too, he better understood the price of controversial engagement unsupported by the sympathy of his constituency.[1]

When he did participate in Senate activities, Lamar concentrated almost exclusively on the politically sure and certain ground of civil rights. He again joined the Democratic majority in defeating a Republican effort to authorize use of troops to police elections.[2] And then on June 14, 1880, he devoted his

1. Lamar first appeared February 16, 1880. See *Congressional Record*, 46th Cong., 2nd Sess., 909. He prefaced his one speech near adjournment time with a declaration that he had meant not to speak at all. See *ibid.*, 4527.

2. *Senate Journal*, 46th Cong., 2nd Sess., 464–67.

single speech of the session to the southern question and the Negro.[3]

This speech followed a controversial committee report on the Negro "exodus" from the southern states to the Midwest. Population movements such as that of 1879–1880 were then an unknown phenomenon and caused great concern on both sides of the question. The migration had been favored by many Republican politicians, and the National Emigration Society had been organized to provide assistance. On the other hand, most southerners anticipated a threat to their economic system, and they resisted. In Lamar's home state, James R. Chalmers, a well-known Democrat, led a group which intimidated Mississippi River ship owners into leaving about 1,500 waiting Negroes stranded along the banks.[4]

When the contagion of flight spread from Mississippi and Louisiana to North Carolina in late 1879, Democrats in both houses of Congress moved to bring about an investigation. In the upper house, Senator Daniel W. Voorhees assumed a prominent role as head of a committee to investigate the Negro movement to Indiana, his home state.

Predictably, the committee returned both a majority and a minority report. Also not surprisingly, bitter debate followed in the Senate. The Democratic report and argument held that Republicans had purposely colonized Indiana, and that the "exodus" had not resulted from maltreatment of Negroes in the South. The Republican retort denied both contentions.

Lamar followed Voorhees' defense of the majority report in a speech not remarkable for its strength of argument or for its eloquence, but moderate enough to draw praise from President Hayes.[5] In measured terms he reiterated the claim that relatively few Negroes had left the South and that these had been

3. Lamar apparently planned an earlier speech in defense of southern election "Outrages" but did not give it. See Wade Hampton to Lamar, September 12, 1879, in Lamar-Mayes Papers.

4. Hirshon, *Farewell to the Bloody Shirt*, 63–68.

5. Lamar to Rutherford B. Hayes, July 24, 1880, in Rutherford B. Hayes Papers.

enticed to Indiana by the Republicans. Lamar further explained away the Democrats' embarrassment by declaring it altogether proper if the Negro's aspirations led him to seek fulfillment elsewhere. He also admitted that some problems in the South encouraged migration, especially the easy credit extended to the improvident by unscrupulous, mostly nonsouthern, merchants. Then, as if by habit, Lamar testified to the general happiness and effectiveness of southern labor and to the benevolent conditions under which men worked: "You may talk, sir, of the dignity of labor, but labor can be put nowhere upon such a dignified and equitable basis as it is in Mississippi." [6]

The remarks hardly squared with a frank and apparently unguarded personal letter written more than two months earlier when Lamar candidly admitted what he could never afford to say in public: that the Negro had small hope in the South and that there existed no prospect for substantial advancement. For his own sake, the Negro should leave. The Negro race ought to escape "such influences as cause it to pervert and poison the civilization on which it has been superimposed." Few plantation-oriented southerners would have agreed, but Lamar declared that "the disappearance of negro labor has no terrors for me. I would hail it as the beginning of a glorious Southern renaissance." [7]

Lamar had achieved little of an official or public nature during the Senate session which ended in June, 1880, but at least he regained his health sufficiently to attend the Democratic nominating convention in Cincinnati—presumably en route to Mississippi since his train normally took him through that city. Lamar favored Thomas F. Bayard of Delaware for the nomination and may have attended the convention in his behalf. Bayard failed to obtain the nomination, however, and Lamar returned to Mississippi to campaign for Winfield Scott Hancock against

6. *Congressional Record*, 46th Cong., 2nd Sess., 4527–33. The New York *Times*, June 22, 1880, took Lamar to task for glossing over the violent condition of life in the South.

7. Lamar to W. B. Montgomery, March 24, 1880, quoted in Mayes, *Lamar*, 415–16.

formidable opposition in a three-way race with Republican James A. Garfield and James B. Weaver, Greenbacker.[8]

The summer proved difficult for Lamar in a personal sense. His own health was yet unsteady; he suffered again from vertigo, as he called it, and he felt some pain and dizziness. And even more depressing, the doctors had found his wife to be seriously ill of "consumption." He found it necessary, so he wrote a friend, to stay at her bedside almost constantly.[9]

Nevertheless, Lamar took the election trail and campaigned hard. In September he traveled to Indiana at the invitation of that state's party, and then in October he toured northern and central Mississippi. The message was everywhere the same. He eulogized Hancock and attacked the opposition, both Republicans and Greenbackers. His approach to the two parties differed, however. According to the partisan Memphis *Daily Appeal*, "he arraigned the Republican Party for its crimes, venality and corruption, his castigation of Garfield being cruel though true." [10] Lamar also attacked James Weaver personally but implored the prodigal Greenbackers to again vote Democratic as an act of patriotism and loyalty to their section. He regretted the defection from Democratic ranks and urged reconciliation in a common cause of defeating Republicans. The Republican threat required a "solid" South, and he insisted that the Democratic party satisfied both sectional and national needs. The national party's goals and Mississippi's goals should be civil service reform, economy in government, a lower tariff, and a reduction in taxation.[11]

During the canvass Lamar's health declined alarmingly. Two- and three-hour speeches in the gruelling Mississippi sun proved too much for his delicate constitution. Late in October he delivered his addresses while sitting in a chair, and on November

8. Lamar to General [Walthall], May 25, 1880, in Lamar Papers, University of Mississippi Library; Wade Hampton to Lamar, May 1, 1880, in Lamar-Mayes Papers; Mayes, *Lamar*, 418–19; Tansill, *Thomas Francis Bayard*, 268.

9. Mayes, *Lamar*, 420; Lamar to J. W. C. Watson, October 1, 1880, quoted, *ibid.*, 419–20. Mrs. Lamar probably suffered from pulmonary tuberculosis.

10. Memphis *Daily Appeal*, October 5, 1880.

11. *Ibid.*, September 12, October 2, 5, 6, 21, November 14, 1880.

14 the *Daily Appeal* regarded him "as an invalid, and fears are expressed for his health." [12] But still he saw the election through.

The Republican presidential victory could hardly have surprised or disconcerted Lamar. By this time he had adapted to Republican control of the national government as long as Democrats maintained their position in Mississippi. He even presumed to advise Garfield in the composition of his cabinet. Blaine, he thought, was eminently qualified to be secretary of state.[13] He also suggested that as a cabinet officer retiring Senator Bruce of Mississippi "would give as much satisfaction to the Southern people as the selection of any white Republican in the Southern States." [14]

When his health allowed, Lamar traveled to Washington for the third session of the Forty-sixth Congress. He first attended on December 20, 1880, two weeks after the session convened.[15] Two days later, on the same day that Congress recessed for Christmas, he pushed through a bill granting a right of way to the Memphis and Vicksburg Railroad Company through public lands near Vicksburg. That piece of Mississippi business out of the way, Lamar joined his colleagues in celebrating the holidays until January 5, 1881.[16]

Lamar reported on schedule in January but again failed to attend with regularity. Throughout the session his voting was sporadic and infrequent, as for instance when he cast no vote on a matter of substance for an eighteen-day period in the middle of February; and indeed, his votes in that month were concentrated in a single day—February 26, 1881. Even if able to keep reasonably informed, he obviously could not maintain the daily contact with his peers that might have made his influence greater.

12. *Ibid.*, November 14, 1880. See also *ibid.*, October 21, 1880.
13. Lamar to James A. Garfield, January 3, 1880 [*sic*], in James A. Garfield Papers.
14. Interview from Washington *Post*, quoted in Jackson (Miss.) *Weekly Clarion*, January 27, 1881. The article stated similar sentiments from other Mississippi congressmen.
15. *Senate Journal*, 46th Cong., 3rd Sess., 68.
16. *Ibid.*, 81–82.

Despite a spotty voting record, Lamar made a large and, in view of his continued illness, exacting effort to enact the rivers and harbors appropriation and other economic legislation important to the Mississippi valley. On February 26, 1881, he voted numerous times to increase the rivers and harbors appropriation against endeavors by the minority to weaken the legislation. These efforts proved to be his most successful of the session, and the bill passed with the changes he favored.[17] On that same day he introduced a bill granting right-of-way through public lands to the New Orleans and Northeastern Railroad Company from New Orleans to Meridian, but it died in committee.[18] On March 3, 1881, just before the session ended, he brought up a bill to allow the Cherokee and Arkansas Railroad access through the Indian Territory. In arguing for the measure Lamar disputed with Henry Dawes, champion of Indian rights, and other senators who believed the legislation contrary to the existing treaty arrangement. Lamar's broad interpretation of the treaty provided that explicit consent from the Indians was not necessary; but he could not push the bill through before the end of the session.[19]

Since debate was sharply curtailed for lack of time, Lamar's attitude toward the complex and confusing Indian question cannot be definitely separated from the economic aspect of the Cherokee and Arkansas Railroad bill. One may only surmise that his support of the railroad may have outweighed any consideration he might have had for Indian rights. Only one other vote of the session and one of the previous session had bearing on this attitude. Late in January, 1881, Lamar had voted with Dawes to give citizenship to the Indians.[20] In the previous ses-

17. *Ibid.*, 327–29, 334–35.
18. *Congressional Record*, 46th Cong., 3rd Sess., 2108.
19. *Ibid.*, 2377–78, 2407, 2416–17; *Senate Journal*, 46th Cong., 3rd Sess., 373, 386, 389.
20. *Senate Journal*, 46th Cong., 3rd Sess., 165. This was a vote against westerners who resisted any change in the Indian's status. As Secretary of Interior in 1885 Lamar opposed immediate citizenship as being dangerous for the Indian's welfare. See *Report of the Secretary of the Interior* (1885), I, 25, hereinafter cited as *Interior Report*.

sion he had voted to open the Ute Reservation in Colorado to white settlement and for distribution of the remaining tribal lands among individual Indians. Since Lamar did not partici- pate in the debates upon the merits of severalty and citizenship, it is not clear whether he at this date looked upon them as re- forms, as some did, or only as measures to open up reservation lands to white settlers. These questions had not been defined by 1881, and Lamar indicated little concern for the interests of the Indians.[21]

Lamar made only one other speech during the session, and that was his single foray on the southern question. Actually he raised the southern banner himself without provocation—per- haps to advance his moderate position or to call attention to his presence. When Republican senators presented a bill retiring U. S. Grant from the army with a pension, all Democratic mem- bers except Lamar opposed the motion. He made a short speech in which he held that the general's military service entitled him to the pension, that it was not properly a political question, and that it had no sectional overtones whatever. These sentiments presumably did not hurt Lamar's now dimming national image as an impartial reconciliator. But at home his critics jumped at the new opportunity to attack.[22]

The inauguration of President Garfield on March 4, 1881, and the calling of Congress in special session began a highly partisan strugggle for control of the Senate's organization. The dispute arose from the Senate's peculiar composition which included

21. *Senate Journal*, 46th Cong., 2nd Sess., 420, 425–26. On the general con- fusion of motives on these issues see Loring B. Priest, *Uncle Sam's Stepchildren: The Reformation of United States Indian Policy, 1865–1887* (New Brunswick, N.J., 1942), 189–92, 208–11. Priest maintains that the enemies and friends of the Indian often voted together during this period for opposing reasons.

22. *Senate Journal*, 46th Cong., 3rd Sess., 156, 161; Lamar to John W. Daniel, March 7, 1881, in John W. Daniel Maunscripts, Duke University Library; *Con- gressional Record*, 46th Cong., 3rd Sess., 901–902; Jackson (Miss.) *Weekly Clarion*, February 9, 1881. After Grant's death Lamar donated $10.00 toward the erection of a memorial. See Lamar to William [———?], n.d., 1885, in Letterbook IV, Lamar- Mayes Papers.

thirty-seven Republicans, thirty-seven Democrats, one Independent (David Davis of Illinois), and one Readjuster (William Mahone of Virginia). Davis sided with the Democrats, leaving Mahone as the pivotal vote since in case of a tie the vice-president would vote Republican. A protracted and bitter quarrel grew out of this situation; and even when Mahone went with the Republicans, allowing them to control the committees, the Democrats demurred and successfully blocked replacement of their own Senate administrative officers with members of the newly installed Republican majority. The Democratic effort was clearly obstructionist and Lamar opposed it in caucus as an unwise course of action. He nevertheless voted regularly with his party to frustrate the Republicans to the exclusion of all other business.[23]

The continuing Democratic filibuster provoked the Republicans to attack southern senators and their state governments, contending that southern elections were based on fraud and intimidation. On April 1 Lamar put aside his misgivings about the filibuster and ignored his failing physical strength to enter the unseemly fray. He castigated Republican tactics as an effort to court the anti-Democratic Readjusters of Virginia by electing one of them to an administrative position. Lamar devoted the balance of this lengthy speech to a defense of the "solid South" which the Republicans, working through the Readjusters and other anti-Democratic elements, were intent on breaking.

Lamar's speech added little to the debate; and even a sympathetic newspaper questioned the wisdom of his having made it, especially since "he was very unwell, and when he finished fell in his chair from exhaustion, his head throbbing with pain and his face bearing marks of intense physical suffering." [24]

Lamar faced another uncomfortable situation when the Senate turned to the appointment of Stanley Matthews of Ohio to the United States Supreme Court. Matthews had been named to the position first by his brother-in-law and close political ally,

23. New York *Times*, March 23, 1881; Mayes, *Lamar*, 426. The Republicans gave way on May 5, 1881. See *Senate Journal*, 46th Cong., 3rd Sess., 486.
24. Aberdeen (Miss.) *Tri-Weekly Examiner*, April 15, 1881.

Rutherford B. Hayes. When the Senate failed to ratify the appointment it was resubmitted by President Garfield. Matthews was again caught between the anti-Hayes Stalwart wing of his own party and the Democrats; but this time he finally won ratification in May, 1881, by only one vote. Lamar was the only member of the Judiciary Committee to vote for confirmation, and then he argued in the full session in Matthews' behalf. This attitude doubtlessly caused Lamar to appear more tolerant than his fellow southerners, but of course it also recalled the still shadowy relationship between the two men during the troubled days of 1876–1877. Lamar's critics in Mississippi cared little for his attitude in this matter.[25]

Even before Congress adjourned on May 20, politics in Mississippi showed signs of turmoil and indications that the coming season might give Lamar trouble. In state politics the year 1881 caused greater concern than the national elections had in 1880. The Democratic party convention would meet in August to choose candidates, and in November both executive and legislative positions would be filled in a general election. The new legislature would, as one of its most important tasks, select Lamar's successor. In some respects, especially for Lamar personally, these events were the most important since the revolution of 1875 when the Democrats first won control of the state and sent Lamar to the Senate.[26]

The election year of 1881 presented one major contrast to 1875. In the latter year Democrats had stood united against the Republican administration. Factionalism stemming from the color line question had not been permitted to disrupt party effort. By 1881 the need for unity seemed less compelling, and the old factionalism, more abrasive than ever, threatened to disrupt the party and retire Lamar from office.

25. New York *Times*, May 10, 13, 1881; Jackson (Miss.) *Weekly Clarion*, February 17, 1881. Stanley Matthews to Lamar, April 1, 1881, in Lamar-Mayes Papers, discusses the subject.

26. Halsell, "Democratic Dissensions in Mississippi," 129–30, discusses the elections and the importance of these events.

Strife over the distribution of offices, difference of opinion over silver and greenbacks, and attitudes toward the federal government all combined to threaten party unity. Not surprisingly, Lamar's personal leadership provided a focus for dispute on all points. As one local politico, an aspirant for a congressional seat, put it: "He has done less, and got more credit for doing nothing, than any man I ever saw. He makes about two speeches a year, votes against us every chance he gets, and habitually represents Wall Street and Boston, instead of Miss." [27]

As usual, Ethelbert Barksdale led the opposition to Lamar and was strongly backed by Congressman James R. Chalmers, editor of the Vicksburg *Daily Commercial*. As early as May, 1881, Barksdale raised the old question of Lamar's failure to obey legislative instructions on the silver bill and made clear the *Clarion's* freedom from commitment in the Senate election. Also in May, Chalmers' *Daily Commercial* suggested that the Lamar faction divide the spoils of office—either the senatorship or governor's office—with the other wing of the party. During the summer, editors throughout the state aligned behind one of the two factions or maintained an uneasy neutrality. [28] Lamar remained publicly aloof but participated in the newspaper war by feeding information to others. [29]

The press dramatized the issues of 1881; but the county and state conventions would actually make the decisions. Local organizations meeting in June and July would pass resolutions binding delegates to the state convention in advance. Barring a deadlock the voice of the counties would be final. [30]

27. W. F. Tucker to Lafayette P. Reynolds, August 11, 1881, in Lafayette P. Reynolds Papers, Duke University Library.

28. Jackson (Miss.) *Weekly Clarion*, May 12, 26, June 16, 1881; Vicksburg (Miss.) *Daily Commercial*, cited in Halsell, "Democratic Dissensions in Mississippi," 131; Aberdeen (Miss.) *Tri-Weekly Examiner*, April 27, May 13, 1881; Memphis *Daily Appeal*, September 3, 1881.

29. Lamar to E. D. Clark, July 15, 1881, in Lamar Papers, University of Mississippi Library, supplied Clark with information to be used against Chalmers and suggested a line of attack. The Jackson (Miss.) *Weekly Clarion*, May 26, 1881, declared that Lamar furnished data to the correspondent "A. B. C." who defended Lamar's course in disobeying the Mississippi legislature on the silver issue.

30. Kirwan, *Revolt of the Rednecks*, 52–53.

In northern Mississippi, Lamar won endorsement without exception, and he carried the string of plantation counties stretching along the Mississippi River in the west. Only scattered opposition appeared in the central and southern parts of the state, so that by August a comfortable majority of the delegates were pledged in his behalf. The gubernatorial nomination was not so clear cut. A number of counties left their delegations uninstructed or threw away votes on weak candidates leaving the issue undecided. The Barksdale and Lamar factions therefore concentrated their efforts on this office, and each moved to compel the convention, the supreme party authority, to do its bidding.[31] While Lamar's own career was not in jeopardy, his influence in the party and his prestige on the home scene were at stake.

Lamar did not travel to Jackson to participate personally in the convention's proceedings. Presumably he had learned a lesson from his setback the previous year. He nevertheless completely supported the candidacy of John M. Stone, who had held the governorship during two terms since 1875. Lamar had preferred E. C. Walthall to Stone for the governorship in 1877, but Stone over the years had been identified with the Lamar faction and now carried the banner against Barksdale.[32]

Stone and Barksdale deadlocked for thirty ballots before Barksdale decided to compromise with a group who opposed Stone because of the third-term issue, but who refused to accept Barksdale himself. The two factions agreed on Robert Lowry and offered his name to the convention. Stone's supporters were caught unawares, and Lowry carried the nomination. Barksdale had not won the office he coveted, but he had stopped the Lamar wing of the party. Lamar, on the other hand, had not been totally vanquished. Lowry agreed in principle with Lamar and could not be considered either an economic liberal or an "unreconstructed Bourbon" of the Barksdale type. The settlement was not

31. *Ibid.*; Halsell, "Democratic Dissensions in Mississippi," 132–33.
32. Halsell, "The Bourbon Period in Mississippi Politics," 528, describes Stone's place in the political spectrum.

unlike that which gave James Z. George a senate seat in 1880.[33]

Lamar seemed somewhat bewildered by it all. He wrote Clark: "My opinion is that the result of the action at Jackson is not a favorable one for me; but it is less unfavorable than the pre-existing conditions were capable of working out." [34] In a second letter to Clark he wrote: "As yet I have not formed a decided opinion about the result of the action of the convention. . . . I am left as yet wholly to conjecture. . . . If you know anything of the influences which are operative upon Lowery [sic] I would like to have them." [35]

These results again attested that Lamar's following in Missis-sippi was primarily a personal one which could not be effectively transferred to another individual. The division of the party be-tween the farmer faction and the planter groups partially ex-plains this. But Lamar also lacked the sagacity in political in-fighting to prevent such a struggle. Stone was vulnerable because of the third-term stigma and could possibly have been dumped prior to the convention for another Lamar man. Or a Lamar-instigated compromise with the anti-third-termers at the con-vention might have made an accommodation with Barksdale unnecessary. And finally, since the Barksdale branch of the party legitimately claimed a share of the spoils as their due for past service, Lamar might well have given in with good grace and avoided the hard feelings which followed.

After the convention, Mississippi Democrats faced their most formidable opposition since 1875. While Democrats fought among themselves, opposition groups banded together to con-test the party's hold on the state government. The Republican party, the Greenback party, Independents, and renegade Demo-crats expediently united to support Benjamin King on a coali-tion ticket. The real threat of the coalition, however, came when it resurrected the Negro's claim to a decisive role in state govern-

33. Memphis *Daily Appeal*, August 4, 5, 6, 1881.
34. Lamar to E. D. Clark, n.d., quoted in Mayes, *Lamar*, 434–35.
35. Lamar to E. D. Clark, August 10, 1881, in Lamar Papers, University of Mississippi Library.

ment. Just as in reconstruction, the freedmen still constituted a potential majority, and power awaited any party which could mobilize that potential. All Democrats appreciated this possibility; and many still felt unmitigated hostility to Negro voting. The challenge resulted in a revival of the rhetoric and, to some degree, the tactics of 1875.

Lamar's response to the coalition threat contrasted markedly to his campaigning of past years. For one thing, he departed from his accustomed stumping grounds along the Mississippi Central Railroad in the northern part of the state and moved into central and southern Mississippi, where his policies had provoked strong opposition. For the first time in his career he made a truly statewide race. This alteration in strategy probably resulted from an appreciation of the limitations of his personal following, as shown in the machinations of preceding months, and perhaps from genuine fear for the party's ticket. The small farmers outside the Black Belt, whose economic and racial views contrasted with Lamar's, clearly threatened rebellion against the establishment. Lamar had long been aloof from the small farmers, even those who helped send him to Congress in 1872, and now he hastily sought to make amends.[36]

The content of Lamar's campaign changed with the location. A new emphasis on race crept into his speeches and communications during these months. While still disclaiming sympathy with illegal deprivation of Negroes' voting rights, his remarks clearly were demagogic in their appeal to white unity and in their suggestion of calamity should defeat come at the hands of a Negro backed party. By comparison, he appeared less moderate in 1881 than he had been in 1875–1876 when trying to hold the rabid "white liners" in check. The disgruntled farmers were highly susceptible to racial rhetoric, and they after all provided

36. Jackson (Miss.) *Weekly Clarion*, September 8, 15, 1881; Memphis *Daily Appeal*, October 4, 1881; Mayes, *Lamar*, 435. Kirwan, *Revolt of the Rednecks*, 40–49, describes the geographic factors involved in agrarian discontent in the 1880s and the reaction of the small farm areas against the established Democratic leadership.

a large part of the support the King forces depended upon. It was Lamar's task to bring the farmers into line.

In a letter to R. H. Henry, editor of the Brookhaven (Mississippi) *Ledger,* Lamar denounced the "shameless partnership" with the Negroes which intended to install "simply *negro government,* to be reestablished by carpetbaggers and a few ambitious natives." [37] His own response to the threat, as he described it in another letter, was "to arouse the white people and to impress them with the necessity of union against negro government." To do so "I have to demonstrate the insulation of the negro as a political element in our system, his refusal to assimilate with out political habitude and methods, and our failure hitherto to get him to unite with us in reaching any equilibrium of power between the two races." [38] But still Lamar attempted to draw the line between illegal disfranchisement and the use of the racial question simply to unite whites: "I make no attack upon the negro race. I insist upon . . . all his rights." But as for the whites "I say that they should combine and unite to prevent, by such means, the negro from grasping the power of the State." [39]

Lamar's white solidarity message also included a specific plea for Lowry. The rift of August could not be allowed to stand in the way of victory, and Lamar made clear his acceptance of the convention's settlement. In one speech he told the crowd that "I do not know whether Lowry is for Lamar for the Senate or not, but I do know, and wish it understood once and for all, that Lamar is for General Lowry for Governor." [40] And of course he also spoke in his own behalf—especially about the old issues of the electoral commission, the Stanley Matthews case, the Grant retirement bill, and the silver bill. He made many more speeches

37. Lamar to R. H. Henry, n.d., quoted in Mayes, *Lamar,* 435–36.
38. Unaddressed letter by Lamar, quoted, *ibid.,* 438.
39. *Ibid.* See examples of his application of these tactics in his speech of September 6, reported in Memphis *Daily Appeal,* September 7, 1881; and his address of November 7, reported in Memphis *Daily Appeal,* November 8, 1881.
40. Memphis *Daily Appeal,* September 7, 1881. *Ibid.,* September 13, 1881, gloried that the "serpent of faction" had been slain.

than was his custom, and although his tour was interrupted during October by a special session of Congress, he carried his message of impending danger to all corners of the state.[41]

The election results thoroughly vindicated the Democrats. Lowry carried the state by a 60 percent majority, and the Democrats won control of the legislature. In the predominantly black areas where "fusion" and fraud were standard practices, the Democratic machine held sway in twenty-seven of thirty-eight counties. Of the thirty-three white counties where rebellion threatened, only three resisted the high pressure campaign conducted by Lamar and his fellow partisans. Once again personal and economic enmity had given way to party loyalty and white supremacy. As for Lamar, the party caucus unanimously nominated him for the Senate, and the legislature obligingly awarded him another six-year term.[42]

Lamar joined the Forty-seventh Congress when it convened on December 5, 1881. The Republicans had now gained control of the Senate, and he suffered the fate of the defeated party. His committee appointments were cut back, and he lost the valued chairmanship of the Mississippi River Committee. Now he would serve on the Railroads and Judiciary committees and on the Select Committee on Epidemic Diseases.[43] And again Lamar sharply reduced his effectiveness by repeated absences. During this session he was almost a member in name only. He rarely voted between the first meeting of Congress on December 5, 1881, and the middle of February. He made one speech and then

41. Memphis *Daily Appeal*, September 2, 7, October 4, November 8, 17, 1881. Mayes, *Lamar*, 435–36, copies a number of newspaper accounts which are no longer available. The Jackson (Miss.) *Clarion* generally ignored Lamar's efforts on the party's behalf, presumably because of the ill will between Barksdale and Lamar. The special session of Congress resulted from James Garfield's death and met from October 10, 1881, to October 29, 1881.

42. Memphis *Daily Appeal*, January 5, 6, 18, 1882. Exact figures as provided by Political Research Consortium: Robert Lowry—76,857, to Benjamin King—51,856. County analysis based on data from Political Research Consortium and *Compendium of the Eleventh Census* (1892), Pt. I, 493–94.

43. *Senate Journal*, 47th Cong., 1st Sess., 29, 71–72.

lapsed again until early April when he requested an official leave due to family illness.[44] From that time until July 10 he did not vote more than two or three times. Not a single vote is recorded for Lamar during the last part of the session from the middle of July until adjournment on August 8, 1882.[45]

Lamar doubtless was frustrated by his impotency, but his wife's worsening condition left him no alternative. As he wrote his "dear friend," E. D. Clark: "She wants me all the time, (I am writing this in the intervals of her fitful and troubled sleep) and cannot bear for me to leave her. The demand upon my care is all through the day and night; for her insomnia yields to no medicine." Besides the grief and emotional strain Lamar felt, he well understood the impact which his situation had upon his career. As he told Clark: "My future as a public man if not cut [sheer(?)] off is indefinitely suspended. I am very sensible of the fact that my continued absence from the Senate, and my silence when there, will excite comments which must pain my friends. But I cannot remedy it at least for the present." [46]

Lamar's single speech in the first session appears to have been insignificant and must certainly have been intended to publicize his presence to a constituency becoming impatient with his delinquency. On February 16 he took the floor for only a brief moment to treat a unique question involving the civil and religious rights of the Mormons, an issue toward which he had shown no previous interest. Lamar denounced the proposed general disfranchisement of Mormons on grounds that such an action by the government would punish all Mormons for an illegal practice (polygamy) engaged in by only a part of the Mormon population.[47] Whatever the merits of the argument Lamar seems

44. *Congressional Record*, 47th Cong., 1st Sess., 2723.

45. *Senate Journal*, 47th Cong., 1st Sess., 1118, shows Lamar voting once on the final day of the session. Possibly that was in error.

46. Lamar to E. D. Clark, May [or August] 12, 1882, in Lamar Papers, University of Mississippi Library.

47. *Congressional Record*, 47th Cong., 1st Sess., 1212. Evidence does not permit an evaluation of Lamar's tolerance for religions other than his own. The only known reference to Jews resulted from an attempt to describe James G. Blaine to a friend. Speculating as to whether Blaine might be Jewish, he

not to have pursued the subject thereafter. Certainly it was not a major concern either to him or to Mississippi.

Despite personal difficulties, Lamar attended to the all important rivers and harbors appropriations. Republican control of the Senate excluded him from membership on the committee which initiated the legislation, but on the floor he helped protect provisions for levee work, and he assisted in gaining additional funds for Potomac River improvements as well as other increases. Congress's extravagance in passing this $18,743,875 bill was such that President Chester A. Arthur, not known for squeamishness in such matters, vetoed it on constitutional grounds.[48]

Later in the summer the Senate passed the bill over Arthur's veto, but Lamar was not there. He most likely left Washington early to see to his wife's health and hopefully to rest himself from what had been a difficult session. The only Mississippi elections to be held in the fall of 1882 were for Congress and should have required no special attention on his part. Such an undemanding visit, in view of Mrs. Lamar's illness, would indeed have been welcome.

Lamar in fact did not campaign during the summer and fall, though the political atmosphere was anything but calm. James R. Chalmers, one of Lamar's antagonists in the intra-party struggle of 1881, bolted the Democratic party and challenged Vannoy H. Manning, the incumbent congressman from Lamar's district. Embittered by his failure to gain a larger role in the Democratic party, and convinced, perhaps with good reason, that Lamar had not supported him against Negro John R. Lynch in a disputed election in 1880, Chalmers determined to seek a new political base outside the Democratic party. When he lost

---

wrote: "Look at his children; they are Jew, all over. I think so because, beyond any American politician except [Judah] Benjamin he has not only the will, the ambition & popular aptitudes of the American Statesman, but also the artistic delicacy of the Jewish mind. You know I think the mixture of that blood is to the human family like a cross of the Jersey on the bovine race." See Lamar to S. A. Jonas, June 15, 1884, in S. A. Jonas Papers, MDAH.

48. *Senate Journal*, 47th Cong., 1st Sess., 939, 946–47, 957–58; George Frederick Howe, *Chester A. Arthur: A Quarter Century of Machine Politics* (New York, 1957), 170–71.

the contested congressional seat to Lynch, and the Democratic
state legislature redistricted the state to his disadvantage, he announced his decision to run on an Independent ticket. Hoping
to unite anti-Lamar forces of all party complexions, Chalmers
moved to Lamar's own district and announced his decision to
run for Congress.[49]

Chalmers intended to take advantage of Chester A. Arthur's
efforts to build up Independent parties in the South as a counter-
balance to the Democrats. Asking for and receiving support from
the national Republican administration, he laid plans to deliver
Mississippi to the Republicans.[50] Probably because of Mrs. Lamar's illness, or perhaps for fear of defeat, Lamar determined
not to intervene. It may be too that he disliked Manning as much
as he did Chalmers and therefore would not support him. Before
the last congressional race Lamar had suggested such an attitude
of disdain: "I have no use for Manning," he said, "but I dont
see the wisdom of making a vain effort to beat him." [51]

Lamar's indifference or negligence matched that of many other
Democrats. Chalmers won by a majority of only 851 votes in an
election which turned out almost 30 percent fewer votes statewide than had been cast in the previous and normally large
presidential year campaign. The drop in the number of voters
was almost exclusively a Democratic loss, and in Lamar's home
county alone the decline since 1880 was over 1,000. This proved
decisive since Chalmers carried the county by 363 votes whereas
in 1880 Manning had won by a majority of 588 votes. Another
Democratic problem was the failure to hold two large black

49. Willie D. Halsell, "James R. Chalmers and Mahoneism in Mississippi,"
Journal of Southern History, X (February, 1944), 37–58, treats the Chalmers movement. See also Jackson (Miss.) *Weekly Clarion*, May 10, 17, 1882. Lamar to E. D.
Clark, December 27, 1880, in Lamar Papers, University of Mississippi Library, suggests that Chalmers may have had good reason to consider Lamar lukewarm in the
dispute with Lynch.
50. DeSantis, *Republicans Face the Southern Question*, 160–61; Halsell, "James
R. Chalmers," 44–45.
51. Lamar to E. D. Clark, May 25, 1880, in Lamar Papers, University of Mississippi Library. Lamar explained his failure to campaign in another district for
Ethelbert Barksdale because of illness in the family—meaning, presumably, his
wife. See Jackson (Miss.) *Weekly Clarion*, September 13, November 1, 1882.

counties—Marshall and Panola—which together gave Chalmers over 4,000 votes or nearly half the total number he received. The result in Marshall and Panola suggested that the fusion combination between blacks and the Democratic establishment was for the moment in abeyance. This was further indicated by the fact that black Republicans ran their own candidate, Ham C. Carter, and at the same time Blanche K. Bruce apparently gave the nod to Chalmers. Corruption of the Negro vote was also widely reported and Democrats unsuccessfully challenged the Independent's victory in a long drawn out legal dispute which continued until June 25, 1884, when Chalmers was seated.[52]

Throughout the state in 1882 an anti-Democratic coalition of white Republicans, Greenbackers, dissident Democrats, and Negroes protested against the ruling clique. Chalmers, running as an Independent, and Republican Elza Jeffords won election to Congress; thirteen counties of seventy-four in the state voted against the Democrats. The election was the strongest challenge to Democrats since reconstruction.

Chastened by the Independent's strong challenge, Lamar returned to the second session of the Forty-seventh Congress prepared for the first time in months to carry out the normal obligations of his position. He voted regularly throughout the session; and while he made only one speech, it was a carefully prepared discourse on the tariff. The tariff question dominated Congress for the first time since Lamar's return to national politics, and thus afforded him an unworn issue on which to make his mark. The only other prominent aspect of the session which concerned Lamar was the debate over the civil service reform bill of 1882, a subject about which he had had no previous opportunity to register an opinion. Otherwise, Congress proved uneventful, without important voting on measures of economic importance to Mississippi or protracted debate on civil rights. In this sense Lamar concentrated less than usual on local matters and more on national affairs.

52. Halsell, "James R. Chalmers," 44, 49–53. Voting figures provided by Political Research Consortium.

Early in December, soon after Congress convened, the question of civil service reform came to a head. The pressure of public opinion and the beating which the Republicans suffered in the by-elections of 1882 caused Arthur to recommend remedial action.[53] Although Lamar favored bringing reform legislation up for consideration, the Republican majority was in a position to write the law, and he made no speeches.[54] Once the amending process began, however, he seemed worried about the political use that the dominant Republican party might make of the supposedly professional civil service system. He accordingly voted for a series of schemes calculated to give Democrats protection from a permanently locked-in Republican government bureaucracy. Failing to gain such absolute assurance, he accepted prohibition of campaign contributions from civil servants and voted for passage. The much amended bill proved, as much as anything else, that Congress cared quite as much about party considerations as about reform. In the end Lamar's vote for passage did not distinguish him as a reformer, and the mutilated bill became law with bipartisan support.[55]

Political exigencies of 1882 also forced Congress to consider the tariff. A Tariff Commission, appointed by Arthur in 1882, returned its recommendations, and serious effort at revision began for the first time since the Civil War. Despite mounting criticism, however, the protectionists held desperately to their system, and long debate and manipulation for special interests followed. Lamar had always favored a low tariff and he rose to speak for downward revision on February 7, 1883, after consideration of the matter had already dragged on since early December.

The tariff speech constituted Lamar's most carefully prepared effort after a long unproductive period in the Senate. The result was remarkably representative of Lamar's ability to combine ar-

53. Ari Hoogenboom, *Outlawing the Spoils: A History of The Civil Service Reform Movement, 1865-1883* (Urbana, 1961), 236-37; Howe, *Chester A. Arthur,* 207.

54. *Senate Journal,* 47th Cong., 2nd Sess., 82, 110.

55. *Ibid.,* 123, 128, 137-38, 140; Hoogenboom, *Outlawing the Spoils,* 238-47.

guments and to absorb and rationalize apparently conflicting economic policies. Nowhere is his peculiar blend of Whiggery (as seen in his position on internal improvements) and agrarian Democratic philosophy more perceptible. The low tariff position established the limit of Lamar's economic nationalism and showed that men of his conviction could not fit into the mold cast for them by industrial minded "New Departure" Republicans. Lamar had favored a positive government role in internal improvements and railroad subsidies; but he could not countenance support of manufacturing through a protective tariff, or the taxation which a tariff in effect levied against the farmer and consumer.

This movement to the farmer's side, inconsistent as it was with industrial nationalism, marked a partial resolution of another of the ideological tensions in Lamar's career. During the currency debate of the 1870s he had been embarrassed by the discrepancy between his own commitment to hard money and Mississippi's pathetic demand for inflation. Happily, Democratic tradition and Mississippi's economic need now coincided to place Lamar in an unassailable political position. A new confidence must have been apparent as he stood before Congress "striking in appearance . . . with a massive head set upon broad and slightly stooping shoulders," [56] his presence belying his fifty-eight years and poor health. His speech rang with renewed assurance and well-being.

Lamar sought to confound his opponents by serving up a generous portion of the agrarian myth as a foil against the protective system and a manufacturing economy in general. Perhaps recalling Solitude plantation on the Tallahatchie, he declared that "there is an instinctive tendency in the Anglo-Saxon blood to landowning. This instinct gives to agriculture a social dignity and personal independence which compensate for its meager profits. . . . The magic of the freehold is more potent than that

56. New York *Times*, February 8, 1883.

of wages of hire. The thrilling associations of the homestead, where wife and children live in security and peace and love, cannot be measured by a scale of dollars and cents." [57]

Lamar's sometime companions, the economic nationalists, really should not have been surprised. Such a comment betrayed idle romanticism less than it reflected Mississippi's continuing agrarian emphasis. The state's largest manufacturing interests included lumber mills, cotton goods, woolen goods, oil, cotton-seed, and cake mills; and these were small and could profit little from a protective tariff. Its aggregate assets in manufacturing industries in 1890 had reached only $14,896,884. The industrial lag was remarkable even among southern states. Economically speaking, Mississippi remained but a poor relative of the "New South." [58]

Lamar mischievously tweaked Republicans about the failure of their protective system to make manufacturing truly independent and self-sufficient. Citing copious evidence provided by the Tariff Commission, he remarked that tax supported industries "are not really industries, but . . . branches of the public service, as much as the army and navy." [59] He then launched into the kind of scholarly review of tariff literature which could cause Henry Watterson to call him "the biggest brained of all the men I have met in Washington." [60] He piled up past and contemporary authorities and concluded that history, economic theory, public opinion, and common sense all decreed a reduction in tariff duties: "Sir, I warn the manufacturers of this country. The handwriting is upon the wall . . . and I trust that they will have the intelligence to comprehend its import." [61]

57. Congressional Record, 47th Cong., 2nd Sess., 2184–94. Lamar also owned a small farm in Mississippi where he planned to retire. See Halsell, "L. Q. C. Lamar's Taylor Farm," 185–96.

58. Eleventh Census, Manufacturing Industry (1890), 482–84.

59. Congressional Record, 47th Cong., 2nd Sess., 2184–94.

60. Henry Watterson, Marse Henry: An Autobiography (New York, 1919), II, 20–21.

61. Congressional Record, 47th Cong., 2nd Sess., 2184–94. Though Lamar did not vote on passage, he consistently voted for reductions whenever he was present.

If Lamar intended the tariff address to herald a comeback on the political scene, he had no call for disappointment. The New York *Times* called it "The Most Striking Effort of the Session on the Tariff Question" and resurrected the faded image of a reticent Lamar who purposely held aloof from debate except on great occasions.[62]

Even more complimentary, the southern press soon began a movement for Lamar as a vice-presidential candidate. The Memphis *Daily Appeal* went so far as to demand his nomination as the South's due recognition for "a generation of silence and subserviency." [63] Throughout September and October, 1883, the *Appeal* reprinted a series of articles advocating this position. Some months later the proud Aberdeen (Mississippi) *Tri-Weekly Examiner* even recommended the famous Mississippian for the presidency.[64]

Amidst praise reminiscent of earlier glory Lamar spent a quiet summer and fall in Mississippi. Since it was one of those rare nonpolitical seasons, he should have rested with unaccustomed ease. The governor had been elected for a four-year term in 1881; Lamar himself had been reelected for six years in 1882, and the threat of the Independents would be quiet in his district at least until Chalmers came up for reelection in 1884. The contining decline of his wife's health, however, hung pall-like over Lamar's spirits and over his career. He returned to Washington in December, 1883, but woefully neglected his duties in the Senate, while Mrs. Lamar remained at home in the family's care.[65]

During the Forty-eighth Congress, Lamar did what he could to promote the policies he favored. Ironically he was appointed

62. New York *Times*, February 8, 1883. Jackson (Miss.) *Clarion*, February 14, 21, 1883, reprinted a series of complimentary articles gleaned from the contemporary press.

63. Memphis *Daily Appeal*, September 25, 1883.

64. *Ibid.*, September 3, 11, 21, 23, 25, 30, October 2, 5, 9, 1883. Aberdeen (Miss.) *Tri-Weekly Examiner*, March 3, 1884.

65. Jackson (Miss.) *Clarion*, January 7, 1885.

to a committee supposedly dedicated to government economy—
the Civil Service and Retrenchment Committee.[66] He nevertheless continued to support prodigious government spending in all
areas from the most insignificant to major grants such as the
Mexican War pension bill and aid to common schools.[67]

Lamar also continued his advocacy of government assistance
for private enterprise. He supported a right-of-way through the
Indian Territory for the Southern Kansas Railroad; aid for the
Atlantic and Pacific Railroad against threatened forfeiture of
land grants; an appropriation to encourage a domestic silk industry; and the establishment of a federal bureau of animal industry. He likewise favored maximum internal improvement appropriations and the mildly nationalistic Interstate Commerce
Commission Act which gave the federal government increased
authority over trade.[68]

Lamar's expanding view of the federal government's responsibilities combined with sectional interest in a curious way in the
Blair bill to provide aid for public schools. In his only important
speech in the Forty-eighth Congress, Lamar put his support of
the Blair bill in a southern context and for a good reason. The
appropriation would be distributed among the states according
to their number of illiterates, and the South might thereby receive as much as two thirds of the total grant.

For this aid Lamar and the southerners who agreed with him
were willing to overlook the bill's Republican sponsorship and
its obviously partisan overtones. The Republicans meant to
spend money on a good cause while, at the same time, ridding
the country of a treasury surplus which they found embarrass-
ing. If the treasury could be depleted then arguments for high
tariff, vital to the Republican program, could be advanced with
some cogency. If, however, a spending scheme such as the Blair
bill were not approved then the low tariff advocates could claim

66. He also served on the Judiciary and Railroad Committees. See *Senate
Journal*, 48th Cong., 1st Sess., 65–66
67. *Ibid.*, 209, 212, 298, 443, 479–80, 493, 830.
68. *Ibid.*, 813, 908–909, 596–97, 665–66, 863, 878; 2nd Sess., 479, 228.

that the treasury surplus removed all justification for high rates. Lamar stood as always for a low tariff, but he did not hesitate to make the best of the Republicans' dilemma.[69]

In this instance Lamar did not make reconciliation the main point of his speech. He concentrated on the fiscal inability of southern states to provide the common school education needed for equality with other sections of the nation. And while including both races in his plea for educational funds, Lamar emphasized the particular requirements of the freedmen. If his support of education for Negroes was sincere and not only a rhetorical appeal to northern sympathies, Lamar reached a high plane of statesmanship that day. He prophetically contended that the education bill would be the most effective measure ever taken by the federal government in support of the freedmen—more so than the wartime amendments. "The problem of race," he said, "in a large part is the problem of illiteracy. Most of the evils, most of the difficulties which have grown up out of that problem have arisen from a condition of ignorance, prejudice, and superstition." Because education would remove these difficulties, he would "go with those who will go farthest in this matter." [70]

While seeking federal money for such a commendable use, Lamar claimed that the funds should be administered by local authorities rather than by the national government. As in all instances involving home rule, he insisted upon local control. Federal administration, he contended, would amount to a declaration of distrust in the South and would lead to discrimination against the white race in favor of the Negroes. But if federal financing be combined with local autonomy, Lamar argued, then such spending would promote national unity; the government's program would stand as an expression of goodwill and would advance the cause of sectional reconciliation. The result would be a happy combination: federal spending, educational

69. Allen J. Going, "The South and the Blair Education Bill," *Mississippi Valley Historical Review*, XLIV (September, 1957), 267; C. Vann Woodward, *Origins of the New South* (Baton Rouge, 1951), 63–64.

70. *Congressional Record*, 48th Cong., 1st Sess., 2368–71. See also *ibid.*, 2470, for further comment by Lamar.

benefits, a reconstructed union, and southern autonomy. When the legislation finally passed the Senate with strong southern support, state control of funds and segregated schools were in fact permitted, but the House refused even to consider the measure.[71]

The political and economic context of Lamar's remarks on the Blair bill obviously raise the question of real motivation. All that he said of the need for aid to black and white education rang true. But the question permits a less flattering interpretation. Federal support for white and black education was sorely needed in the poor southern states; and at the same time education, unlike the franchise, did not seem an immediate or direct threat to white supremacy. Thus the South could afford to share the funds with the freedmen. And of course Lamar knew that federal aid without federal supervision would accrue to the whites more than to the Negro.[72]

Actually Lamar's motives were not exclusively humanitarian or exclusively political. The duality which often characterized his attitude toward Negro rights and the desire for home rule and economic relief for the South again prevailed. He did want to assist in the effort to educate both blacks and whites and apparently held the belief that education might correct many of the social evils of the time. He also insisted upon control of funds by the white Democratic governments with the almost certain knowledge that this control would treat the Negro unfairly, at least to some extent. In his mind these positions were not contradictory.

The issue of the South's right to freedom from political intervention played a more obvious role in Lamar's endless fight against supervision of southern elections and in his defense of former Confederates against government reprisal. To this end he unsuccessfully opposed investigation of alleged election ir-

71. *Ibid.*, 2368–71; Going, "Blair Education Bill," 272–75

72. The bill allowed separate education facilities for white and Negro so long as no discrimination resulted. See Woodward, *Origins of the New South*, 63. Southern senators, Democratic and Republican, provided the bill's main support in the Senate. Black Belt leadership was most enthusiastic for the bill. See Going, "The South and the Blair Education Bill," 288–89.

regularities in Mississippi and Virginia in 1883 and voted against amending the Mexican War pension to exclude persons disabled in Confederate service.[73] On January 12, 1885, he once again spoke in defense of Jefferson Davis against the perennially repeated charge of treason and conspiracy and against the rather academic contention that Davis had intended suppressing any state which might have attempted to secede from the Confederate States of America.[74] For the most part these were old issues rehashed. Lamar's southernism had become rather monotonous.

The most vital matter before Congress during these days was not legislative. The approaching presidential election overshadowed all such questions, and despite personal difficulties Lamar took a keen interest. He reacted with pleasure when he heard of the nomination of James G. Blaine by the Republicans and affirmed to a friend that "as far as I am personally concerned I 'couldn't have been better suited if called upon to arbitrate at Chicago.' "[75] The relationship between Lamar and the Republican standard-bearer who had often befriended the South was warm enough to convince Blaine that "Mr. Lamar will see that I get a fair count in Mississippi." The politically astute John Lynch knew better and replied that Lamar " 'would not if he could and could not if he would, secure a fair count in Mississippi. The State will be returned against you.' "[76]

The gathering of the Democratic party at Chicago affected Lamar more directly. An enthusiastic home town paper, the Oxford *Falcon*, reported that Lamar himself would make an ideal presidential candidate and regretted that the sectional issue ex-

73. *Senate Journal*, 48th Cong., 1st Sess., 230, 816.

74. *Congressional Record*, 48th Cong., 2nd Sess., 627; Lamar to Jefferson Davis, February 28, 1885, in Louisiana Historical Association Collection: Jefferson Davis Collection, Tulane University Library.

75. Lamar to S. A. Jonas, June 15, 1884, in S. A. Jonas Papers.

76. Conversation quoted in Lynch, *The Facts of Reconstruction*, 224–25. Lynch did not intend this as an indictment, since he reflected that "to expect any ambitious man to make such a sacrifice as this was contrary to human nature."

cluded him.[77] Presumably admitting to his disqualification, Lamar actively supported Thomas Bayard of Delaware just as he
had in 1880.[78] Lamar had doubts that Bayard could carry the
convention, however, and believed that some Democratic senators would oppose him. Grover Cleveland, he thought, would
make the "strongest man could he get the nomination," but opposition among the New York Irish might make that difficult.
The prospect of Cleveland as president did not satisfy him completely even if the Irish could be silenced. He regretted that
the "Southern section . . . is practically ineligible to [sic] the
presidency"; and "northern men are incapable of leadership." [79]
Nevertheless, when Cleveland carried the convention Lamar announced at a reception in Oxford that the nomination was the
best possible under the circumstances. He seemed eager for the
contest, went right to work on Blaine, and then "had a friendly
handshaking all around." [80]

Early in October Lamar launched a vigorous campaign. He
and other Democrats meant not only to work in Cleveland's behalf but also to redeem Lamar's congressional district from Independent James R. Chalmers. Congressional candidate James B.
Morgan joined with Lamar, Governor Lowry, E. C. Walthall,
and ex-Congressman Manning at Holly Springs on October 6
to open the battle. In a long speech, variations of which he repeated throughout the canvass, Lamar attacked the opposition
on all fronts. He singled out corruption, election interferences,
and financial assessments on federal employees by Republicans,
and praised Cleveland as a reformer who would correct the mess
in government. In this and in speeches which followed, Lamar
addressed himself to the farmers with more care than usual. The
high tariff and taxes, he said, were hurting Mississippi's economy. Although manufacturing held a place of importance within
the state, agriculture must continue to come first. A protective

77. Oxford (Miss.) *Falcon*, February 7, May 17, 1884.
78. Lamar to Thomas Bayard, n.d., 1884, quoted in Tansill, *Thomas Francis Bayard*, 321–22.
79. Lamar to S. A. Jonas, June 15, 1884, in S. A. Jonas Papers.
80. Oxford (Miss.) *Falcon*, July 26, 1884.

tariff only served manufacturing interests and the monopolies while oppressing the masses. Intending to offset the appeal of Chalmers' Independents and Republicans who solicited the Negro vote, Lamar warned white men to stand together for safety and civilization. At the same time he denied any intention of disfranchising the Negro or any ill will toward the black race. Whites must stand together, he said, because the Negro's ignorance made him vulnerable to exploitation.[81]

The results of the campaign, unlike that of 1882, reflected the all out effort of the Democrats. Cleveland carried the state by almost 64 percent of the vote, and the party carried every congressional district. The Independent movement had been extinguished in its infancy. Every county but one in Lamar's district returned Democratic majorities; Chalmers won only Panola. The appeal to the farmer's interest and to racial solidarity, besides the large turnout normally associated with a presidential race, effectively reversed the trend of two years earlier. Republican appeal again carried ten counties (only nine of the thirty-nine black counties) despite fusion and other Democratic tactics, but this showing did little to dampen Democratic elation. Lamar must have once again considered the congressional district and the state to be his own.[82]

Before the jubilation in Oxford completely subsided, Lamar suffered a terrible personal loss. On December 29, 1884, Virginia Longstreet Lamar, his wife of almost forty years, died of the lung disease which had tormented her since 1880. The blow was devastating. Even in his most triumphant hours Lamar's life seemed dogged by tragedy.[83]

81. Memphis *Daily Appeal*, October 7, 14, 22, 25, 26, 30, 1884; Jackson (Miss.) *Clarion*, October 22, 1884.

82. Election figures provided by Political Research Consortium.

83. Jackson (Miss.) *Clarion*, January 17, 1885.

Cabinet, Court, and Reunion

News came first from John B. Gordon who telegraphed Lamar: "Thank God! Cleveland is elected. Turn the rascals out." [1] As confirming reports arrived from other sources, Democrats looked forward to a new era. A quarter of a century of waiting for the highest office in the land had whetted their taste for victory.

Gordon proved accurate, if somewhat over sanguine, in his belief that a new age had dawned. In Congress, Republican numbers and conscience had already suffered as the old radicals died off. Perhaps this, even more than Cleveland's election, showed the weariness of northern voters with issues born of war time. "Bloody shirt" tactics would reappear and sometimes succeed, but still the atmosphere had changed. No pretense of success remained for the reconstruction program as conceived by the abolitionists. The haggard protective policy of the federal government toward the freedmen would certainly be further eroded, and all hope of winning national elections with southern help seemed lost to the Republicans. It made little impact and not much sense thereafter either to harangue against the party of treason and slavery or to suggest that Confederates in office would somehow subvert the national will.

These implications were obvious enough for white southern Democrats. They knew that Cleveland's victory would end effective hostility emanating from Washington and that south-

---

1. John Gordon to Lamar, n.d., quoted in Mayes, *Lamar*, 460.

erners might again participate in the executive branch of government and prove their loyalty to the union. Southerners or persons not unfriendly to the South would control vital executive agencies such as the Justice Department, which supervised elections, and the War Department, with its control over troop deployment. There could be little doubt about it since the South gave Grover Cleveland 107 of his total 219 electoral votes with not a single vote going to James G. Blaine.[2]

L. Q. C. Lamar became an instrument and symbol of the new order which returned former Confederates to hitherto proscribed areas of government. He joined Cleveland's cabinet as Secretary of Interior and remained there three years relatively unchallenged as evidence of the South's regained national stature.

Ironically he proved more durable than the Democratic hold on the presidency. The 1888 elections unseated Cleveland and placed the Republicans in control of both houses of Congress. Meanwhile Lamar had become, after a hard confirmation struggle in 1888, a justice of the Supreme Court of the United States— the first Confederate to gain a place on that last unbreached Republican stronghold. Thus he survived the Democratic defeat and still served on the Court when Cleveland regained the presidency in 1892.

Lamar's achievement could not be undone by an election. As secretary and justice he represented the permanent installation of the Democratic South as a participant in the highest reaches of government, and he lived as proof that Confederate antecedents were not an insurmountable disqualification. And just as importantly, his conduct in these offices embodied the terms upon which the sectional conflict had reached this advanced stage of settlement. Lamar's presence, after his Court confirmation in 1888, created no stir. He seemed altogether compatible with the temper of the time. Occasional resurgence of sectional

2. Svend Petersen, *A Statistical History of the American Presidential Elections* (New York, 1968), 52–53. Mississippi voted 63.75 percent for Cleveland. The New York *Tribune*, December 12, 1884, quoted Lamar as saying that the Cleveland administration would be the first friendly to the South since the Civil War.

disputes notwithstanding, reunion had become an accomplished fact in the cabinet and on the Court.

The Cleveland years also marked a new era for Lamar personally. Appointment to the executive and judicial branches of government separated him from the political base of support he had maintained for thirty years in Mississippi. In a spirit tempered by resolution, he admitted to Jefferson Davis in 1885 "that it puts a terminus to my political career." [3] And the chances were of course very good then, as he told E. C. Walthall, that "I close my career in Congress, and will go into private life at the close of four years, perhaps sooner." [4] Since Lamar was sixty years old in 1885 and had no real financial security to cushion his retirement, this posed an important consideration. Still ambition and habit of service to party and section were decisive, and Lamar did not hesitate to accept a new and uncertain status in place of security and familiarity. [5]

Immediately after the Democratic victory in 1885 Lamar entered into the discussions concerning the appointment of Cleveland's cabinet. He gave qualified recommendations for several southerners including Augustus Garland of Arkansas and John B. Gordon of Georgia. [6] But, as he explained to Garland, " an active support of one friend on such an occasion as this is apt to involve an ungracious disservice to another friend." [7] His unstinted support went to his friend and ally in Mississippi, Ed-

3. Lamar to Jefferson Davis, February 28, 1885, in Louisiana Historical Association Collection: Jefferson Davis Collection.

4. Lamar to E. C. Walthall, February 3, 1885, quoted in Mayes, *Lamar*, 469–70.

5. Savannah (Ga.) *Morning News*, January 17, 1888, cited an interview with E. C. Walthall who estimated Lamar's worth at $15,000 to $20,000. Aberdeen (Miss.) *Tri-Weekly Examiner*, February 6, 1884, called Lamar a poor man incumbered by old debts. See Halsell, "L. Q. C. Lamar's Taylor Farm," 185–96, for an account of Lamar's retirement plans and his Mississippi farm. The extent of Lamar's investments is not known; but see John B. Gordon to Lamar, October 1, 1881, in Lamar-Mayes Papers.

6. Lamar to A. H. Garland, November 15, 1884, in Grover Cleveland Papers, Manuscript Division, Library of Congress; Lamar to Grover Cleveland, January 1, 1885, *ibid.*; Lamar to Cleveland, February [6?], 1885, *ibid.*

7. Lamar to A. H. Garland, November 15, 1884, *ibid.*

ward Cary Walthall. He declared that "if Mr. Cleveland will put Walthall in his cabinet, he would link me to his administration by a bond as strong as steel and as soft as silk." [8] However, Lamar's support of the little-known Walthall and lukewarm advocacy of Garland and Gordon probably masked personal aspirations. He feigned indifference to friends, but when Cleveland decided upon him for the Interior Department, he immediately accepted.[9]

The appointment made good political sense. Cleveland needed representation from the South for geographical balance, and, in fact, he appointed his attorney general from the same area. Also, on a number of major issues including currency, the tariff, and civil service reform, Lamar and Cleveland were in absolute agreement. These shared views, combined with Lamar's reputation for moderation on sectional issues, made him palatable to the northern wing of the party. There were, of course, drawbacks to Lamar's appointment, and Cleveland might have avoided criticism had he chosen someone not identified with secession and the Confederacy. Questions were also raised about Lamar's capacity for an administrative post and especially for the Interior portfolio. He had no experience to speak of, and the Republican press also noted Lamar's absentmindedness and reputed disdain of detail work. These shortcomings notwithstanding, confirmation followed without difficulty.[10]

After taking office Lamar turned first to the question of appointments. As a congressman he had espoused reform in government. Cleveland had campaigned in a similar vein, and the

8. Lamar to Mr. [?] Bates, December 18, 1884, *ibid.*; Burton N. Harrison to Lamar, February 16, 1885, quoted in Mayes, *Lamar*, 471.

9. Lamar to E. C. Walthall, February 3, 1885, quoted in Mayes, *Lamar*, 469–70; Lamar to "My Dear Sister" [Mrs. M. A. Ross], February 14, 1885, quoted *ibid.*, 470; Lamar to Grover Cleveland, February 21, 1885, in Grover Cleveland Papers.

10. Mobile (Ala.) *Daily Register*, March 7, 1885; New York *Times*, March 6, 1885. Cleveland doubtless knew, as perhaps the newspapers did, that Lamar's absences and his distractedness resulted partially from disturbing difficulties at home. In fact it is unlikely that Lamar could have been considered for a cabinet position except for the death of his wife just after the presidential election.

two men happily agreed that civil service reform should be of primary importance in the Interior Department. From the first, however, Lamar found the pressure for jobs from long-deprived Democrats irresistible. On March 10, 1885, a few days after taking over his department, he wrote: "I am nearly drowned in an inundation of ink . . . from all parts of the country." [11] And the evidence certainly sustains his charge; in fact, the first several months were given over largely to appointments. The new secretary moreover was not entirely unsympathetic to personnel changes. "The thirst for a general 'turn out' all over the country is almost fearful," he wrote. "The proscription and intolerance of the Republican party . . . are constant provocations . . . and I cannot blame the feverishness of our people for a change under such circumstances." [12]

Civil service reform, even so far as politically desirable, proved difficult. Lamar struggled against the endless demand for offices and refused applicants over and over again. He also sought to maintain publicly the standards professed by Cleveland and the party.[13] In numerous letters to Carl Schurz, interior secretary under Hayes and self-appointed gadfly, Lamar explained his appointments and justified his actions. He claimed to be cooperating fully in the administration of the civil service law and told Schurz a year and a half after he took office that "I am to-day surrounded with men of the opposite party . . . and have retained them against the protest of my personal and political friends." "Moreover, the fact that the great body of the clerical force is still Republican is due not so much to the compulsory power of the law as to a sincere cooperation with its intent and purpose." [14]

Expectant southerners pressed especially hard. Requests came

11. Lamar to Mr. Pope Barrow, March 10, 1885, in Letterbook I, Lamar-Mayes Papers.

12. Lamar to Brevet Maj. General G. Pennypacker, July 11, 1885, *ibid.*

13. *E.g.*, Lamar to Dorman B. Eaton, Chairman, Civil Service Commission, quoted in New York *Times*, July 30, 1885.

14. Lamar to Carl Schurz, October 2, 1886, in Carl Schurz Papers, Manuscript Division, Library of Congress. But he admitted to Schurz that he had in instances yielded to the importunities of political friends.

from every conceivable source including acquaintances and innumerable family connections throughout the South. To a
"Cousin," Lamar painfully wrote: "I confess to you a reluctance
towards appointing my own relatives to office. It is proper to
state here that the applications from this source are numerous
and distressing to me." [15] Other requests came from southern
"ladies" who were down on their luck and asked for clerical jobs
in Washington. Once more Lamar demurred, saying that the
work was really not suitable for persons of gentle southern background and that "I am troubled to death by their constant revolt from the authority of their superiors." [16]

Lamar compromised—as did the entire Cleveland administration—before these supplications. He dismissed Republican officials to make way for Democrats and even appointed members
of his immediate family to office. Most notably, he named his
thirty-two-year-old son, L. Q. C. Jr., as his personal stenogra-
pher.[17] He also assisted southern women on occasion, as for example when he wrote Miss Kitty Carr of Georgia, saying "oh, no,
Miss Kitty: I have not forgotten you by any means," and "*I have
not been able to forget you*. I have got from Mr. Vilas a place for
you, and a pretty good one." [18]

The importance of Lamar's appointive power did not stop
with paupers and poor relations. He also assisted southern party
leaders who urged the placement of large numbers of Democrats in office. In this he tried to move cautiously so as not to

15. Lamar to "Cousin," May 13, 1885, in Letterbook I, Lamar-Mayes Papers.
Presumably the burden of kinship increased when Lamar remarried into an
old Georgia family with the innumerable connections which that implied. The
second Mrs. Lamar was the widow of William Holt, late president of the
Southwestern Railroad Company. See Mayes, *Lamar*, 507.
16. Lamar to Mrs. R. R. [Grasty?], October 2, 1885, in Letterbook I, Lamar-
Mayes Papers.
17. Lamar to Kate [his daughter-in-law], May 16, 1885, *ibid.* Young Lamar
also served on occasion as special Indian agent. See Lamar, Jr., to Lamar, July
19, 1886, in Letterbook III, *ibid.*; and Lamar to Senator George G. Vest, June
26, 1885, in Letterbook I, *ibid.* There is almost no information on Lamar's
relationship to his children except during these years in the interior department. He seemed then to be considerably burdened financially by their needs.
18. Lamar to Miss Kitty Carr, June 1, 1885, in Letterbook I, *ibid.*

excite suspicion or to offend the civil service reformers. He wrote
Wade Hampton in South Carolina explaining his position: "But
you must give me time. I do not want to hurry southern appointments, especially when they involve removals of northern
men." [19] And he asked Mississippi party leader and friend E. C.
Walthall to carefully select men for jobs as "you know we profess, and, I think, sincerely, to make appointments with reference to the competency of the agents and employees of the
government." [20]

Lamar gave particular attention to the needs of the Mississippi Democratic organization. Indeed the first assistant secretary, Henry L. Muldrow, was a Mississippian and a former Confederate colonel. Generally, however, he followed his practice of
many years and left most details to others closer to the local situation. His chief instrument in this was Walthall, whom he had
successfully promoted as his successor in the senate and as head
of the Lamar wing of the Democratic state organization. In a
letter of May 28, 1885, Lamar wrote that he would make no
appointments in Mississippi save those desired by Walthall, and
that he would intercede with Postmaster General William Vilas
in Post Office appointments.[21]

Lamar had in the past enhanced his political position in Mississippi by cooperating with Negro Republican leaders. He continued to do this through appointments within the Interior Department's Washington staff and other nonsouthern posts. His
agents in this matter were Republican state leaders John R.
Lynch and Blanche K. Bruce. According to Lynch, Lamar offered him a post as special agent of public lands in the West
with the single condition that Lynch not embarrass the Democratic administration by becoming conspicuously active against
the government. When Lynch declined the offer, Lamar accepted

19. Lamar to Wade Hampton, March 10, 1885, *ibid.* See also Lamar to H. S.
Van Eaton, September 11, 1885, *ibid.*
20. Lamar to "My Dear General" [Walthall], May 28, 1885, *ibid.*
21. *Ibid.* Lamar asked E. D. Clark to be assistant secretary, but his reply is
unknown. See Lamar to Clark, n.d.; Lamar to Clark, March 2, 1885; and Clark
to Mrs. Clark, n.d., in Lamar Papers, University of Mississippi Library.

his proposal to retain a number of Negro clerks in office instead. Lamar took exception to only two of Lynch's recommendations: a Negro man married to a white woman and a white man married to a Negro woman. In these cases the political danger seemed too great for Lamar.[22]

Lamar finally turned from the "inundation of ink" to the proper business of the Interior Department. Responsibility, of course, rested ultimately with the president, who determined overall policy and appointed the department's division heads (bureaus of land, patents, pensions, and Indian affairs). Lamar approached the Interior Department's expansive structure through this bureaucratic framework.

The Pension Bureau presented one of the toughest and politically most important situations. Opponents of Lamar's appointment had professed horror that Union veterans should be dependent upon a Confederate secretary.[23] Neither the Democratic administration nor Lamar, the advocate of reconciliation, could afford that kind of criticism. Cleveland had to prove the loyalty of the Democratic party to the Union veterans, and Lamar wanted to demonstrate the South's goodwill in acceptance of the postwar settlement.

Actually Lamar's record gave no cause for alarm. In Congress he had stood aloof of southern attacks on pension bills; and he had forcefully endorsed a retirement pension for U. S. Grant. Cleveland further neutralized charges of indifference to veterans by naming a Union veteran, John C. Black, commissioner of pensions. As a reformer Black eliminated hundreds of fraudulent applications. Meanwhile Cleveland vetoed congressional efforts to extend the pension privilege to veterans with as little as three months service and rejected over two hundred private pension bills. Lamar remained inconspicuous and probably inactive in this field. In the official *Annual Report* he projected a

22. Lynch, *The Facts of Reconstruction*, 235–50; Blanche K. Bruce in Boston *Herald*, January 28, 1893, quoted in Mayes, *Lamar*, 593.
23. New York *Times*, March 6, 1885.

politically desirable attitude of uncorrupted liberality toward
veterans.[24]

The Indian Bureau offered a much larger opportunity and
better illustrated the way in which a southern spokesman might
adapt his principles and experience outside his own province.
Unfortunately, however, the bureau had been pathetically mis-
managed in the past, and the new secretary had no special qualifi-
cations in this area and had shown no particular interest in Indians during his congressional tenure. Realizing this deficiency, he
turned for advice to men of more training—notably, the Senate
champion of a liberal Indian policy, Henry L. Dawes, and Herbert Welsh, secretary of the Indian Rights Association. To Dawes
he wrote: "I shall depend upon you largely in trying to do something for the Indians"; and to Welsh: "The only difficulty that
I see in the way [of reform] is my own want of familiarity with
the details of the best methods to accomplish this purpose." [25]

Years of concentration upon southern interests did not prepare
Lamar in any real sense for administering the Indian service, but
it did provide a political and intellectual orientation in problems of racial and cultural minority groups. Lamar thought that
he understood Negroes and that he had treated them justly in
matters of public policy. He turned to Indian affairs with pater-
nalistic benevolence nurtured by this concept of his experience
in the South. In retrospect, however, his approach to reservation
problems seemed much more generous than his record on Negro rights.

Lamar opposed the western policy of dissolving the reserva-
tions and opening tribal lands to homesteaders. He feared that
abuse of the Indian would result, and he compared prospects for

24. William Henry Glasson, *History of Military Pension Legislation in the
United States* (New York, 1900), 109, 123; *Interior Report* (1885), I, 56. Mayes,
Lamar, 497, credits Lamar with the choice of Black, but no other evidence of this
has come to light. The number and cost of pensions continued to increase through-
out the Cleveland years. See the tabulation provided by Glasson, *Military Pension
Legislation*, 133.

25. Lamar to Henry L. Dawes, November 13, 1885, in Letterbook I, Lamar-
Mayes Papers; Lamar to Herbert Welsh, April 16, 1885, *ibid.*

assimilation of the reservation population with the Negro's piti-
ful situation during reconstruction. Relying on that experience,
he couched his recommendations for caution and gradual change
in humanitarian terms. The reservation system, he believed,
must be continued until the Indian could reach an advanced
state of development.[26]

Lamar's scruples exceeded those of Congress and the general
public, but he persisted. He held the federal government ultimately responsible for the welfare of the reservation population
and opposed any relinquishment of power by national authorities. At first glance this attitude appears inconsistent with his
position on the southern Negro, whose control he had helped
remand to the local whites. But on the other hand, he had argued
eloquently for federal aid in educating the Negro for participation in American society. Of course the similarity of the two
problems was less real than apparent. As Lamar himself noted,
the Indian in no way presented a danger or an obstacle to be
removed. The problem was moral rather than political.[27]

In this patronizing context Lamar concluded that the Indian's
salvation required a drastic change in traditional policy. Assimilation should, he felt, be gradual and preceded by several conditions. The Indian ought first to accept the idea and habit of
individual property holding as opposed to tribal ownership; he
should become acquainted with English, arithmetic, and the
practical arts; and he should accept law as a substitute for superstition and force. Lamar recommended that a commission visit
the Indians and report on their needs in respect to these objectives. And he strongly urged that Congress in the meantime go
ahead with a general law for allotting reservation lands in severalty while the tribal organization remained intact. In his third

26. Lamar to Henry L. Dawes, November 13, 1885, *ibid.*; Lamar to John T.
Morgan, November 2, 1885, *ibid.*; *Interior Report* (1885), I, 24–27. Lamar's indefinite attitude toward the Indian while in Congress has been noted in a preceding chapter.

27. *Interior Report* (1885), I, 24. In his report Lamar struck a moralistic
note by referring to Helen Hunt Jackson's characterization of past policy as a
"century of dishonor."

and last *Annual Report* the secretary commended Congress for its passage of the Dawes Severalty Act. He also suggested as a further step toward assimilation that the question of compulsory education of Indian youths be considered.[28] In sum, his report offered a statesmanlike approach. Inevitably, and unanswerably, one wonders whether Lamar might have favored a program of planned rehabilitation for freedmen if it were not for the supreme political considerations in the reconstructed South.

Lamar's experience with territories and public lands resembled that with Indian policy in a number of ways. Here again, he lacked depth in practical training for the job. His interest had been confined to the question of slavery expansion prior to the Civil War and to railroad construction during the postbellum period. The latter provided certain insights but hardly amounted to a well-rounded education in territorial government.

Actually, the territories were almost free of direct control from Washington. Poor communications, political considerations, and lack of vital concern all combined to give territorial officials a virtually free hand, except for rare occasions when the secretary or the president wished to depart from this pattern. Lamar acted on more such occasions than previous secretaries. Here Cleveland left him considerable administrative freedom and encouraged his advice on legislation.[29]

Probably the most notable thing about Lamar's administration was his emergence as a conservationist. With certain exceptions arising from political and legal considerations, he departed from his long-time affinity with economic largess and federally stimulated laissez-faire and placed himself in the role of public guardian against these same principles.

In making this adjustment Lamar became much more nationalistic in terms of federal authority over local matters. During the

28. *Ibid.* (1886), I, 4–6; *ibid.*, (1887), I, 25–30.

29. Earl S. Pomeroy, *The Territories and the United States, 1861–1890* (Philadelphia, 1947), 23–27. For an example of this strong role, see Lamar to Thomas C. McRae, Committee of Public Lands, House of Representatives, April 5, 1886, in Letterbook II, Lamar-Mayes Papers.

antebellum period he had narrowly construed the government's authority over the territories, and after the Civil War he had always fought for unhampered home rule. In the Interior Department he initially pursued the home rule concept with consistency and appointed bona fide residents of the territories to high office. He quickly learned that residents were likely to favor more or less restrained development of natural resources by private enterprise. Faced with conflict between local autonomy and public interest, he moved toward the latter. With land, as with the Indian, Lamar believed that the federal government must retain a measure of authority in order to arrest exploitation.[30]

Lamar's program basically sought to conserve public lands and resources for the legitimate freeholder. He therefore became a staunch defender of the Homestead Act of 1862, which granted 160 acres from the public domain to any citizen or applicant for citizenship who occupied the land for five years. This law, offering easy acquisition of a single family sized farm, seemed to him the backbone of the land system, and he therefore opposed efforts to weaken it. At the same time he advised repeal of all other laws contrary to the spirit of the Homestead Act. Preemption laws, timber culture acts, cash-entry laws, and the desert-land law should all be discarded because of their susceptibility to fraud. To rectify past abuse of the land laws, Lamar and his even more aggressive land commissioner, William Andrew Jackson Sparks, handed down decrees to drive speculators and poachers off Indian lands and to remove unlawful enclosures of public domain.[31]

Lamar stated his case for land reform in terms of the demo-

30. *Interior Report* (1887), I, 20; Pomeroy, *The Territories and the United States*, 27, classifies Lamar with Carl Schurz as a true conservationist in contrast to the political minded secretaries such as Columbus Delano and Zachariah Chandler. Lamar also proposed legislation in support of national parks. See *Interior Report* (1886), I, 73–77; and *ibid.* (1887), I, 71 ff.

31. Lamar to Thomas C. McRae, Committee on Public Lands, House of Representatives, April 5, 1886, in Letterbook II, Lamar-Mayes Papers; *Interior Report* (1885), I, 33, 38–41; *ibid.* (1886), I, 30; *ibid.* (1887), I, 5–7. These reforms, it should be noted, were foreshadowed by the work of Secretary Schurz of the Hayes administration.

cratic virtues of small freeholding units as opposed to massive
exploitation of natural resources. The phraseology is striking by
comparison to Lamar's antebellum association with the cotton
aristocracy and postbellum sympathy for railroad corporations.
Equality, he now maintained, depended on the government's
success in controlling the land monopolies; for, "nothing can be
a surer safeguard in a free community against the dominating
influences of powerful corporations and combinations of capital
than a body of independent small land owners living upon their
own freeholds." [32]

Beset by opposition from vested interests and western congressmen, Congress refused to enact the legislation called for by
Lamar, and reform continued to be a purely administrative policy. The Interior Department nevertheless took vigorous action
through existing laws to restore vast areas of public domain. By
October, 1887, Lamar could boast reclamation of over forty-five
million acres, and the total might have gone even higher if he
had given the less cautious Commissioner Sparks free rein. [33]

A great deal of land was taken from western railroad corporations. The land commissioner's strategy against railroads called
for a suspension of land patents—which would have granted final
title—while the department investigated and Congress prepared
legislation for forfeiture. In this way he and Lamar sought to
prevent companies from claiming land for which they had not
fulfilled requirements laid down in the original grants. [34]

This policy most affected the transcontinental giants, especially the Atlantic and Pacific, the Northern Pacific, and Southern Pacific railroads. But the Interior Department did not limit
its actions to the trans-Mississippi area. In the South where La-

---

32. *Interior Report* (1887), I, 3. For another statement see *ibid.* (1885), I, 38.
Lamar had in fact made similar references to the noble yeoman in the antebellum Congress.

33. *Ibid.* (1887), I, 4.

34. Leslie E. Decker, "The Railroads and the Land Office: Administrative
Policy and the Land Patent Controversy, 1864–1896," *Mississippi Valley Historical
Review*, XLVI (March, 1960), 695–96; John B. Rae, "Commissioner Sparks and
the Railroad Land Grants," *ibid.*, XXV (September, 1938), 211–12.

mar had also worked for railroad expansion as a congressman, land patents of the New Orleans, Baton Rouge, and Vicksburg Railroad were suspended.[35]

Lamar and Sparks generally worked together for the reform of land policy until November, 1887. By that time it had become evident that Lamar was less zealous than Sparks and more concerned with legal precedents and political considerations. The difference in point of view became crucial when Lamar certified, despite Sparks's objection, 200,000 acres of land claimed by the Chicago, St. Paul, Minneapolis, and Omaha Railroad. Sparks refused to compromise and quit the department.[36]

Aside from Sparks's zeal, there is also reason to believe that he had become a political liability. Since Lamar would leave the cabinet for the Court in two months, he might have agreed to get rid of Sparks and thus to divert from Cleveland some of the criticism certain to come from Sparks's defenders.

By the time Lamar left the Interior Department in January, 1888, he had established a record as a reasonably competent secretary, and certainly he had done nothing to outrage northern opinion. He had given southern Democrats a piece of the pork barrel, but the civil service merit system had at least gotten a start. The Pension Bureau had dealt leniently with Union veterans, while many blatantly outrageous claims had been denied. And public resources had been secured to some degree by a conservation minded secretary.

In all these matters Lamar had shown a concern for reform and seems to have honored in general the pledges of the president. He also demonstrated a growing proclivity for extending the national government's responsibility for the execution of its laws. As a congressman his nationalism usually had been limited

35. *Interior Report* (1885), I, 43.
36. *Ibid.* (1887), I, 4; Lamar to W. A. J. Sparks, November 11, 1887, in New York *Times*, November 12, 1887; W. A. J. Sparks to Grover Cleveland, November 15, 1887, in New York *Times*, November 16, 1887; New York *Times*, November 13, 14, 15, 1887; Rae, "Commissioner Sparks and the Railroad Land Grants," 226–27; Harold Dunham, "Crucial Years of the General Land Office, 1875–1890," *Agricultural History*, II (April, 1937), 136–37.

to economic matters. In dealing with western rather than southern problems, however, he favored a patronizing federal government committed to the protection of the public's rights. Mercifully freed of the need to invoke states' rights in defense of the South, his Whiggish inclinations carried him further away from the antebellum compact theory of government and toward a type of nationalism becoming more and more characteristic of the late nineteenth century.

Lamar's bureaucratic encounter with nationwide issues provided a useful apprenticeship for the bench of the United States Supreme Court.[37] And there was ample justification for the appointment on other grounds. The deceased justice William B. Woods, whom Lamar succeeded, had resided in the South, and the section had had no other appointment since before the Civil War. Ironically, Woods was a Republican carpetbagger from Ohio who had marched with Sherman to the sea, and his presence in such a highly esteemed office offended many southerners. Therefore the selection of an individual like Lamar dramatically demonstrated the reunionist designs of the Democratic party. Finally, Lamar's constitutional views were not unlike Cleveland's own, and it could be argued that his congressional service and the legal duties of the Interior Department provided some of the needed preparation.

The appointment of the secretary also raised many legitimate questions and doubts. Lamar was somewhat advanced in age, his health was always fragile, and his legal background was not all that it might have been. Lamar had never served as a judge and

37. Two articles by Willie D. Halsell discuss in detail the questions of Lamar's Court appointment and his contribution on the Court. See Willie D. Halsell, "The Appointment of L. Q. C. Lamar to the Supreme Court," *Mississippi Valley Historical Review*, XXVIII (December, 1941); and "L. Q. C. Lamar, Associate Justice of the Supreme Court," *Journal of Mississippi History*, V (April, 1943). A somewhat different interpretation may be found in Arnold Paul, "Lucius Quintus Cincinnatus Lamar" in Leon Friedman and Fred Israel (eds.), *The Justices of the Supreme Court, 1789–1969* (New York, 1969), II, 1431–51. Another account is Samuel Sibley, *Georgia's Contribution to Law: The Lamars* (New York, 1948).

had not engaged in regular private practice since his early manhood. His experiences as a professor of law during the reconstruction era should have counted for something in theoretical law, but no one mentioned it during the discussion which surrounded his nomination to the Court.[38]

All things considered, the news was well received in June, 1887, when speculation about Lamar's appointment began. The press, including Republican papers, and the Republican-dominated Senate showed signs of satisfaction that a southern reconciliator would be honored. In a short time, however, pressures arising from the coming presidential election campaign—still a year off—caused partisans to launch an attack upon the administration. Republican newspapers, congressional leaders, and local party organizations turned against Lamar even before Cleveland placed his name before the Senate in December, 1887. The examination of Lamar's credentials by the Senate Judiciary Committee and by the press quickly deteriorated into a purely partisan exercise. Many Republican leaders damned Lamar, the South, and the Democratic party, claiming that all were tainted by treason.[39]

The attack became blatantly personal and vitriolic on one occasion. An article in the New York *Evening Post*, December 23, 1887, supported by a letter to the Judiciary Committee, charged Lamar with unethical conduct in office and with moral turpitude. The story clearly implied that Lamar had entered into an improper liaison with a Mrs. Mary McBride of Mississippi, and that he had favored her in obtaining jobs in the government printing office and in the Interior Department. The enterpris-

38. On the considerations surrounding Lamar's appointment see: Halsell, "The Appointment of L. Q. C. Lamar to the Supreme Court," *passim*. According to Meador, "Lamar and the Law at the University of Mississippi," 227, Lamar was the first justice to have had an academic background.

39. Halsell, "The Appointment of L. Q. C. Lamar to the Supreme Court," 400, 402–405; Lamar to Mrs. Kate Freeman, December 23, 1887, quoted in Mayes, *Lamar*, 525. Surveys of the Republican press by the following friendly newspapers also draw these conclusions about the changing nature of Republican reaction: New Orleans *Daily Picayune*, January 7, 1888; and Mobile *Daily Register*, January 14, 1888. See New York *Times*, December 23, 30, 1887.

ing Mrs. McBride then allegedly operated a Washington rooming house which she maliciously set on fire. She was arrested for her crime, but vowed that she would never be convicted, because of Lamar's influence. Happily for Lamar, Mrs. McBride wrote the Judiciary Committee denying the charges and contending that her benefactor in finding employment had in fact been a Mississippi Republican. The episode seems never to have caused serious difficulty.[40]

Usually the criticism proved less fanciful and more telling. Lamar's advanced age (sixty-two and at that time the second oldest appointee ever proposed) and lack of experience were cited; but mostly opponents charged political offenses arising from the sectional issue. His states' rights, secessionist, and Confederate careers all received comment along with his defense of important southern leaders such as Davis and Calhoun. It was also asserted that he had gained political office by fraud and intimidation, and that he opposed the franchise for Negroes—indeed that he opposed all the war amendments to the Constitution. As Secretary of Interior, Lamar had, it was claimed, failed to treat Union soldiers fairly while bestowing honor on former Secretary Jacob Thompson of Mississippi by lowering the flag to half mast when he died.[41]

Not all Republican correspondents with the Judiciary Committee opposed Lamar. An ex-postmaster of Mobile, Alabama, testified that he considered Lamar to be the most liberal man in the South, "a man who will take the broader and more national view of all questions that may arise than any Southern man with whom I am acquainted." [42] A former United States marshal in Mississippi echoed that sentiment.[43] In Tennessee, a judge fa-

40. J. W. Hubbard to Judge Edmunds, n.d., in Senate file relating to L. Q. C. Lamar's appointment to the Supreme Court, SEN50B–A3, Record Group No. 46; Mrs. Mary McBride to the Senate Judiciary Committee, January 9, 1888, *ibid.*; New York *Evening Telegram*, December 22, 1887, *ibid.*

41. SEN50B–A3, *passim.*

42. James E. Slaughter to George E. Edmunds (chairman), January 11, 1888, *ibid.*

43. J. H. Pierce (unaddressed), December 31, 1887, *ibid.*

vored confirmation on grounds of political expediency. Believing that Republicans would suffer in the South for Lamar's defeat, he commented that "the highest considerations of the public interest demand, in my judgment, his confirmation . . . and thereby advance the party's interest in this section of the country." [44] And outside the South, discretion in the Pensions Bureau yielded an assertion from a local official of the Grand Army of the Republic that Secretary Lamar "has always recognized the true Soldier." [45]

In balance, however, outspoken Republicans condemned Lamar and made clear their intention of seriously seeking his defeat in the Senate. Under this pressure Lamar decided to quit his Interior post. On January 7, 1888, he gave Cleveland his resignation with the explanation that he feared to embarrass the administration if he should remain in the government. Three days later the Judiciary Committee reported an adverse recommendation.[46]

The full Senate vote did not at first look much more promising. Membership at that time included thirty-seven Democrats, thirty-eight Republicans, and one Independent. Before the Senate went into executive session, however, it became apparent that party lines might not hold. Then when final action came on January 16, Republicans William M. Stewart of Nevada and Leland Stanford of California crossed over; H. H. Riddleberger, the Independent from Virginia, also voted with the Democrats. The breach in Republican discipline gave Lamar a thirty-two to twenty-eight victory.[47]

The critics had stung Lamar in reviling his broken and limited legal background. He wrote letters prior to the Senate's ac-

44. Honorable Eli Shelby Hammond, District Judge, United States Court-Western District of Tennessee to George Edmunds, December 27, 1887, *ibid.*

45. H. J. Crouch to Chairman of the Judiciary Committee, December 11, 1887, *ibid.*

46. Lamar to Grover Cleveland, January 7, 1888, in Grover Cleveland Papers; Cleveland to Lamar, January 7, 1888, *ibid.*; Mobile (Ala.) *Daily Register*, January 11, 1888.

47. New York *Times*, January 3, 9, 17, 1888; Mobile (Ala.) *Daily Register*, January 17, 1888. The *Daily Register*, January 21, 1888, suggests that the contest was not so close as it seemed and that other Republicans would have crossed party lines if it had been necessary to confirm Lamar.

tion telling friends of his feelings of inadequacy,[48] and indications of insecurity appeared later in his correspondence. After more than a year in office he wrote his lifelong friend Burton N. Harrison saying: "I would be an imposter . . . if I were to allow you to believe that I am doing any thing useful or with even moderate ability." [49] And to Justice Joseph Bradley he explained his failure to read an opinion in much the same tone: "I suspect my breakdown was somewhat due to a misgiving as to how it would be received. It is however the best I can do." [50] After discounting for characteristic modesty, Lamar's uncertainty seems real enough. The lack of confidence and stability of his early career, exacerbated by the bitter struggle for confirmation, returned to plague him. Stronger men might again shape his destiny; and in these circumstances the uncertain temperament would be no virtue.

Certain aspects of Lamar's Supreme Court record may reflect his uncertainty. He dissented from the opinion of the Court only thirteen times in four years of active service, and in only two instances did he dissent alone. Only Justice Samuel Blatchford, who never dissented at all, returned fewer contrary opinions. Equally striking is the fact that Lamar's opinions almost never provoked dissent from his colleagues. There were dissents on only four of his ninety-six decisions, and in at least two of those the difference of opinion was minor. This high level of agreement indicates that Lamar either sympathized entirely with the trend of the Court, or his colleagues' arguments completely overshadowed him. The lack of opposition to Lamar's opinions also suggests that he could have been assigned cases which evoked little discussion and thus probably were not of great consequence in the Court's history.[51]

48. Lamar to E. C. Walthall, July 30, 1887, quoted in Mayes, *Lamar*, 521; Lamar to Mrs. Kate Freeman, December 23, 1887, quoted, *ibid.*, 525; Lamar to Edward Mayes, December 13, 1887, quoted, *ibid.*, 541.
49. Lamar to Burton N. Harrison, April 11, 1889, cited in Halsell, "L. Q. C. Lamar, Associate Justice of the Supreme Court," 77.
50. Lamar to Justice Bradley, November 30, 1889, in Joseph P. Bradley Papers, New Jersey Historical Society, Newark.
51. For a comparative table (with totals slightly different from those of the

Lamar's diffidence may have reflected an exaggerated sense of awe, but it also indicated accord with the Court in certain large areas. His philosophy, wrought from years as congressman and bureaucrat, blended with that which had characterized the national judiciary since the 1880s. To a striking extent Lamar and the Court had taken similar approaches in the effort to resolve issues growing from the economic needs of the late nineteenth century.

The most obvious and least complicated agreement came in the field of internal improvements. Since his return to Congress in 1872 Lamar had always promoted governmental appropriations for transportation and other public services. The court had likewise moved steadily toward an unqualified acceptance of an expanded role for Congress in this field. Lamar and the other judges extended still further their common view and laid to rest, in *California v. Central Pacific Railroad* (1888), a constitutional question dating back to the early days of the Republic. In this decision the Court, with Justice Lamar concurring, definitely confirmed the government's right to build interstate highways and bridges.[52]

Similarly, Lamar's background determined the attitude he took in respect to the more complicated and relatively new question of property rights and interstate commerce regulation. As a powerful member of congressional railroad committees he had espoused generous subsidy programs for transportation enter-

---

present author) see Willard L. King, *Melville Weston Fuller: Chief Justice of the United States, 1888–1910* (New York, 1950), App. I, 340–41. See also Halsell, "L. Q. C. Lamar, Associate Justice of the Supreme Court," 76; and Charles Fairman, *Mr. Justice Miller and the Supreme Court 1862–1890* (Cambridge, 1939), 386. Lamar returned no decisions after May, 1892, although he continued as justice until January, 1893.

Albert Blaustein and Roy Mersky surveyed sixty-five scholars as a means of ranking justices from the founding of the court until the Nixon appointments. The survey gave twelve men status as "great," fifteen were listed as "near great," six as "below average," eight as "failures," and fifty-five were classified "average." Lamar was one of the "average" performers. See Albert P. Blaustein and Roy M. Mersky, "Rating Supreme Court Justices," *American Bar Association Journal*, LVIII (November, 1972), 1183–89.

52. Charles Warren, *The Supreme Court in United States History* (Boston, 1937), II, 625, 637; *California v. Central Pacific Railroad*, 127 U.S. 1 (1888).

prises. An undoubted friend of railroad corporations in this regard, he might logically oppose restrictive and shortsighted legislation. In the Interior Department Lamar and Sparks had taken
the railroads to task, but that did not indicate antagonism to
railroads as such. He ultimately curbed Sparks's enthusiasm and
largely confined himself to action against evasion of proper governmental requirements. Lamar proved reform minded but not
the enemy of propertied interests, except perhaps in the matter
of land laws.

Here again Lamar's philosophy of economic expansion supported by a sympathetic national government paralleled the
trend of the Court. Two years before his appointment the Wa-
bash decision (1886) had virtually declared that a state might not
regulate railroad rates involving interstate transportation. That
marked a great step toward exempting commerce from state interference, but the Court, including Lamar, went much further.

Lamar's opinion for the majority in *Kidd* v. *Pearson* defined
state and federal relationship to commerce and also clearly de-
lineated the bounds of his commitment to centralized economic
responsibility. He made two basic points which anticipated the
Court's position for years to come. The power of the national
Congress over interstate commerce, he said, was absolute, leaving
no place for state legislatures. But he described commerce so
that it excluded manufacturing from federal authority—in effect
leaving that aspect of the economy without regulation. These
categories figured prominently after Lamar's death in the more
famous E. C. Knight case of 1895. Then the Court reiterated that
"commerce succeeds to manufacture and is not a part of it." This
interpretation stood well into the twentieth century when the
economy and its regulation acquired proportions inconceivable
during Lamar's tenure.[53]

53. *Kidd* v. *Pearson,* 128 U.S. 1 (1888). Later in *Leisy* v. *Hardin,* 135 U.S. 100
(1890), Lamar concurred in the reiteration of this position. However, in *Chicago,
Milwaukee and St. Paul Railway Company* v. *Minnesota,* 134 U.S. 418 (1890), which
interpreted the Fourteenth Amendment, he thought that state legislatures, and
not the judiciary, might decide on the reasonableness of rates fixed by a regulatory
commission. Lamar did not write his opinion, but Arnold Paul, "Lucius Quintus

Although Lamar's opinions fostered an economic system largely outside the control of state legislatures, he did not favor the Court's similar approach in other areas. State responsibility for social rights, criminal proceedings, and local elections was basic to his creed. In this sense Lamar's final career—that of judge—ran curiously true to his antecedents. The peculiar dichotomy which had characterized his political life stayed with him to the end. As in Congress and to a lesser degree in the Interior Department, he successfully fused the justification of a federally stimulated economy with an unalterable commitment to political states' rights.

In several of the most important cases of this era Lamar opposed enlargement of the national government's power, especially in the area of implied rather than legislatively granted authority. In *Cunningham* v. *Neagle*[54] Lamar denied that the federal government had authority over a United States marshal assigned to protect Justice Stephen A. Field and who, in pursuance of this duty, had killed a man. Since no national law provided for appointment of such a bodyguard, Lamar maintained that state officials had jurisdiction. The majority, however, held that the marshal's appointment fell within the implied power of the executive branch, and that jurisdiction therefore belonged to the federal government.[55]

The majority made a similarly sweeping decision for federal power in *Corporation of Latter Day Saints* v. *United States,*[56]

Cincinnatus Lamar," II, 1446, considers him to be a traditionalist resisting the trend toward substituting judicial review for legislative responsibility. There were few economic cases under the Fourteenth Amendment at this time, and Lamar seldom spoke on the subject. It appears, according to Paul, that the Court was moving away from Lamar in this area. In *McCall* v. *California*, 136 U.S. 104 (1890); *Norfolk and Western Railroad* v. *Pennsylvania*, 136 U.S. 114 (1890); and *Maine* v. *Grand Trunk Railway Company*, 142 U.S. 217 (1891), Lamar advocated exemption of interstate commerce from state taxation.

54. *Cunningham* v. *Neagle*, 135 U.S. 1 (1890). Warren, *The Supreme Court*, II, 697, called it "the broadest interpretation yet given to implied powers of the National Government."

55. Chief Justice Fuller concurred with Lamar.

56. *The Late Corporation of the Church of Jesus Christ of Latter Day Saints* v. *United States*, 136 U.S. 1 (1890).

which sustained congressional action in annulling the Mormons' church charter. Claiming that Congress possessed unlimited power over the territories, the Court upheld the government's seizure of property as punishment for the criminal practices of that church. Chief Justice Melville Fuller, joined by Lamar and Justice Field, protested that Congress' authority to acquire property and suppress crime was not sufficient to include confiscation. Lamar did not write the opinon, but he had argued the question of congressional power over property in the territories before, in antebellum times.[57]

Only one of Lamar's dissents dealt directly with federal protection of freedmen's rights. Standing alone on this question without even the support of Democratic justices Fuller and Field, Lamar simply recorded his objection without offering an opinion of his own. The case of *Logan* v. *United States*[58] arose from a federal statute prohibiting conspiracy against civil rights. Lamar denied the jurisdiction of the federal court over an attack by "conspirators" upon the prisoner of a federal marshal.

Lamar's failure to write an opinion in *Logan* v. *United States* could have indicated his hopelessness on the question, or he may have wished to avoid the acrimonious political discussion sure to follow such an opinion by the ex-rebel justice. In the different circumstances of *Cunningham* v. *Neagle*, Lamar definitively stated his attitude on the state's control over its political functions. In denying federal jurisdiction over Marshal Neagle, he deprecated the effect of "this decision upon the autonomy of the States, in divesting them of what was once regarded as their exclusive jurisdiction over crimes committed within their own territory, against their own laws, and in enabling a federal judge or court, by an order in a habeas corpus proceeding, to deprive a State of its power to maintain its own public order or to protect the security of society and the lives of its own citizens, whenever

57. Lamar held a moderate position on the Mormon question while in the Senate. Fuller, Lamar, and Field were the only Democrats on the Court and frequently voted together on issues of federal political authority.

58. *Logan* v. *United States*, 144 U.S. 263 (1892).

the amenability to its courts of a federal officer or employee or agent is sought to be enforced." [59]

In this ringing declaration, the last phase of a highly varied career and its achievements can be traced to the earlier antebellum and reconstruction stages. Unification and nationalism had been established as Lamar had hoped, but his compromise on states' rights continued to the last to be only veiled acquiescence. The irate Lamar who struck down a United States marshal in an Oxford courtroom seems not so far removed from the old justice who disputed federal authority over an assault on the prisoner of a federal marshal. Lamar had not deviated far from the road he had chosen while teaching and practicing law in Oxford. He knew the price paid by the South, in terms of cherished autonomy, for its return to a northern dominated union. He accepted the cost, but his principles did not change.

Justice Lamar wrote no additional opinions after the spring of 1892. While the Court remained in session, he suffered a recurrence of the ill health which plagued most of his adult life. Although it seems unlikely that Lamar's physique could ever have fully recovered from the paralytic attacks which he suffered intermittently after 1861, there is no way to connect the last illnesses with the earlier ones. Apparently he began for the first time in the spring to experience lung hemorrhaging which left him almost helpless. This symptom suggested tuberculosis, but he failed to respond to the healthy mountain climate where he went for a cure.[60] One physician thought that he had suffered gradual deterioration of the arteries and kidneys over a period of years. Other doctors believed him afflicted with Bright's kidney disease. Lamar's correspondence confirmed symptoms of both a kidney ailment and lung hemorrhaging.[61]

59. *Cunningham* v. *Neagle*, 135 U.S. 1 (1890).
60. Lamar to Grover Cleveland, April 3, 1892, in Grover Cleveland Papers; Lamar to N. T. A. Robinson, April 14, 1892, in Hampton L. Carson Collection; Lamar to William H. McCardle, May 18, 1892, in William H. McCardle Papers, MDAH; Lamar to Mrs. M. A. Ross [his sister], September 9, 1892, quoted in Mayes, *Lamar*, 568.
61. Opinion of William Pepper, March 8, 1892, quoted in Mayes, *Lamar*, 568;

Looking forward to the Court's recess to bring renewed energy, Lamar traveled South with the intention of returning for the next session of Court. En route to Mississippi by way of Georgia, he suffered another attack; and on January 23, 1893, he died at age sixty-eight not far from the place where he was born.[62]

Lamar to William H. Hardy, January 10, 1893, quoted, *ibid.*, 569. The New Orleans *Daily Picayune*, January 24, 1893, obituary credited the death to "Bright's disease, with apectoris."

62. Oxford (Miss.) *Eagle*, January 26, February 2, 1893.

Epilogue

By 1885 Lamar had come to represent certain qualities and policies of national importance which were appreciated by both friends and political adversaries. During his long career he had first been known for sectionalism and then for reconciliation and nationalism. As an active participant in the period divided by the Civil War, he became identified with both historical eras. He had not altogether earned the dubious credit he sometimes received as a secessionist leader, but after the war he did in fact make a measurable contribution to historic developments. But beyond Lamar's advocacy of sectional reconciliation, the last eight years of his life acquired significance because his personal career provided a battleground where sectional conflicts could still be fought and resolved.

It is probable that Lamar knew his place in history when he decided to leave Congress in 1885. He wrote Jefferson Davis on February 28, 1885: "I know that I am not well fitted to be a Cabinet officer. But I think it best for me to undertake the task which has been pressed upon me. . . . If I can administer the department with honesty & efficiency & fairness to all parts of the country I think I may go far towards convincing the people that the South desires to serve the best & highest interests of a common country." [1]

1. Lamar to Jefferson Davis, February 28, 1885, in Louisiana Historical Association Collection: Jefferson Davis Collection. See also Lamar to E. C. Walthall, February 3, 1885, quoted in Mayes, *Lamar*, 469–70.

He showed the same preoccupation with historical implications when appointed to the Supreme Court in 1887. After Republican opposition rose to block his confirmation, he expressed anxiety to a fellow cabinet member: "I have determined . . . not to allow those Senators to raise the sectional issue on *my* name. I won't let my name remain before them if they start a sectional angry debate." [2] Even if Lamar did not actually contemplate withdrawing, it is noteworthy that he thought and spoke in terms of his effect upon the South's future.

Lamar had cause to fear that his appointment would call up emotional rhetoric. Partisans immediately saw the possibilities in treating him as the embodiment of the Confederate cause. If the public mind had not already personified the whole sectional question in him since the Sumner eulogy (which was often mentioned during the controversy), then the newspapers would have provided the idea during the winter of 1887–1888.[3] Even Republican senator Stewart, who voted for confirmation, phrased his support in sectional terms, explaining that "the rejection of Mr. Lamar will be construed, both in the north and in the south, as a declaration that his participation in the war disqualified him." [4]

In equating the justice-designate with the southern question the press simply legitimized an image artfully cultivated over the years. From the date of the carefully planned Sumner eulogy he had kept up appearances as the harbinger of peace and slipped from this pose only in a few instances. There is every reason to believe that he consciously saved himself to present the best face of the South. His reticence in Congress can be partially explained by an unwillingness to tax the interest of those who might listen to his message of reconciliation. When he did speak, Lamar gen-

2. Unaddressed note, n.d., [but about December 1, 1887], in Thomas F. Bayard Papers. Interestingly, the recipient of this note scribbled at the bottom that Lamar's fears were groundless and that his nomination was intended to quiet the sectional issue rather than to raise it.

3. *E.g.*, see New York *Times*, December 20, 23, 1887; New York *Tribune*, December 25, 1887, January 4, 12, 1888; New Orleans *Daily Picayune*, January 10, 1888; and Mobile (Ala.) *Daily Register*, January 10, 13, 17, 1888.

4. New York *Times*, January 9, 1888.

erally prepared with care and chose lofty topics evoking patriotic sentiments—such as the Centennial Celebration in 1876, the
electoral commission bill, and Grant's retirement pension.[5] Lamar even made a virtue of his disregard of the Mississippi legislature's instructions on the silver issue; and in all instances he
attempted to project himself as a paragon of virtue and honesty.[6]

Lamar's more or less self-consciously prepared image enabled
him to achieve his immediate purposes, and it proved sufficiently
well done to persist beyond his own life. He joined the galaxy of
southern folk heroes of the Civil War era, and thus earned the
right to carry his message to later generations in the South. Publications such as the *Confederate Veteran*, organ of the United
Confederate Veterans, regularly mentioned him for years after
his death. More important to the romantic memory of Lamar, the
Sumner eulogy and other speeches were preserved and passed on
to school children in anthologies and in "southern readers." And
the South, especially his home state, has contributed to his reputation for eminent statesmanship by giving his name to a variety
of worthy landmarks.

Perpetuation of Lamar's good name has not been reserved
for the nostalgic alone. Since the turn of the twentieth century,
scholars have generally assigned Lamar the role he chose for himself. His early biographer, Wirt Armistead Cate, wrote in that
vein in 1935. Twenty years later, in 1955, Lamar still seemed an
admirable subject for such a popular work on political heroism
as John F. Kennedy's *Profiles in Courage*. In 1969, a distinguished group of southern scholars, public officials, editors, and
businessmen committed to the social and economic development

---

5. Lamar made these claims himself in Lamar to Hampton L. Carson, April
24, 1891, in Hampton L. Carson Collection. See also Gaines, *Southern Oratory*,
54–56.

6. After leaving the Senate, Lamar made only one major address, and he
did not fail to present once more the theme of his career. In speaking at the
unveiling of a statue of John C. Calhoun, Lamar said that if Calhoun were alive
he would say to South Carolina that she should "seek the happiness of her
people . . . in the greatness and glory of the American Republic." See Ladies
Calhoun Monument Association, *A History of the Calhoun Monument* (Charleston, 1888), 72.

of the region, organized in Durham, North Carolina, as the
L. Q. C. Lamar Society. Lamar was chosen as namesake because
"the Society believes that the type of behavior exemplified by his
struggle for reconciliation between the races and regions of this
country in the divisive 1870s is worthy of emulation by his fellow southerners in the 1970s." [7]

This is not to say that either the South or the nation came to
accept the whole of Lamar's position: certainly not all those who
respect his name today. But well into the twentieth century the
South embraced and the nation adopted his synthesis of nationalism and sectionalism. While the federal government looked on,
the South preserved to a large degree its political autonomy and
latitude for dealing with social and racial questions.

Indeed, Lamar's view of the black man's role in America was
already in the 1890s becoming the national view. Public opinion,
Congress, and the Supreme Court agreed that the war amendments had not after all been intended to guarantee political
equality. By the turn of the century Lamar's contention that
whites ought to lead Negroes in their political activities seemed
humane and liberal in a society growing accustomed to disfranchisement and segregation. With good reason the South came to
appreciate Lamar's conviction that compromise with the Union
would secure many substantive objectives which were otherwise
unobtainable. Lamar had charted the narrow course between
nationalism and sectionalism until the two sentiments became
compatible. The ends of reconstruction were renounced by most
Americans, and fifty years would pass before they reemerged to
be viewed as a noble dream unfulfilled.

7. Material provided by Thomas H. Naylor, Executive Director, L. Q. C.
Lamar Society, Durham, North Carolina.

Bibliography of Sources Cited

PRIMARY SOURCES

Manuscript Collections in Library of Congress

Thomas F. Bayard Papers.
A. T. Bledsoe Papers.
Grover Cleveland Papers.
Confederate States of America Papers.
James A. Garfield Papers.
Burton N. Harrison Papers.
Carl Schurz Papers.
A. H. Stephens Papers.
Henry Watterson Papers.

Other Manuscript Collections

Balch Papers. The Historical Society of Pennsylvania, Philadelphia, Pennsylvania.

Joseph P. Bradley Papers. New Jersey Historical Society, Newark, New Jersey.

Blanche K. Bruce Papers. Howard University Library, Washington, D.C.

John Emory Bryant Papers. Duke University Library, Durham, North Carolina.

Hampton L. Carson Collection. Free Library of Philadelphia, Philadelphia, Pennsylvania.

C. C. Clay Papers. Duke University Library, Durham, North Carolina.

Howell Cobb Papers. University of Georgia Library, Athens, Georgia.

John W. Daniel Manuscripts. Duke University Library, Durham, North Carolina.

Lamar to A. Y. Donaldson, August 12, 1872. In the possession of Miss Mary Donaldson, Box 84, Oakland, Mississippi.

Rutherford B. Hayes Papers. Hayes Memorial Library, Fremont, Ohio.

S. A. Jonas Papers. Mississippi State Department of Archives and History, Jackson, Mississippi.

L. Q. C. Lamar Letters. Miscellaneous Collection, Emory University Library, Atlanta, Georgia.

L. Q. C. Lamar Letters. Southern Historical Collection, University of North Carolina Library, Chapel Hill, North Carolina.

L. Q. C. Lamar Papers. University of Mississippi Library, Oxford, Mississippi.

Lamar-Harper Letters. Lunsford Collection, Georgia State Department of Archives and History, Atlanta, Georgia.

Lamar-Mayes Papers. Mississippi State Department of Archives and History, Jackson, Mississippi.

Louisiana Historical Association Collection: Jefferson Davis Collection. Tulane University Library, New Orleans, Louisiana.

William H. McCardle Papers. Mississippi State Department of Archives and History, Jackson, Mississippi.

New York Historical Society Papers. New York Historical Society, New York, New York.

Charles Nordhoff Papers. Houghton Library, Harvard University, Cambridge, Massachusetts.

A. J. Phillips Papers. Houghton Library, Harvard University, Cambridge, Massachusetts.

Lafayette P. Reynolds Papers. Duke University Library, Durham, North Carolina.

Senate file relating to L. Q. C. Lamar's appointment to the Supreme Court. SEN50B–A3, Record Group No. 46, National Archives, Washington, D.C.

William Henry Smith Papers. On microfilm, Hayes Memorial Library, Fremont, Ohio.

Alonzo Snyder Papers. Louisiana State University Library, Baton Rouge, Louisiana.

Governor's Papers: John M. Stone. Mississippi State Department of Archives and History, Jackson, Mississippi.

John M. Stone Papers. Mississippi State Department of Archives and History, Jackson, Mississippi.

Harvey Walter Papers. Southern Historical Collection, University of North Carolina Library, Chapel Hill, North Carolina.

War Department Records. Record Group No. 109, National Archives, Washington, D.C.

Published Correspondence

Ames, Blanche Butler, comp. *Chronicles from the Nineteenth Century.* 2 vols. N.p., 1957.

Brooks, Robert P., ed. "Howell Cobb Papers." *Georgia Historical Quarterly,* VI (March, 1922), 35–84.

Halsell, Willie D., ed. "Advice from Michael C. Kerr to a Reconstructed Rebel Congressman." *Indiana Magazine of History,* XXXVII (September, 1941), 257–61.

Phillips, U. B., ed. *The Correspondence of Robert Toombs, Alexander H. Stephens, and Howell Cobb.* American Historical Association, *Annual Report, 1911,* II. Washington, 1913.

Rowland, Dunbar, ed. *Jefferson Davis, Constitutionalist: His Letters, Papers, and Speeches.* 10 vols. Jackson, 1923.

Russell, Mattie, ed. "Why Lamar Eulogized Sumner." *Journal of Southern History,* XXI (August, 1955), 374–78.

Strode, Hudson, ed. *Jefferson Davis: Private Letters, 1823–1889.* New York, 1966.

Unpublished Records

Catalogue of the Officers & Students in Emory College, Ga., and the Report of the Board of the Trustees to the General Conference, 1839, 1845, 1846. Emory University Library, Atlanta, Georgia.

Deed Books, Lafayette County Courthouse, Oxford, Mississippi.

Election Data. Inter-University Consortium for Political Research, Ann Arbor, Michigan.

L. Q. C. Lamar Subject File. Mississippi State Department of Archives and History, Jackson, Mississippi.

Minutes of the Board of Trustees of the University of Mississippi. University of Mississippi Library, Oxford, Mississippi.

Mortgage of the Mississippi Central on May 1, 1872. Illinois Central Archives, Newberry Library, Chicago, Illinois.

Official Documents Relating to the Mission of L. Q. C. Lamar, Com-

missioner of the Confederate States of America to Russia. Mississippi State Department of Archives and History, Jackson, Mississippi.

Personal Tax Rolls, Lafayette County, Mississippi. Mississippi State
Department of Archives and History, Jackson, Mississippi.

Record Book of the Faculty of the University of the State of Mississippi. University of Mississippi Library, Oxford, Mississippi.

Record Book of the Treasurer of Emory College, 1836–1839. Emory
University Library, Atlanta, Georgia.

Southern Railroad Association Ledger, II, III, IV. Illinois Central
Archives, Newberry Library, Chicago, Illinois.

The Statutes of Emory College and the Bye-Laws of the Faculty, 1839.
Emory University Library, Atlanta, Georgia.

Tax Digest, Newton County. Georgia State Department of Archives
and History, Atlanta, Georgia.

Tripartite Agreement of April 11, 1872. Illinois Central Archives,
Newberry Library, Chicago, Illinois.

Published Records

*Annual Report of the President and Directors of the Mississippi Cen-
tral Railroad Company*, 1867, 1868. Mississippi State Department
of Archives and History, Jackson, Mississippi.

*Annual Report of the President and Directors of the Mississippi Cen-
tral Railroad Company*, 1873. Illinois Central Archives, Newberry
Library, Chicago, Illinois.

Report of the Secretary of the Interior, 1885, 1886, 1887.

Candler, A. D., ed. *The Confederate Records of the State of Georgia.*
Atlanta, 1909–1911.

*Chicago, St. Louis and New Orleans Railroad Company Laws and
Documents*, 1881. Illinois Central Archives, Newberry Library,
Chicago, Illinois.

Compendium of the Eleventh Census, 1892.

Congressional Globe, 1858–1873.

Congressional Record, 1873–1885.

Eleventh Census, Manufacturing Industry, 1890.

Historical Catalogue of the University of Mississippi, 1849–1909.
Nashville, 1910.

"Journal of the Congress of the Confederate States of America."
Senate Documents, 58th Cong., 2nd Sess., No. 234, XXV–XXXI.

Journal of the House of Representatives of the State of Georgia, 1851–1864.

Journal of the House of Representatives of the United States, 1857–1877.

Journal of the Senate of the United States, 1877–1884.

Journal of the State Convention and Ordinances and Resolutions Adopted in January, 1861. Jackson, 1861.

Ninth Census, 1870.

Official Records of the Union and Confederate Navies in the War of the Rebellion. 31 vols. Washington, 1894–1927.

"Paroles of the Army of Northern Virginia." *Southern Historical Society Papers,* XV (1887).

"Report of the Investigation of the Presidential Election of 1876." *House Miscellaneous Documents,* 45th Cong., 3rd Sess., No. 31.

Richardson, James D., ed. *A Compilation of the Messages and Papers of the Confederacy, Including the Diplomatic Correspondence, 1861–1865.* 2 vols. Nashville, 1905.

Richardson, James D., ed. *A Compilation of the Messages and Papers of the Presidents, 1789–1897.* 10 vols. Washington, 1894–1899.

"Testimony Taken by the Joint Select Committee to Inquire into the Conditions of Affairs in the Late Insurrectionary States." *Senate Reports,* 42nd Cong., 2nd Sess., No. 41.

United States Reports, 1888–1892.

The War of the Rebellion: A Compilation of the Official Records of the Union and Confederate Armies. 128 vols. Washington, 1880–1901.

Newspapers

Aberdeen (Miss.) *Tri-Weekly Examiner,* 1881–1884.

Atlanta *Southern Confederacy,* 1864.

Brandon (Miss.) *Republican,* 1874–1875.

Chicago *Tribune,* 1879.

Hernando (Miss.) *Press and Times,* 1872.

The Index: A Weekly Journal of Politics, Literature and News, 1863.

Jackson (Miss.) *Clarion,* 1883–1885.

Jackson (Miss.) *Daily Clarion,* 1867–1880.

Jackson *Daily Mississippi Pilot,* 1875.

Jackson (Miss.) *Weekly Clarion,* 1872–1882.

Jackson *Weekly Mississippi Pilot,* 1872–1875.

Louisville (Ky.) *Courier-Journal*, 1874.
Macon *Georgia Journal and Messenger*, 1855.
Macon *Georgia Telegraph*, 1847–1855.
Memphis *Daily Appeal*, 1851–1883.
Milledgeville (Ga.) *Confederate Union*, 1864.
Milledgeville (Ga.) *Federal Union*, 1853.
Milledgeville (Ga.) *Southern Recorder*, 1864.
Mobile *Daily Register*, 1885–1888.
New Orleans *Daily Picayune*, 1874–1893.
New York *Times*, 1858–1888.
New York *Tribune*, 1858–1888.
Oxford (Miss.) *Constitution*, 1851.
Oxford (Miss.) *Democratic Flag*, 1852.
Oxford (Miss.) *Eagle*, 1893.
Oxford (Miss.) *Falcon*, 1866–1871.
Oxford (Miss.) *Intelligencer*, 1860–1861.
Oxford (Miss.) *Organizer*, 1850.
Oxford (Miss.) *Signal*, 1856.
Savannah (Ga.) *Morning News*, 1888.
Washington *Union*, 1877.

Published Contemporary Writings

Adams, Henry. *The Education of Henry Adams*. Boston, 1918.
Barnard, Dr. F. A. P. "Autobiographical Sketch of Dr. F. A. P. Barnard." *Publications of the Mississippi Historical Society*, XII (1912), 107–21.
Blaine, James G. *Twenty Years in Congress*. 2 vols. Norwich, Connecticut, 1884.
Chesnut, Mary B. *A Diary from Dixie*. Edited by Ben Ames Williams. Boston, 1949.
Claiborne, John F. H. *Life and Correspondence of John A. Quitman*. 2 vols. New York, 1860.
Clay, Mrs. Clement C. *A Belle of the Fifties*. New York, 1889.
Curry, J. L. M. *Civil History of the Government of the Confederate States*. Richmond, 1900.
Davis, Jefferson. *Rise and Fall of the Confederate Government*. 2 vols. New York, 1881.
Davis, Reuben. *Recollections of Mississippi and Mississippians*. Boston, 1891.

Davis, Varina Howell. *Jefferson Davis . . . A Memoir by His Wife.*
2 vols. New York, 1890.

Fielder, Herbert. *Life, Times and Speeches of Joseph E. Brown.*
Springfield, 1883.

Fitzgerald, Oscar Penn. *Judge Longstreet, A Life Sketch.* Nashville,
1891.

Foote, Henry S. *Casket of Reminiscences.* Washington, 1874.

Fulkerson, Horace S. *A Civilian's Recollections of the War Between
the States, 1886.* Edited by P. L. Rainwater. Baton Rouge, 1939.

Govan, Gilbert E., and James W. Livingood. *The Haskell Memoirs:
John Cheves Haskell.* New York, 1960.

Harris, Wiley P. "Autobiography." *Courts, Judges, and Lawyers of
Mississippi, 1798–1935.* Edited by Dunbar Rowland. Jackson, 1935.

Harrison, Mrs. Burton. *Recollections, Grave and Gay.* New York,
1911.

Harrison, Fairfax, ed. *Aris Souis Focisque . . . The Harrisons of
Skimino.* N.p., 1910.

Hegel, G. W. F. *The Philosophy of History.* Translated by J. Sibree.
Prefaces by Charles Hegel and J. Sibree. Revised edition. New
York, 1944.

Hemleben, Sylvester J., and Richard T. Bennett. "A Historical Sketch
of the Early Law School of the University of Mississippi: A New
Found Memoir." *Mississippi Law Journal,* XXXVII (December,
1965), 28–54.

Henderson, Dwight Franklin, ed. *The Private Journal of Georgiana
Gholson Walker, 1862–1865, With Selections from the Post-War
Years, 1865–1876.* Tuscaloosa, 1963.

Hesseltine, William B., ed. *Three Against Lincoln: Murat Halstead
Reports the Caucuses of 1860.* Baton Rouge, 1960.

Hill, Walter B. "L. Q. C. Lamar." *The Green Bag,* V (April, 1893),
153–65.

Hodgson, Joseph. *The Cradle of the Confederacy: Or the Times of
Troup, Quitman and Yancey.* Mobile, 1876.

Johnston, Joseph E. *Narrative of Military Operations Directed During the Late War Between the States.* Introduction by Frank Van-
diver. Bloomington, 1959.

Ladies Calhoun Monument Association. *A History of the Calhoun
Monument.* Charleston, 1888.

Lamar, L. Q. C., *et al.* "Ought the Negro to be Disfranchised." A symposium. *North American Review*, CXXVIII (March, 1879), 225–83.

Lamar, Lucius Quintus Cincinnatus. *Speech of Hon. L. Q. C. Lamar, of Miss., on the state of the country.* New York, 1972.

Leftwich, George J. "Lucius Q. C. Lamar." *The Methodist Review*, XLIV (1896), 65–73.

Lynch, John R. *The Facts of Reconstruction.* New York, 1915.

Mayes, Edward. *History of Education in Mississippi.* Edited by Herbert B. Adams. Washington, 1899.

————. *Lucius Q. C. Lamar: His Life, Times, and Speeches.* Nashville, 1896.

Miller, Stephen F. *The Bench and Bar of Georgia.* Philadelphia, 1858.

Nordhoff, Charles. *The Cotton States in the Spring and Summer of 1875.* New York, 1876.

Robertson, James I., Jr., ed. *The Diary of Dolly Lunt Burge.* Athens, Georgia, 1962.

Sorrel, G. Moxley. *Recollections of a Confederate Staff Officer.* Edited by Bell Irvin Wiley. Jackson, Tennessee, 1958.

Sparks, W. H. *The Memories of Fifty Years.* Philadelphia, 1882.

Spencer, Edward. *Public Life and Services of Thomas F. Bayard.* New York, 1880.

Waddell, John N. *Memorials of Academic Life.* Richmond, 1891.

Watterson, Henry. *Marse Henry: An Autobiography.* 2 vols. New York, 1919.

Williams, T. Harry, ed. *Hayes, The Diary of a President, 1875–1881.* New York, 1964.

Wilson, Henry. *History of the Rise and Fall of the Slave Power.* 3 vols. Boston, 1875–1877.

SECONDARY SOURCES

Biographical Articles

Allen, John R. "Bishop Paine in Texas." Extract from the *Texas Methodist Historical Quarterly*, I (October, 1909), 172–74. In L. Q. C. Lamar Letters. Southern Historical Collection, University of North Carolina Library, Chapel Hill, North Carolina.

Caldwell, Robert G. C. "Mirabeau Buonaparte Lamar." *Dictionary of American Biography.* Edited by Allen Johnson and Dumas Malone. 23 vols. New York, 1928–1958, X, 553–54.

Cooper, William J. "A Reassessment of Jefferson Davis as War Leader: The Case from Atlanta to Nashville." *Journal of Southern History*, XXXVI (May, 1970), 189–204.

Dickey, Dallas C., and Donald C. Streeter. "Lucius Q. C. Lamar." *A History and Criticism of American Public Addresses.* Edited by Marie K. Hochmuth. 3 vols. New York, 1955, III, 175–221.

Halsell, Willie D. "The Appointment of L. Q. C. Lamar to the Supreme Court." *Mississippi Valley Historical Review*, XXVIII (December, 1941), 399–412.

————. "The Friendship of L. Q. C. Lamar and Jefferson Davis." *Journal of Mississippi History*, VI (July, 1944), 131–44.

————. "L. Q. C. Lamar, Associate Justice of the Supreme Court." *Journal of Mississippi History*, V (April, 1943), 59–78.

————. "L. Q. C. Lamar's Taylor Farm: An Experiment in Diversified Farming." *Journal of Mississippi History*, V (October, 1943), 185–96.

————. "Note on a Phase of L. Q. C. Lamar's Career." *Journal of Mississippi History*, IX (January, 1947), 21–29.

————. "Prelude to a Career: L. Q. C. Lamar Tries Politics." *Journal of Mississippi History*, VII (April, 1945), 75–90.

Hansen, Vagn K. "Jefferson Davis and the Repudiation of Mississippi Bonds: The Development of a Political Myth." *Journal of Mississippi History*, XXXIII (May, 1971), 105–32.

Harris, William C. Introduction to John R. Lynch, *The Facts of Reconstruction.* Indianapolis, 1970.

Lamar, William Harmong. "Thomas Lamar of the Province of Maryland and a Part of his Descendants." *Publications of the Southern History Association*, I (July, 1897), 203–10.

Meador, Daniel J. "Lamar and the Law at the University of Mississippi." *Mississippi Law Journal*, XXXIV (May, 1963), 227–56.

Mims, Edwin. "Albert Taylor Bledsoe." *Dictionary of American Biography.* Edited by Allen Johnson and Dumas Malone. 23 vols. New York, 1928–1958, II, 364–65.

Paul, Arnold. "Lucius Quintus Cincinnatus Lamar." *The Justices of the Supreme Court, 1789–1969.* Edited by Leon Friedman and Fred Israel. 4 vols. New York, 1969, II, 1431–51.

Sibley, Samuel. *Georgia's Contribution to Law: The Lamars.* New York, 1948.

Sydnor, Charles S. "Jacob Thompson." *Dictionary of American Biography.* Edited by Allen Johnson and Dumas Malone. 23 vols. New York, 1928–1958, XVIII, 459–60.

Urofsky, Melvin I. "Blanche K. Bruce: United States Senator, 1875–1881." *Journal of Mississippi History,* XXIX (May, 1967), 118–41.

General Articles

Blaustein, Albert P., and Roy M. Mersky. "Rating Supreme Court Justices." *American Bar Association Journal,* LVIII (November, 1972), 1183–89.

Decker, Leslie E. "The Railroads and the Land Office: Administrative Policy and the Land Patent Controversy, 1864–1896." *Mississippi Valley Historical Review,* XLVI (March, 1960), 679–99.

Dodd, W. E. "The Principle of Instructing U.S. Senators." *South Atlantic Quarterly,* I (October, 1902), 326–32.

Donald, David. "The Scalawag in Mississippi Reconstruction." *Journal of Southern History,* X (November, 1944), 447–60.

Dunham, Harold. "Crucial Years of the General Land Office, 1875–1890." *Agricultural History,* II (April, 1937), 117–41.

Eaton, Clement. "Southern Senators and the Right of Instruction, 1789–1860." *Journal of Southern History,* XVIII (August, 1952), 303–19.

Ellem, Warren A. "Who Were the Mississippi Scalawags?" *Journal of Southern History,* XXXVIII (May, 1972), 217–40.

Garner, James W. "The First Struggle Over Secession in Mississippi." *Publications of the Mississippi Historical Society,* IV (1901), 89–104.

Going, Allen J. "The South and the Blair Education Bill." *Mississippi Valley Historical Review,* XLIV (September, 1957), 267–90.

Graebner, Norman A. "Northern Diplomacy and European Neutrality." In *Why the North Won the Civil War.* Edited by David Donald. Baton Rouge, 1960. Pp. 55–78.

Greene, Helene. "Politics in Georgia, 1853–1854: The Ordeal of Howell Cobb." *Georgia Historical Quarterly,* XXX (September, 1946), 185–211.

Halsell, Willie D. "The Bourbon Period in Mississippi Politics." *Journal of Southern History,* XI (November, 1945), 518–37.

_____. "Democratic Dissensions in Mississippi, 1878–1882." *Journal of Mississippi History*, II (July, 1940), 123–35.

_____. "James R. Chalmers and Mahoneism in Mississippi." *Journal of Southern History*, X (February, 1944) 37–58.

Hearon, Cleo. "Mississippi and the Compromise of 1850." *Publications of the Mississippi Historical Society*, XIV (1914), 6–230.

Johnson, Guion Griffis. "The Ideology of White Supremacy." In *The South and the Sectional Image*. Edited by Dewey W. Grantham, Jr. New York, 1967. Pp. 56–78.

Kendel, Julia. "Reconstruction in Lafayette County." *Publications of the Mississippi Historical Society*, XIII (1913), 223–64.

Legan, Marshall Scott. "Mississippi and the Yellow Fever Epidemics of 1878–1879." *Journal of Mississippi History*, XXXIII (August, 1971), 199–217.

McNeily, J. S. "The Enforcement Act of 1871 and the Ku Klux Klan in Mississippi." *Publications of the Mississippi Historical Society*, IX (1906), 109–71.

_____. "War and Reconstruction in Mississippi, 1863–1890." *Publications of the Mississippi Historical Society*, Centenary Series, II (1918), 165–535.

Rae, John B. "Commissioner Sparks and the Railroad Land Grants." *Mississippi Valley Historical Review*, XXV (September, 1938), 211–30.

Smith, Samuel D. "The Negro in the United States Senate." In *Essays in Southern History Presented to Joseph Gregoire de Roulhac Hamilton*. Edited by Fletcher M. Green. Chapel Hill, 1949. Pp. 49–66.

Biographical Books

Appleton's Cyclopedia of American Biography. Edited by James Grant Wilson and John Fiske. 6 vols. New York, 1888–1889.

Barnard, Harry. *Rutherford B. Hayes and His America*. Indianapolis, 1954.

Biographical Directory of the American Congress, 1774–1961. Washington, 1961.

Biographical Encyclopedia of Ohio of the Nineteenth Century. Cincinnati, 1876.

Cate, Wirt Armistead. *Lucius Q. C. Lamar: Secession and Reunion.* Chapel Hill, 1935.

Davis, Charles S. *Colin J. McRae: Confederate Financial Agent.* Tuscaloosa, 1961.

Davison, Kenneth B. *The Presidency of Rutherford B. Hayes.* Westport, Connecticut, 1972.

Fairman, Charles. *Mr. Justice Miller and the Supreme Court, 1862–1890.* Cambridge, 1939.

Govan, Gilbert E., and James W. Livingood. *A Different Valor: The Story of General Joseph E. Johnston, C.S.A.* New York, 1956.

Hay, Thomas R., and Donald B. Sanger. *James Longstreet: Soldier and Politician.* Baton Rouge, 1952.

Hill, Louise Biles. *Joseph E. Brown and the Confederacy.* Chapel Hill, 1939.

Howe, George Frederick. *Chester A. Arthur: A Quarter Century of Machine Politics.* New York, 1957.

King, Willard L. *Melville Weston Fuller: Chief Justice of the United States, 1888–1910.* New York, 1950.

LeMar, Harold Dihel. *History of the Lamar or Lemar Family in America.* Omaha, 1941.

Mayes, Edward. *Genealogy and History of Lamar and Related Families.* Hattiesburg, Mississippi, 1935.

Nevins, Allan. *Abram S. Hewitt, with Some Account of Peter Cooper.* New York, 1935.

Pereyra, Lillian A. *James Lusk Alcorn: Persistent Whig.* Baton Rouge, 1966.

Ranck, James B. *Albert Gallatin Brown: Radical Southern Nationalist.* New York, 1937.

Ross, Ishbel. *First Lady of the South: The Life of Mrs. Jefferson Davis.* New York, 1958.

Smith, T. C. *The Life and Letters of James Abram Garfield.* 2 vols. New Haven, 1925.

Strode, Hudson. *Jefferson Davis: Tragic Hero—The Last Twenty-Five Years, 1864–1889.* New York, 1964.

Tansill, Charles C. *The Congressional Career of Thomas Francis Bayard, 1869–1885.* Washington, 1946.

Wade, John Donald. *Augustus Baldwin Longstreet: A Study of the Development of Culture in the South.* New York, 1924.

Wilson, Beckles. *John Slidell and the Confederates in Paris, 1862–1865*. New York, 1932.

General Books

Alexander, Thomas B. *Sectional Stress and Party Strength*. Nashville, 1967.

Avery, I. W. *The History of the State of Georgia from 1850 to 1881*. New York, 1881.

Bettersworth, John K. *Confederate Mississippi: The People and Policies of a Cotton State in Wartime*. Baton Rouge, 1943.

Bryan, T. Conn. *Confederate Georgia*. Athens, Georgia, 1953.

Buck, Paul H. *The Road to Reunion, 1865–1900*. Boston, 1937.

Bullock, Henry Morton. *A History of Emory University*. Nashville, 1936.

Cabaniss, James A. *A History of the University of Mississippi*. University, Mississippi, 1949.

Carpenter, Jesse T. *The South as a Conscious Minority*. New York, 1930.

Cash, W. J. *The Mind of the South*. New York, 1941.

Coulter, E. Merton. *The Confederate States of America, 1861–1865*. Baton Rouge, 1950.

Craven, Avery O. *The Coming of the Civil War*. Chicago, 1966.

DeSantis, Vincent P. *Republicans Face the Southern Question: The New Departure Years, 1877–1897*. Baltimore, 1959.

Dunning, W. A. *Reconstruction, Political and Economic, 1865–1877*. New York, 1907.

Eaton, Clement. *The Freedom of Thought Struggle in the Old South*. New York, 1964.

Gaines, Francis Pendleton. *Southern Oratory: A Study in Idealism*. Tuscaloosa, 1946.

Garner, James W. *Reconstruction in Mississippi*. New York, 1901.

Glasson, William Henry. *History of Military Pension Legislation in the United States*. New York, 1900.

Hamilton, Holman. *Prologue to Conflict: The Crisis and Compromise of 1850*. New York, 1966.

Harris, William C. *Presidential Reconstruction in Mississippi*. Baton Rouge, 1967.

Haynes, George H. *The Senate of the United States: Its History and Practice.* 2 vols. Boston, 1938.

Hirshon, Stanley P. *Farewell to the Bloody Shirt: Northern Republicans and the Southern Negro, 1877–1893.* Bloomington, 1962.

Hoogenboom, Ari. *Outlawing the Spoils: A History of the Civil Service Reform Movement, 1865–1883.* Urbana, 1961.

Jenkins, William Sumner. *Pro-Slavery Thought in the Old South.* Chapel Hill, 1935.

Johnston, James Houston, comp. *Western and Atlantic Railroad in the State of Georgia.* Atlanta, 1931.

Jordan, Donaldson, and Edwin J. Pratt. *Europe and the American Civil War.* Boston, 1931.

Kennedy, John F. *Profiles in Courage.* New York, 1964.

Kirwan, Albert D. *Revolt of the Rednecks: Mississippi Politics, 1876–1925.* New York, 1965.

Logan, Rayford W. *The Betrayal of the Negro from Rutherford B. Hayes to Woodrow Wilson.* New York, 1965.

Mims, Edwin. *History of Vanderbilt University.* Nashville, 1946.

Montgomery, Horace. *Cracker Parties.* Baton Rouge, 1950.

Moore, Albert Burton. *Conscription and Conflict in the Confederacy.* New York, 1924.

Nichols, R. F. *The Disruption of American Democracy.* New York, 1962.

Owsley, Frank L. *King Cotton Diplomacy.* Chicago, 1931.

————. *States' Rights in the Confederacy.* Gloucester, Massachusetts, 1961.

Petersen, Svend. *A Statistical History of the American Presidential Elections.* New York, 1968.

Phillips, U. B. *Georgia and State Rights.* Washington, 1902.

————. *A History of Transportation in the Eastern Cotton Belt to 1860.* New York, 1908.

Pomeroy, Earl S. *The Territories and the United States, 1861–1890.* Philadelphia, 1947.

Priest, Loring B. *Uncle Sam's Stepchildren: The Reformation of the United States Indian Policy, 1865–1887.* New Brunswick, New Jersey, 1942.

Rainwater, Percy L. *Mississippi, Storm Center of Secession, 1856–1861.* Baton Rouge, 1938.

Rowland, Dunbar. *History of Mississippi: The Heart of the South.* 2 vols. Chicago, 1925.

————, ed. *Mississippi: Comprising Sketches of Counties, Towns, Events, Institutions, and Persons, Arranged in Cyclopedic Form.* 3 vols. Atlanta, 1907.

Shryock, Richard Harrison. *Georgia and the Union in 1850.* Durham, 1926.

Smith, Henry Nash. *Virgin Land: The American West as Symbol and Myth.* New York, 1950.

Stampp, Kenneth M. *The Era of Reconstruction, 1865–1877.* New York, 1966.

Unger, Irwin. *The Greenback Era: A Social and Political History of American Finance, 1865–1879.* Princeton, 1964.

Warren, Charles. *The Supreme Court in United States History.* 2 vols. Boston, 1937.

Wharton, Vernon L. *The Negro in Mississippi, 1865–1890.* Chapel Hill, 1947.

Woodward, C. Vann. *Origins of the New South.* Baton Rouge, 1951.

————. *Reunion and Reaction.* Boston, 1951.

Unpublished Theses and Dissertations

Baxter, James E. "Congressional Redistricting in Mississippi from 1817 to 1938." M.A. thesis, Duke University, 1938.

Campbell, Florence E., transc. "Journal of the Minutes of the Board of Trustees of the University of Mississippi, 1845–1860." M.A. thesis, University of Mississippi, 1939.

Folmar, John Kent. "The Erosion of Republican Support for Congressional Reconstruction in the House of Representatives, 1871–1877." Ph.D. dissertation, University of Alabama, 1968.

Hathorn, John Cooper. "A Period Study of Lafayette County from 1836 to 1860." M.A. thesis, University of Mississippi, 1939.

Jenkins, William T. "Ante Bellum Macon and Bibb County, Georgia." Ph.D. dissertation, University of Georgia, 1966.

Moore, Ross H. "Economic and Social Conditions during Reconstruction in Mississippi." Ph.D. dissertation, Duke University, 1938.

Sallis, Charles. "The Color Line in Mississippi Politics, 1865–1915." Ph.D. dissertation, University of Kentucky, 1967.

Summers, Mary F. "Edgar Wilson: The Mississippi Eagle, Journalist of the New South." Ph.D. dissertation, Mississippi State University, 1962.

Index